PEG CONTRUCCI is president of InFormat Communications, a home-based business that provides editorial/production services, and has served as managing editor for a nationally distributed monthly magazine.

```
658.041    Contrucci, Peg.
C             The home office : how to set it up, operate
           it, and make it pay off! / Peg Contrucci. --
           Englewood Cliffs, NJ : Prentice-Hall, c1985.
              214 p.
              ISBN 0-13-393026-2 (pbk.) : 12.95
              1. Home-based businesses--Management.
           2. Office layout. 3. Small business--Data
           processing.

       MELVINDALE PUBLIC LIBRARY.
           18650 ALLEN RD.                  13235              Je86
       MELVINDALE, MI 48122
              381-8677
```

PEG CONTRUCCI

THE HOME OFFICE

How to Set It Up, Operate It, and Make It Pay Off!

A SPECTRUM BOOK   PRENTICE-HALL, INC., Englewood Cliffs, New Jersey 07632

Library of Congress Cataloging-in-Publication Data

Contrucci, Peg.
  The home office.

  A Spectrum Book.
  Includes index.
  1. Home-based businesses—Management.
  2. Office layout 3. Small business—
  Data processing. I. Title.
  HD62.7.C66 1985   658'.041   85-12145
  ISBN 0-13-393034-3
  ISBN 0-13-393026-2 (pbk.)

This book was designed by the author to provide accurate, helpful guidelines on the subject matter covered. This notwithstanding, the author and those who have assisted her are not engaged in rendering any legal, accounting, financial, or other professional or expert advice in this book and disclaim any responsibility therefor. Competent professional assistance should be sought on any matter possibly requiring any such advice.

ISBN 0-13-393034-3

ISBN 0-13-393026-2 {PBK.}

©1985 by Prentice-Hall, Inc., Englewood Cliffs, New Jersey 07632.
All rights reserved. No part of this book may be reproduced
in any form or by any means without permission in writing
from the publisher.

A SPECTRUM BOOK. Printed in the United States of America.

10 9 8 7 6 5 4 3 2 1

Editorial/production supervision by Claudia Citarella
Manufacturing buyer: Carol Bystrom

This book is available at a special discount when ordered
in bulk quantities. Contact Prentice-Hall, Inc.,
General Publishing Division, Special Sales, Englewood Cliffs, NJ 07632.

Prentice-Hall International (UK) Limited, *London*
Prentice-Hall of Australia Pty. Limited, *Sydney*
Prentice-Hall Canada Inc., *Toronto*
Prentice-Hall Hispanoamericana, S.A., *Mexico*
Prentice-Hall of India Private Limited, *New Delhi*
Prentice-Hall of Japan, Inc., *Tokyo*
Prentice-Hall of Southeast Asia Pte. Ltd., *Singapore*
Whitehall Books Limited, *Wellington, New Zealand*
Editora Prentice-Hall do Brasil Ltda., *Rio de Janeiro*

Contents

PREFACE ix

1 THE PRESIDENT WORKS AT HOME—
WHY SHOULDN'T YOU? 1

2 THE IRS WANTS YOU TO WORK AT HOME! 7

Meeting the Home Office Test, 9
What Can't Be Deducted for a Home Office, 14
What Can Be Deducted for a Home Office, 15
Sale of the Home Office, 23
Other Tax Strategies for the Home Office, 27

3 THE MARKET ECONOMY WANTS YOU
TO WORK AT HOME 29

Higher Productivity, 31   Lower Overhead, 31
Opportunity, 32   Dissemination of Technology, 32

4 BREAKING OUT ON YOUR OWN   35

The Independent Subcontractor, 36
Work-at-Home Employees, 48

5 CREATING YOUR HOME WORK SPACE   53

What Makes the "Right Space"? 55
Six Sites for the Home Office, 63
Home-Office Furnishings, 67

6 EQUIPPING THE HOME OFFICE   73

Telephones, 76   Telephone Answering Machines, 79
Typewriters, 81   Dictating and Transcribing Equipment, 83
Photocopiers, 83   Postage Meters, 86

7 THE HOME OFFICE COMPUTER   89

Software: The Electronic Intellect, 91
The Computer Shopping List, 99   Computer Hardware, 102
Selecting Computer Equipment, 109
How (and How Not) to Cut Computer Costs, 110
The Computer in the Home Office, 111

8 SUPPLIERS AND SERVICERS: IMPORTANT MEMBERS OF YOUR HOME-OFFICE TEAM   115

The Five "Cs", 117
Stocking Up—Typical Office Supply Needs, 119
Storing Supplies, 122   Local Telephone Service, 122
Long-Distance Telephone Service, 125
Telephone Answering Service, 127   Electronic Mail, 127
U.S. Postal Service, 129   United Parcel Service, 134
Air and Ground Couriers, 135   Airlines, Trains, and Buses, 136
Repair Services, 136   Miscellaneous Services, 139

9 INFORMATION RESOURCES: YOUR HOME-OFFICE LIFELINE   141

Five Reference Books Every Office Should Have, 143
Print Publications, 144
Trade and Professional Associations, 145
Person-to-Person Networks, 145
Computer-to-Computer Networks, 147
Information Utilities, 150

10 ORGANIZING YOUR HOME OFFICE   157

Four Things to Do Every Morning, 160
Five Things to Do Every Evening, 161
Setting Up the Filing System, 162   Computer Files, 165

Logs, 167   Addresses and Telephone Numbers, 168
The Daily Mail, 168   Work in Process, 170
Finances, 172   Housecleaning, 175

11 HOME-OFFICE INSURANCE   177

What the Standard Homeowner's Policy Doesn't Cover, 179
Home-Office Riders, 180   Separate Business Coverage, 180
Additional Types of Insurance Coverage for the Home Office, 181
Twelve Precautions that Help Protect the Home Office, 183

12 THE HOME OFFICE AND THE COMMUNITY, STATE, AND NATION   185

Zoning Laws and Home-Based Occupations, 187
Other State and Local Regulations Affecting
the Home Office, 192   Labor Law Restrictions, 192
Contractual Restrictions on the Home Office, 194

13 A MATTER OF PERSONAL STYLE   195

Habits, 197   Solitude, 200
Other Members of the Household, 201
Employees in the Home Office, 203
The 24-Hour Partnership, 204

APPENDIX   207

INDEX   212

To Joseph and Jean Jones, who said "You Can!";
to Joe Contrucci, who said "You Will!";
and to Angus and Morgan MacAroni, who never said
a mumbling word.

Preface

**SNOWSTORM EXPECTED TO CAUSE MASSIVE RUSH-HOUR DELAYS
SMALL BUSINESS FAILURES AT RECORD RATE
GROWING CONCERN FOR THE PLIGHT OF LATCHKEY CHILDREN
RENT INCREASES FOR DOWNTOWN OFFICE SPACE AT ALL-TIME HIGH
ECONOMISTS DEBATE LOW WORKER PRODUCTIVITY**

These are just a few of the grim realities confronted by most American workers and small businesses—but not by all. Not by the millions of independent professionals, entrepreneurs, moonlighters, and telecommuters who work out of a readily available, economical, alternative work place: their home offices. They are freed from tedious commutes, rigid work schedules, and exorbitant office rents. Their home offices provide them with significant financial and tax advantages, along with a competitive edge in their businesses and in their personal finances.

If you have ever dreamed of breaking away from the workaday world and working at home, then this book will show you how—and how not—to realize your dream. It will provide you with the tested strategies, know-how, technology, techniques, and resources essential to making the most out of a home office.

The Home Office will help you to take the highest possible tax deductions for your home office; to get your present employer to hire you as an independent subcontractor; to create, furnish and equip your home office; to select a home-office computer; to deal with suppliers and servicers; to tap into the information resources necessary to keep you on top; to organize yourself and your office; to make sure your home office investment is adequately insured; to deal with zoning restrictions; and to successfully juggle your work life with your home life. You will also find valuable resource and reference listings especially designed for the home-office worker.

The Home Office is based on my five years' experience working out of a home office. I am deeply grateful to Joe Contrucci for being my home-office partner. I am also grateful to our many clients who have become our good friends; to Diane, Corinne, and Michelle for putting up with Angus and Morgan; to the Avalon Post Office, town merchants, repair persons, suppliers, delivery persons, and insurance agents; to our neighbors and friends in the community; and to our families, especially my mother-in-law, Betty Contrucci. All of them have been essential to the success of our home office.

Can you succeed in a home office? Only you can answer that question. But if you have a desire for independence, if you think your full potential is untapped in your current job, if you want to capitalize on your resources, then a home office could well be your springboard to financial self-reliance.

1

The President Works at Home—
Why Shouldn't You?

Something's happening in your neighborhood. Oh, you can't tell by walking down the street: On the outside, the houses and apartment buildings on your block look pretty much the same as they always have. But inside something's going on that you should know about. Your neighbors—executives, owners of small businesses, clerical workers, managers, innovators—have abandoned their business suits, long rush-hour commutes, and downtown office buildings. If you could peer behind some of those doors and windows, you would see them busy making a living in their own home offices.

Of course, there have always been the neighborhood eccentrics who worked at home: the local snake-oil distributor next door; the sometimes writer across the street; and the inventor tinkering in his garage down the road (after all, Baron von Frankenstein did some of his best work in his home laboratory). But who could take them seriously?

Well, consider this: The President of the United States works at home. Why? What is it the President and your neighbors know that you don't?

First, they know that working out of a home office provides significant income tax advantages to homeowners and renters alike. Additionally, they know that businesses benefit. A home office means increased productivity and lower overhead, which together make a competitive edge if there ever was one.

Perhaps this is why home offices are so attractive to new businesses and independent professionals like lawyers, agents, consultants, accountants, and doctors. For example, 50 percent of the members of the American Institute of Architects use their homes as their principal place of business. And according to the Small Business Administration, in 1984 20 percent of the new businesses started each year were home-based, and the percentage was climbing. Almost any type of business or profession that doesn't require a storefront or a large support staff is an immediate candidate for a home office—and the tax and financial advantages it brings.

Moonlighters like home offices, too, especially since 1981, when Congress expanded the rules concerning home-office income tax deductions to include business expenses associated with secondary sources of income. This means that the millions of people who are direct-sales representatives for Amway, Mary Kay, Avon, Shaklee, Tupperware, and so on in their spare time can deduct that part of their household expenses directly related to the home office. The tax deductions also apply to moonlighting businesses that are spun off from primary jobs, such a freelance typing service run by a secretary or a sideline bookkeeping business operated by an accountant.

Large businesses like home offices even better. More than 450 American corporations, including American Express, Blue Cross and Blue Shield, and Control Data, are operating or experimenting with programs that allow employees to work on home terminals or personal computers linked to the main office. Telecommunication experts forecast that by 1994 18 million employees will telecommute to work from home offices at least part-time. Their home offices will become "satellites" of the central offices, similar to those now run by some real estate agents and insurance agents who are employed by national networks and who also benefit from home-office tax deductions.

All totaled, in 1984 an estimated 11 million people worked at home either full- or part-time. Certainly, not all of them do so only for the financial and tax advantages. Many are motivated by necessity, such as the physically disabled who are permanently homebound or who are temporarily recuperating from surgery or illness. Others must stay at home to care for young children or, as we will see much more of in the future, infirm elderly parents. For these people, a home office is the only way they can be productively engaged in the work force.

A lack of capital also may require that a business be located in a home office. For an entrepreneur starting a new business, the initial cash flow may not support rent for commercial office space, or the space may not be available nearby at any cost. Professionals who move to rural areas quickly discover the complete dearth of office facilities outside the county seat. The home office is their only way to pursue business opportunities.

Lifestyle considerations lead some workers into a home office. By being at home and accessible during the day, parents can discover, for better or worse, a new closeness with their children. The same holds true for neighbors and community organizations, which, like children, will assume you can find time in your day for them.

The freedom to wear jeans all day, not having to hassle with rush-hour traffic, determining your own work schedule—these are some of the big convenience factors associated with home offices.

So there are many reasons why many different types of people find a home office desirable. But no matter what the reason, all can realize significant financial advantages if they design and operate their home offices with specific business and tax matters in mind.

For instance, under certain conditions defined by the IRS, running your own business out of a portion of your home or apartment allows you to turn some of your currently nondeductible household expenses into deductible ones. Percentages of utility bills, rents, and insurance costs suddenly become business expenses and can be deducted as a cost of doing business. The self-employed homeowner can shift portions of other deductible expenses, such as mortgage interest and real estate taxes, from Schedule A, the taxpayer's itemized deductions, to Schedule C, Profit or Loss from a Business or Profession. By reducing the net profit from the business, the self-employed taxpayer reduces his or her self-employment tax. (If federal income tax laws are revised so local real estate taxes are no longer deductible on Schedule A, the percentage of real estate taxes allocated to operating a home office will *still* be a deductible expense, one more reason establishing a home office is a desirable tax strategy.)

Furthermore, commuting from your principal place of business (home) to meet with clients and customers is a tax-deductible travel expense. Thus, what before was a nondeductible commute to the office becomes a deductible business expense.

A significant business factor associated with home offices is the amazingly high level of productivity achieved by working at home. Control Data reports that its home-based employees realize an average *40 percent* increase in work productivity, primarily as a result of higher morale. The increased productivity, combined with the lowered overhead—no need to rent and furnish office space for a home-based employee—mean that home offices can be an important element in a company's competitive strategy.

This book explains in detail how businesses and individuals can take advantage of the home-office strategy. It advises you how to break out of the going-to-work routine, including how to get your current employer to let you work out of a satellite office at home and how to become an independent subcontractor. It also covers in detail how to obtain the highest legal tax advantages from a home office and how to maximize professional and business gains.

To ensure that your home office is operated efficiently and effectively, this book includes valuable information on how to locate the best space in the home for the office; how to furnish and equip the work space, with special emphasis on the newest computer technology; how to choose business suppliers and servicers; how to keep in touch with the latest business developments; and how to organize your office and your workday. There are also chapters on insuring the home office and office equipment, plus how to deal with your neighbors, landlord, and governmental officials.

Since you can't ignore the "home" part of your home office, Chapter 13 discusses some of the personal and lifestyle concerns often involved in operating out of a home office: questions on developing work habits, dealing with solitude, balancing domestic and work responsibilities, maintaining good employee relations, and the case of two or more professionals working out of the same home office.

Finally, since the person working out of a home office encounters unique problems and opportunities in buying business services and products, the resources listed in the Appendix should prove handy. In it are also included references for other published materials and informal networks that can provide you with more specific information on the legal, financial, and marketing requirements of starting a new business, something this book will only cover insofar as the home-office location is concerned.

Oh yes, there is one brief section of philosophy, and this is it: Most people get up in the morning five days a week and go to work in some impersonal downtown office building. Never mind that what they do doesn't really require them to be physically present at any specific work place. Overlook the fact that rush-hour commutes are a waste of employees' time and the nation's energy resources. Forget that high downtown office rents can cripple businesses, especially start-ups. And ignore the troublesome number of latchkey children spawned by the phenomena of two-career families and single working parents. Common wisdom says "work" must be done under someone else's direction, on someone else's schedule, and someplace other than home.

But common wisdom isn't always right, as those working out of a home office can attest. They don't go to work in the same sense as traditional office workers. Instead, their work comes to them. This one simple difference offers home-based workers a greater degree of control over their time, production, resources, and opportunities. They have taken an important step toward financial and personal independence. You can, too.

2

The IRS Wants You to Work at Home!

"The IRS wants you to work at home"?

Well, not exactly. Actually, the IRS starts off with the premise that a home *by definition* is not a place of business, and any taxpayer claiming otherwise must bear the burden of proof.

On the other hand, in 1981 Congress liberalized the home-office tax deductions, making them available to many more taxpayers. This means that if you plan to take deductions for a home office, be prepared to support your expenses with *more* evidence than would be required if your office were located elsewhere. Although this may seem unfair, the tax savings from legitimate home-office deductions are well worth it.

For example, some types of home-related expenses, such as mortgage interest, are already deductible for homeowners on Schedule A, Itemized Deductions. But if the homeowner is self-employed and has a home office that qualifies under IRS requirements, a portion of these expenses can be moved to Schedule C, Profit or Loss from Business or Profession. This means that the net income realized from the business or profession is lower, and the self-employed taxpayer pays a lower Social Security self-employment tax, which in 1985 was 11.8% of net business income.

In addition, a portion of other home-related expenses that are normally not deductible, like electricity, heating, repairs, insurance, and rent, can be subtracted from gross income to the extent that they relate to the operation of a home office. A homeowner can also take depreciation deductions for that portion of the structure occupied by the office. Finally, if the home office is the principal place of business, then mileage and other costs associated with trips from the home office to visit business clients or suppliers are deductible travel expenses. The cost of commuting to a regular job is not deductible.

MEETING THE HOME OFFICE TEST

All of these tax advantages can add up to a significant savings for the taxpayer *if* the home office qualifies under *each* of four major IRS requirements: A home office must be used

1. exclusively and
2. regularly for
3. activities related to a trade or business, and
4. be either
   a. the principal place of business or
   b. a place to meet and deal with patients, clients, or customers or
   c. located in a separate, free-standing structure.

If the taxpayer is not self-employed but works as someone else's employee, the home office must *in addition* be a condition of employment and must be for the employer's convenience, not the employee's.

Exclusive Use

This simply means that the section of the home set aside for business cannot be used for any personal purposes. A dining room that doubles as a work area in between family meals will not qualify. Neither will a media room where a business's computer, files, and furnishings are mingled with children's video games, a personal stereo, and a VCR. Nor will a spare room that houses an office and, even though only occasionally, a mother-in-law.

The first step to passing the exclusive-use test is to have some way of physically defining where the personal, private part of the home ends and the home office begins. Until 1981, when Congress liberalized the tax laws relating to the home office, this was interpreted by the IRS to mean that a home office must be completely closed off from the rest of the house or apartment, such as in a separate room or on a separate floor. The 1981 rules, however, allow less severe divisions. Bookcases and screens used as room dividers, self-contained groupings of furniture, even changes in lighting and wall coverings can help define the boundaries between the office and the rest of the home.

In addition, the home-office furnishings help indicate the type of use. Typical contents showing business use are desks, filing cabinets, computers, typewriters, copiers, drafting boards, and reference books. Not typical of exclusive business use are beds, televisions and stereos, exercise equipment, and toy chests. It's best to keep these things out of the home office, even if they are not in active use. It's a good idea to take pictures of the home office, showing its arrangement, contents, entrance sign, and any other evidence that supports your claim of exclusive business use.

There are two exceptions to the exclusive-use rule. First, if the business being run out of the home is a qualified day-care service, then the area can be used for both business and personal purposes. This means that a basement recreation room where preschoolers are cared for during the day can still be used by the family in the evenings. Second, inventory for retail and wholesale businesses that are run out of the home can be stored in areas that also double for personal use, such as utility rooms and garages.

Regular Use

In addition to exclusive use, the space must be subject to regular—not incidental or occasional—use. What does "regular" use mean? Would an accountant who moonlights at home during March and April each year preparing tax returns qualify for home-office deductions? Probably not, unless the home office was used regularly during the rest of the year to market tax services, review professional magazines and newsletters, counsel clients, train bookkeepers, etc.

What about an interior designer who spends two hours each morning at home preparing sketches, making telephone calls, and handling correspondence before leaving to visit clients and construction sites? Would this qualify as regular use? Probably, if it could be proven. For this purpose, the interior designer should keep a detailed activity log showing what projects he or she worked on at home and when.

In general, activity logs are essential for self-employed business people and professionals. A log is the best method to record hours spent on a specific project for estimating and billing purposes and to keep track of travel expenses.

Activity logs can be kept in custom-designed daily ledgers or store-bought appointment books—whatever works best for you. But they should be kept on a daily basis to ensure accuracy and have the appearance of a contemporaneous record, not one created at a later date to support a tax deduction. Other types of evidence of regular use for a home office are telephone logs, long-distance phone bills, and chronological correspondence files.

Activities Related to a Trade or Business

This requirement doesn't mean that you are simply trying to turn a buck at home. Most stock market investors, no matter how large their portfolios and how much of their income is derived from dividends and capital gains, are not in the stock brokerage business and cannot deduct home-office expenses.

On the other hand, owning and managing rental property is the sort of investment that might support a home-office deduction. For example, imagine you own a five-unit apartment building and manage it from your home office. You must, on an ongoing basis, advertise for and interview potential tenants, receive rent payments, arrange for repairs and cleaning, pay bills associated with the rental property, and file reports required by the city. Such activities would constitute a "trade or business" under IRS requirements.

Before 1981 the IRS took the position that a person could have only *one* valid trade or business. No home-office deductions were available for people moonlighting out of their homes in the evenings and on weekends. Thanks to Congress, however, the tax law now acknowledges that people can and, in increasing numbers, do supplement their nine-to-five jobs with home-based sideline businesses.

Evidence to meet the trade-or-business test includes such things as: printed letterhead stationery and cards showing the home as the business address; business telephone service, Yellow Page listing, and other forms of advertising and promotion for the business; a businesslike manner of operating, including maintaining complete and accurate books and records; the taxpayer's work history (is this an activity that the taxpayer could reasonably expect to make a living from?); shipping and billing receipts showing the home-office address; state and municipal business registrations, licenses, filings, reports, etc.; and, most importantly, evidence of some sort of profit within the first five years of operation. For sideline businesses in particular, this ability to show a profit can be crucial to differentiate a valid business effort from a hobby pursuit.

Principal Place of Business

Although a taxpayer may have more than one trade or business, each trade or business has only one principal place of activity. For example, a criminal trial lawyer maintains a legal office downtown, but in his spare time he writes a murder mystery in his home office. The mystery is published and immediately zooms to the top of the best-seller list. His home office is his principal place of business for his writing career, and certain expenses associated with its operation can be deducted from his royalty income.

If the trade or business has *no* other location outside of the home, then the home office is clearly its principal place of business. If there is another location, it is necessary to prove which one is the main location. The principal place of business is determined by comparing such things as the amount of income generated by the various locations, the time spent and type of activity performed at each.

Consider the case of the owner-operator of a deli who uses her home office for bookkeeping, storing files, writing letters and promotional copy, ordering supplies, and the other administrative responsibilities associated with the business. Although these are all necessary activities for the successful operation of her business, and although they cannot be performed at the store, she would not be able to take home-office deductions under the principal-place-of-business test. This is because (a) all of the business's income is derived from the deli location, (b) the business is basically in retail sales, and the deli is the retail outlet, and (c) the owner spends far more time at the deli than in the home office.

Sometimes determining the principal place of business isn't quite so clear-cut, and sometimes the various standards used in the determination produce conflicting results. A doctor may realize far more income from a few hours spent each day in a fancy, uptown clinic than from the six to seven hours spent in her home clinic treating low-income, elderly patients. She would be able to qualify her home office under the next test, however.

Meeting and Dealing with Patients, Clients, or Customers

Even if the doctor in the case just mentioned spent more time and received more income from her uptown clinic, she would still be able to deduct expenses related to her home clinic if she regularly received patients there in the normal course of her practice. It need not be her principal place of business.

The meeting-and-dealing test is especially relevant to service professionals (doctors, dentists, attorneys, architects, accountants, designers, engineers) who maintain numerous places of business in order to serve as wide a range of clients as possible. But there has been some confusion regarding what constitutes "meeting and dealing," specifically over whether the contact with the patient, client, or customer has to be in person or whether it can be over the telephone.

In 1983 the United States Tax Court ruled that a real estate development executive, who was required by his firm to spend several hours every week night at home telephoning prospective clients and business associates, met the meeting-and-dealing requirement for taking home-office deductions. However, the IRS appealed, and the Ninth Circuit reversed the decision. The Ninth Circuit reasoned that the law intended the deductions to offset the substantial expense incurred in making a home office presentable to the public. Conducting telephone calls did not fall within this interpretation.

Given the continuing trend in the use of telecommunications, it's highly doubtful that this restrictive interpretation will remain. The rapid spread of conference calling and computer networks is eliminating the need for people to physically travel to appointments and meetings. Even in large corporate offices, much business interaction takes place over computer networks, and it really doesn't matter whether the people involved are across the hall or across town from each other.

Separate Structure

Finally, the home office need not meet either the principal-place-of-business or the meeting-and-dealing tests if it is located in a separate garage, studio, barn, or other free-standing structure. The separate structure can even be a boat or mobile home, as long as it is on the same property as or contiguous with the taxpayer's "dwelling." It can simply be a secondary location where a valid business or professional activity takes place on regular and exclusive bases.

Convenience of Employer

If the taxpayer is not self-employed but works on someone else's payroll, the home office must be required as a condition of employment, and not simply because the employee decides he or she doesn't want to commute anymore and the employer agrees to this eccentricity.

The major criterion by which this requirement is met centers on whether or not the employer makes a suitable work space available. For example, a philosophy professor is required to write and do research in addition to teaching three courses a semester. But the college does not supply adequate office space, and the professor must work at home on his articles and books. Because the home office is necessary to perform his job, the professor qualifies for home-office tax deductions.

In another example, a national insurance company requires an agent to operate an office to service a small, isolated community. The agent sets up the office in her home, while remaining on the insurance company's payroll and being reimbursed for certain office expenses by the company. She qualifies for the home-office deduction.

A taxpayer running a home office while remaining someone else's employee should have a written agreement stating that the arrangement is at the convenience of the employer, not the employee. If the employee is an outside salesperson paid on a commission basis, home-office expenses are deducted on Form 2106. An employee who is not an outside salesperson must deduct unreimbursed home-office expenses on Schedule A, Itemized Deductions. This means that if the taxpayer doesn't itemize tax deductions, he or she won't be able to take the home-office deductions.

The Home Office as Rental Property

One way to possibly get around the convenience-of-employer requirement is for the employer to rent a portion of the employee's home for use as an office. The employee reports the rental income on Schedule E, Supplemental Income, and deducts expenses associated with the home office as expenses incurred to maintain rental property. The net income to the employee is taxable but not subject to Social Security tax.

The amount of rental income must be "reasonable." That is, it must be close to the fair-market rental value. The arrangement must also serve some valuable business purpose for the employer. A written lease agreement is recommended.

It is also possible that an incorporated business operating out of a home office could make the same arrangement, with the corporation renting the home office from the homeowner or subleasing it from a rentor.

One big note of warning: The IRS opposes taxpayers' use of such rental agreements in order to qualify for home-office deductions. Check with a qualified tax advisor before you attempt to use this tax strategy.

WHAT CAN'T BE DEDUCTED FOR A HOME OFFICE

Before discussing what can be deducted for a home office, let's look at what can't. First, anything related to the private, personal-use section of the residence is not deductible as a home office expense. This may seem obvious; after all, who would try to claim a business-related expense for refinishing the kitchen? Well, someone who lets an employee fix and eat lunch in the kitchen every day might try. But it's not allowed. The minute any facility is used for personal reasons, it fails the exclusive-use test and cannot be deducted. Also, expenses incurred for the upkeep of the lawn and for landscaping are not deductible, even though the main reason for such improvements may be to make the entrance more attractive to the public.

Second, there's a limit: Deductions related to the business use of a home cannot be greater than the gross income derived from such a business. Or more to the point, *home-office deductions cannot be used to shelter income from other sources*. The IRS has a somewhat involved formula concerning this limit and in what order home-office deductions can be taken, which will be covered after we look at the types of expenses that are deductible.

WHAT CAN BE DEDUCTED FOR A HOME OFFICE

There are four major categories of deductions related to a home office. Items in the first category, which we'll call *straight business expenses*, have nothing to do with the fact that your office is in your home rather than in a downtown office building. They include such things as pens, pencils, paper clips, and other office supplies; stationery; advertising; car expenses; business equipment rental and depreciation; dues and publications; travel (remember, if the home office is the principal place of business, all trips to visit clients and servicers are deductible); entertainment; bank service and check charges; salaries and payroll taxes; legal and professional fees; filing fees; and so on. Straight business expenses are *not* subject to the home-office deduction limitation.

The second category includes operating expenses that do relate to the fact that the office is in the home but which are related *only* to the office area and not the personal areas. We'll call these *direct home-office expenses*. They include such things as repairing a broken windowpane or light switch in the office, hiring someone to clean the office, and any special riders required for your home-owner's insurance because of the office. Direct home-office expenses, because they relate only to the business activity, are wholly deductible but are subject to the home-office deduction limitation.

Allocating Indirect Expenses

The third category is also subject to the limitation and includes items that are *indirect home-office expenses*; that is, they are derived from general expenses incurred to maintain the entire structure, such as utilities, real estate taxes, casualty losses, mortgage interest, or rent. The portion of these expenses that can be taken as a business deduction is calculated according to how much of the home is used for business purposes versus how much is used for personal purposes. The proportioning is usually done on the basis of square footage.

If, for example, your entire house encloses 2,500 square feet, and you convert your attic, which measures 500 square feet, into a qualified home office, you could allocate 20 percent of your general home maintenance and operating costs to the home office. If you saw numerous clients in your home office, and they had to enter through the same front hall and walk up the same set of stairs that you and members of your family used to gain access to personal sections of the residence, then you could increase this percentage by using what's called the *net square footage calculation*. This method of calculation allows you to subtract those areas that are used for both personal *and* business purposes from the house's total square footage. The remainder, or "net square footage," is then used to compute the percentage of square footage occupied by the home office.

For example, if the stairs and hallway areas equal 200 square feet, then your percentage allocation increases to 21.74 percent (2,500 sq. ft. minus 200 sq. ft. = 2,300 sq. ft. ÷ 500 sq. ft. = 21.74%).

Because home-based day-care businesses are exempt from the exclusive-use requirement, they must further calculate the amount of *time* the facilities are used for business purposes. If 50 percent of the structure is used ten hours a day, five days each week for qualified day-care services and the rest of the time for personal use, then the taxpayer can deduct 15.15 percent of the general expenses associated with maintaining the residence (10 hours × 5 days per week = 50 hours per week/168 total hours in each week = 29.76 percent × 50 percent calculation of space = 14.88 percent allocated to business use).

The square-footage calculation may be an equitable way to apportion such expenses as mortgage interest and real estate taxes, perhaps even more than equitable for the taxpayer because both are based on the value of the structure and the land. But what about utilities? A highly electronic office or home-based manufacturing business, for example, may account for far more of the monthly electric bill than a square-footage calculation would reflect.

Take, for example, the case of a single artist who creates fine ceramic plates and bowls in addition to teaching several pottery classes. His studio is in a converted garage attached to his home and represents approximately 20 percent of the structure's square footage.

His studio is equipped with five electrically driven wheels for throwing clay, a humidity-controlled drying room, a gas-fired kiln, and two window air conditioners. He works eight hours a day on his own creations and two hours at night conducting classes. When he is not working, he likes to go out. He doesn't often eat at home and doesn't even own a TV set.

Obviously, he should not use the square-footage method to calculate his business's utility expenses. While square footage is the most common and most recommended way of apportioning indirect home-office expenses, it is not required by law. Other methods can be used, as long as they can be clearly substantiated.

The above example on allocating utilities is just one more reason to try to separate the business operation from the general household expenses as much as possible. Electricity consumption measured on a *separate* meter and billed directly to the business is a direct home-office expense and need not be allocated on a square-foot percentage basis. A *separate* business telephone line is a straight business expense and not subject to the home-office limitation.

Depreciation

Depreciation is the last type of home-office deduction available. The homeowner can depreciate that portion of the building and capital improvements associated with the home office (real property). Both the homeowner and the renter can depreciate furniture and equipment used at home in connection with work (personal property). The depreciation of personal property is a straight business expense.

Depreciation is a tax device that spreads the cost of a business asset (called a *capital expenditure*) over the useful life of the asset. Normally, you couldn't depreciate your home because it isn't a business asset and doesn't generate any income. At the point you create and put into service a home office, however, that portion of your residence becomes income-producing commercial property, and along with any capital improvements to the office area (including permanent improvements like repainting, remodeling, rewiring, and so forth) can be depreciated. Portions of capital improvements relating to the entire structure, such as repainting or re-siding the exterior, and putting on a new roof, can also be depreciated.

Office furniture and equipment can be depreciated even if you don't qualify for the home-office deduction. For example, you purchase a computer to use at home for business purposes on weekends and late nights, rather than staying at the office. You can depreciate the cost of the equipment based on the percentage of time it is used for business.

However, personal computers used at home in connection with business fall under what is called the *50 percent rule*, meaning that if the business use isn't more than 50 percent of the total use at home, the purchase of the computer is not eligible for the investment-tax credit and cannot be depreciated under an accelerated depreciation schedule (which will be explained later in this chapter). The same test holds true for stereos, VCRs, TVs, and other entertainment-type equipment. Meticulous logs must be kept of *all* use to determine the percentage of business use.

(The 50 percent rule doesn't apply to computers in home offices that qualify for the home-office tax deductions, since they are, by definition, used *exclusively* for business purposes. Any personal use would not only affect the depreciation on the computer but could jeopardize the tax status of the home office.)

Rather than depreciate the cost of business equipment and furnishings, you can take a straight business-expense deduction for up to $5,000 of the cost of assets bought before 1988, $7,500 for assets bought in 1988 or 1989, and $10,000 for assets bought after 1989.

Methods of depreciation. Depreciation is a very complex and rapidly changing area of the tax code. Always consult a tax advisor before taking a depreciation deduction for a home office to find out what the current laws are and how they affect you.

Presently, there are two methods of figuring the depreciation deduction for your home office and for equipment and furniture used in connection with business. The first is the Accelerated Cost Recovery System (ACRS) and *must* be used for property acquired and placed into service after December 31, 1980. In the case of real property, "placed into service" means the date you first occupied the residence, not the date you converted a portion of it into a home office.

If you owned the property prior to January 1, 1981, then you are *not* eligible for ACRS and must use the depreciation rules that were in effect on the date you acquired and first used the property. You also may not use ACRS to depreciate personal property if a related party (such as a parent, spouse, sibling, grandparent, grandchild or partnership or corporation in which you or your relatives held more than a 10 percent interest) owned or used the property before 1981.

There are exceptions to the prior-to-1981 ACRS exclusion. The first improvement or separate "component" (for example, new plumbing or rewiring) placed into service after 1980 on buildings acquired and used prior to 1980 qualifies for ACRS depreciation. Also, substantial improvements are treated as separate buildings and can qualify for ACRS if placed into service after 1980. A "substantial" improvement refers to an improvement whose cost is 25 percent or more of the original building's adjusted basis, is spent within a two-year period, and is undertaken not less than three years after the original building was placed in service.

Regulations common to ACRS and earlier depreciation methods are:

1. Land cannot be depreciated; only the structures located on the lot can be. To calculate the relative values of the land and the building, use the proportionate breakdown provided in a tax assessor's statement, an independent appraisal, or any specific allocation spelled out in the agreement of sale. This percentage must further be multiplied by the percentage of the building actually occupied by the home office.

For example, based on a tax assessment, 75 percent of the value of Mrs. Beacon's home is allocated to her house and 25 percent to the land. Her home office occupies 15 percent of the house's square footage. Mrs. Beacon can depreciate 11.25 percent of her basis in her real property over its "useful life," or recovery period.

2. Depreciation deductions are not based on cash expenses. The fact that an asset is leveraged (purchased with a loan) does not reduce the amount that can be depreciated. If you borrowed $2,000 to buy a $2,500 copier, you can use the entire $2,500 to calculate your depreciation, not just the $500 you put up in cash.

3. If you fail to claim a depreciation deduction in the first year it is allowable, you may not claim it in subsequent years. Your only recourse is to file amended tax returns.

The major *differences* between ACRS and the earlier depreciation methods are:

1. Under ACRS, property is classified as having either a three-year, five-year, ten-year, fifteen-year, or eighteen-year recovery period. Under prior depreciation methods there were no standardized recovery periods, and taxpayers attempted to justify whatever they could claim was the property's "useful life."

2. Under ACRS you may (but are not required to) use an accelerated method of calculating depreciation deductions. Accelerated depreciation percentages allow a greater recovery of the property's cost earlier in the recovery period (see Figure 2-1). Under prior "straight-line" depreciation methods, the percentages spread out the amount of the deduction equally over the recovery period.

In spite of the obvious advantage of being able to take larger deductions, and thus pay less taxes, early in the recovery period, electing the accelerated depreciation schedule under ACRS potentially can result in very unfavorable tax consequences for the homeowner when the time comes to sell a residence that contains a home office. These are covered under the section entitled "Gain from the Sale of the Home Office" later in this chapter.

3. ACRS uses the unadjusted basis of property to calculate depreciation. (The unadjusted basis is cost plus any capital-improvement expenditures and, for property purchased in 1983 and afterward, less 50 percent of any investment credit allowed on personal property.) The older, straight-line method uses the *lesser* of these values: the fair-market value at the time you convert the property to business use, or the adjusted basis, meaning cost plus capital improvements minus any deductions previously claimed, such as casualty losses.

4. Under ACRS, all property in the same recovery-period class acquired in the same year must be treated the same; that is, depreciated on the same schedule. You couldn't elect to depreciate a computer acquired in 1985 using the accelerated schedule and a typewriter also acquired in 1985 using the straight-line method, since they both are five-year property. The prior depreciation methods allowed each piece of property, and even different components of real property, to be treated separately.

5. ACRS does not distinguish between new and used property nor consider the salvage value of property to calculate basis. Salvage value is assigned the first year depreciation is claimed and is estimated as the rock-bottom amount below which the value of the property will never fall.

Depreciating personal property used in your trade or business. In order to understand the varied and complex world of depreciation deductions, we will first examine depreciation claimed on business-related personal property, including office furnishings, computers, typewriters, telephones, and other equipment. (Keep in mind that instead of depreciating personal property, you have the option of taking a straight business expense deduction for the property's cost up to certain dollar limits based on the year of purchase. However, if you elect the straight business expense route, you are not entitled to the investment tax credit,

Figure 2-1 Accelerated Cost Recovery Percentages

3-Year Assets: Includes automobiles, light-duty trucks, R&D machinery and equipment, special tools, etc.

5-Year Assets: Includes all personal property, including office furnishings and equipment.

10-Year Assets: Includes mobile and manufactured homes.

Recovery Year	3-Year	5-Year	10-Year
1	25%	15%	8%
2	38%	22%	14%
3	37%	21%	12%
4		21%	10%
5		21%	10%
6			10%
7			9%
8			9%
9			9%
10			9%

15-Year Assets: Includes low income housing real estate; real property placed into service between January 1, 1981, and March 15, 1984; and "transitional 15-year class property," which is real property placed into service after March 15, 1984 and before January 1, 1987, and for which either (a) the taxpayer before March 16, 1984, entered a binding contract to buy or construct the property or (b) the construction of such property was begun by the taxpayer before March 16, 1984.

The applicable percentage is: (Use the column for the month in the first year the property is placed in service)

Recovery Year	1	2	3	4	5	6	7	8	9	10	11	12
1	12	11	10	9	8	7	6	5	4	3	2	1
2	10	10	11	11	11	11	11	11	11	11	11	12
3	9	9	9	9	10	10	10	10	10	10	10	10
4	8	8	8	8	8	8	9	9	9	9	9	9
5	7	7	7	7	7	7	8	8	8	8	8	8
6	6	6	6	6	7	7	7	7	7	7	7	7
7	6	6	6	6	6	6	6	6	6	6	6	6
8	6	6	6	6	6	6	5	6	6	6	6	6
9	6	6	6	6	5	6	5	5	5	6	6	6
10	5	6	5	6	5	5	5	5	5	5	6	5
11	5	5	5	5	5	5	5	5	5	5	5	5
12	5	5	5	5	5	5	5	5	5	5	5	5
13	5	5	5	5	5	5	5	5	5	5	5	5
14	5	5	5	5	5	5	5	5	5	5	5	5
15	5	5	5	5	5	5	5	5	5	5	5	5
16	—	—	1	1	2	2	3	3	4	4	4	5

18-Year Assets: Includes all real property placed in service after March 15, 1984, which is not low income housing or "transitional 15-year class property." (Note: Property placed in service after March 15, 1984, but before June 23, 1984, will use a slightly different table. Ask your accountant for the applicable table that assumes no mid-month convention.)

The applicable percentage is: (Use the column for the month in the first year the property is placed in service)

Recovery Year	1	2	3	4	5	6	7	8	9	10	11	12
1	9	9	8	7	6	5	4	4	3	2	1	0.4
2	9	9	9	9	9	9	9	9	9	10	10	10
3	8	8	8	8	8	8	8	8	9	9	9	9

(Subsequent years' percentages not available as of printing.)

which may be more desirable depending on your tax situation. Thus, for this example, assume you opt to depreciate the entire amount of the property's cost.)

On December 1, 1985, you purchase a copier for $2,000 and place it into service in your home office. Under ACRS, it is classified as five-year property (along with most other office equipment and furnishings). In the year of purchase you are entitled to a $200 investment credit on the purchase of the copier. This reduces your basis to $1,900.

If you select the accelerated depreciation schedule, in 1985 you can deduct 15 percent of your unadjusted basis in the copier, or $285. If you were to select the straight-line schedule, you would be entitled to a $190 deduction in the first year. Under the straight-line schedule it actually takes six years to completely write off five-year property. This is because in the first year you are entitled to only half the percentage allowed for the following four years; the remaining half-year percentage is taken in the sixth year. Under both the accelerated and straight-line schedules, it doesn't matter when in the year you actually place the copier in service, whether in January or December. Each schedule assumes the property was placed into service in July. In addition, under ACRS you are not entitled to any depreciation deduction in the year you sell personal property.

Now instead of acquiring new equipment and furnishings for your home office, what happens if you convert personal property that you used prior to 1981 into business property; that is, property that is not subject to ACRS? For instance, what would be your depreciation deductions for a desk that you paid $800 for in 1979, used in your den, and want to convert to a business asset in 1985?

First, although you may have paid $800 in 1979, the adjusted basis is the *lesser* of cost versus fair-market value at the time of conversion in 1985. Unless the desk is an antique, the odds are it has already depreciated in value considerably. Based on research into sales of comparable used furniture, you can only reasonably assign a fair-market value of $150 in 1985. Thus, with a basis of $150 spread out over six years, you will be able to take only a $15 depreciation deduction in 1985.

Depreciating real property. Now let's look at possible depreciation situations connected with real property (your home) based on a qualified home office.

In the first example, Mr. and Mrs. McAroni buy a house in April 1983 for $120,000, spend an additional $25,000 finishing the basement, and convert it into a home office, where they publish a financial newsletter. The renovations are finished September 1, and they move in.

Based on the appraisal made at the time of sale, the lot their house sits on is valued at $40,000. This means their unadjusted basis in the property is $105,000, and since the home office occupies 50 percent of the home's square footage, the McAronis are entitled to depreciate $52,500.

As shown in Figure 2-1, under ACRS most real property now falls into an eighteen-year recovery period. The McAronis' property, however, was purchased before March 15, 1984, and thus falls into the fifteen-year asset category. Unlike in the case of personal property, the actual time of year the property is converted to business use *does* affect the percentage used to calculate the first year's depreciation deduction. In this example, the McAronis' property was put into service on the date it was inhabitable, meaning after the extensive renovations were completed on September 1.

Thus, if the McAronis elect to use the accelerated depreciation schedule, they would be entitled to a $2,100 depreciation deduction in 1983, $5,775 in 1984, $5,250 in 1985, and so forth. If they choose a straight-line schedule, they would take a $1,050 deduction in 1983, $3,675 in 1984, $3,675 in 1985, and so forth.

In our second example, Mr. Joyce retires in 1984 after 35 years as an Army procurement officer. Rather than be idle, he decides to start a consulting business advising manufacturers how to obtain military contracts.

On January 1, 1985, he sets up an office in two spare bedrooms in his home, which he bought in 1961 for $35,000 and in which he has invested approximately $17,000 over the years. Based on the recent sale of his neighbor's house, he knows his property is actually worth at least $150,000, with $40,000 for the lot alone.

Unfortunately, Mr. Joyce's depreciation must be calculated on his adjusted basis, since it is less than the fair-market value. Because his house accounts for approximately 73 percent of the property's value, and because his home office occupies approximately 30 percent of the house, his adjusted basis is $12,765 ($35,000 × 73% plus $17,000 × 30%).

Also, since under the old depreciation rules the recovery period is based on some realistic calculation of useful life, Mr. Joyce must spread his depreciation out over 30 years. This means his depreciation deduction in 1985 is $425.50, in 1986 $425.50, etc.

Home-Office Deduction Limitation

As we have seen, there are four kinds of deductions associated with a home office: straight business expenses; direct home-office expenses; indirect home-office expenses; and depreciation of commercial property. But as stated before, there is a limit to how much you can deduct in connection with the home office, and this limitation is based on the gross income derived from the business use of a part of your home.

"Gross income derived" means the income after straight business expenses are deducted. Therefore, it is possible to have a loss from a business operated out of the home. You just can't manipulate and exploit the home-office deductions to generate that loss.

In addition, there is a priority of home-office deductions: After you figure your gross income derived, you must then deduct those indirect home-office expenses that would be deductible on Schedule A even if you didn't have a home office. These include a percentage of home mortgage interest, casualty losses, and—depending on the current tax law—local real estate taxes. If you have any income left, then you deduct the rest of your indirect home-office expenses (such as the percentage of electricity and heating) and your direct home-office expenses. If you have anything left after that, then you may deduct the depreciation of the portion of your residence occupied by the home office.

The worksheet for Mr. Joyce (Figure 2-2) illustrates the various types and order of deductions associated with his consulting business. Note that because of the limitation, Mr. Joyce deducted only $287 of the $426 he calculated was his 1985 depreciation deduction.

SALE OF THE HOME OFFICE

Whenever an asset that was used for both personal and business purposes is sold, it is treated as two sales. Thus, in the case of the sale of a residence that includes a qualified home office, two assets are sold: the residence and the commercial property occupied by the office. This fact is crucial when the time comes to calculate the tax on any gain realized from the sale.

First we will explore the tax rules governing the sale of the private residence. If you had not established a home office, the capital gain that you would realize upon the sale of your principal residence would be eligible for either the "rollover" exclusion or the $125,000 lifetime exclusion. The rollover exclusion allows you to defer all income taxes on the capital gain realized from the sale of

Figure 2-2 Mr. Joyce's Tax Worksheet

Gross Income from Consulting Business:		$ 8,689
Straight Business Expenses:		
Office supplies	$ 146	
Business telephone line	1,450	
Professional fees	600	
Travel	2,112	
Subscription to trade newsletter	150	
Service contract on computer	110	
Depreciation on computer	291	
	4,859	−4,859
Gross Income Derived from Home-Based Business:		3,830
Home-Office Expenses:		
Percentage of home-office deductions that would otherwise be deductible on Schedule A		
Mortgage interest (30% × $2,438)	$ 731	
Real estate taxes (30% × $3,504)	1051	
	1,782	−1,782
Limitation on Home-Office Deduction		2,048
Other Indirect and Direct Home-Office Deductions:		
Insurance, separate rider for equipment & liability	$ 65	
Insurance (30% of structure loss)	240	
Electricity (30%)	388	
Heating (30%)	560	
Water & sewer (30%)	288	
Office repairs	95	
Office cleaning	125	
	1,761	−1,761
Limitation on Home-Office Deduction		287
Depreciation		
Straight-line method based on 30 years, $12,765 adjusted basis in home office	426	
Depreciation amount above Home-Office Deduction Limitation	−139	
	287	−287
Net Income from Consulting Business		-0-

your old home *if* you purchase and occupy a new residence within 24 months of the sale and *if* that new residence cost more than the amount you received from the sale of your old home. The $125,000 exclusion applies to taxpayers age 55 and over and allows them to realize $125,000 in capital gain tax-free from the sale of their principal residence—no need to buy another, more expensive home within 24 months. This exclusion can only be taken once in a lifetime, and the taxpayer must have owned and occupied the home for three of the preceding five years before the sale.

Even if you do not qualify for either of the exclusions, if you owned the property for more than six months, the gain from the sale of the personal residence is taxed as long-term capital gain, meaning tax is calculated on only 40 percent of the gain.

However, the sale of commercial property (i.e., the home office) falls under different rules due to a tax concept called "recapture." Recapture is the flip side of depreciation. The government figures that if you are allowed to deduct part of your income to account for a depreciating asset, and then you sell that asset, any gain that "recaptures" the amount you depreciated should be taxed as income. Seems fair enough.

For the taxpayer with a home office, the problems come in two forms: First, it doesn't matter whether or not you actually claimed a depreciation deduction on your home office; the fact that you are allowed to claim such a deduction will be taken into account when calculating your basis. Second, depending on the type of depreciation calculation you used, the recaptured depreciation may be taxed as ordinary income rather than at the lower capital-gains rate.

If you used an accelerated depreciation schedule under ACRS, and you realize a gain on the sale of the residence containing a home office, *all* your earlier write-offs are recaptured as ordinary income in the year of sale. On the other hand, if you had used a straight-line percentage calculation, the recapture would be taxed as capital gains, which in the case of property held for more than six months, would be based on only 40 percent of the gain.

To illustrate the significance of the tax differential under the two situations, look at the case of Mr. and Mrs. McAroni, who decided to sell their home three years after they converted the basement into a home office. If you remember, they were entitled to depreciate a total of $13,125 for those three years under the accelerated method, reducing their basis in the house to $131,875. In 1988 they sold the house for $200,000, allocated at $60,000 for the land and $140,000 for the structure. The house occupies approximately 60 percent of the land.

Following the worksheet in Figure 2-3, you will see that total gain on the sale is $68,125, $44,000 for the residence and $24,125 for the home office. The McAronis roll over the gain on the residence and thus pay no taxes on the $44,000. However, they must pay taxes on the $24,125, partially at regular income rates (the $13,125 in recaptured depreciation) and partially at long-term

Figure 2-3 Gain on Sale of Home Office

In 1983 Mr. and Mrs. McAroni buy a two-story rancher for $120,000, spend $25,000 converting the basement into a home office, and start publishing a newsletter. In 1986 they sell the house for $200,000. The office occupies 50% of the structure and the structure covers 60% of the lot.

Proceeds from the sale	Total	Residence	Home Office
Building	140,000	70,000	70,000
Land	60,000	42,000	18,000*
Allocations	200,000	112,000	88,000
Original purchase price			
Building	+80,000	+40,000	+40,000
Land	+40,000	+28,000	+12,000
Improvements	+25,000		+25,000
	145,000	68,000	77,000
Depreciation	−13,125	—0—	−13,125
Adjusted Basis	131,875	68,000	63,875
Proceeds from sale	200,000	112,000	88,000
Adjusted Basis	−131,875	−68,000	−63,875
Gain on Sale of Property	68,125	44,000	24,125

Tax on Gain:

$44,000 Long-term gain on residence deferred under rollover exclusion		—0—
100% of recaptured depreciation taxed as ordinary income		13,125
Long-term gain on home office	11,000	
Less 60% deduction	6,600	
	4,400	4,400
		17,525
McAronis' tax rate		×.46
Tax on sale of home office		8,062

If the McAronis had depreciated the home office under the straight-line schedule, they would have only been entitled to $8,400 total depreciation deductions over the three years. However, the entire gain on the home office would have been taxed at the long-term capital-gains rate, and their tax bill would only have been $3,570.

*The value of the land must be allocated between the residential and commercial property. If the structure occupies 60% of the lot and the office occupies 50% of the structure, the office must assume 30% of the land value.

capital-gains rate. At their tax bracket (46%), they must pay $8,062 in taxes on the sale of the home office.

If, however, they had used the straight-line percentage schedule, they would have been entitled to depreciation deductions totaling only $8,400 over the three years. The gain from the sale of the commercial property (their home office) would have resulted only in a $19,400 gain, *all* taxable as long-term capital gains. Their tax bill for the sale would have amounted to only $3,570. Thus, it would seem prudent to elect straight-line recovery for depreciating a home office if you want to avoid recapturing the gain as ordinary income.

There is a way out of the recapture problem altogether. And the same escape route also allows you to apply all the gain from the sale of the property to any capital-gains residential exclusion you may be entitled to. It's simple: Convert the home office back to personal use in the year of sale.

The tax laws provide that if property does not *qualify* for the home-office deduction in the year of sale, then the entire gain is classified as arising from the sale of a personal residence and not commercial property, no matter how great a depreciation deduction may have been claimed in prior years. The key thing to remember is that it isn't sufficient simply to not *claim* the home-office deduction in the year of sale; the home office must in some way actually fail to meet the crucial tests for qualifying for the deduction, such as not being used exclusively for business. So in the year of sale you should consider undoing your carefully executed separation of the business and personal use of your home. Move a bed in and let the office double as a guest room; move a TV in and play video games; take up some hobby activity, such as sewing or model shipbuilding, and center it in the office—just use your imagination and document the change with photographs the same way you documented the absence of any personal activity to qualify the office.

OTHER TAX STRATEGIES FOR THE HOME OFFICE

You should keep two other possible tax advantages in mind when establishing a home office. First, just because you are now working at home doesn't mean that you are ineligible for the child and disabled-dependent care credits. Under this tax program, you can receive a tax credit based on the expenses you incur to have someone provide care for a young child or a physically or mentally disabled dependent.

Second, if you hire your spouse or dependent children to help out in the home office, you will realize two significant tax savings: you will be able to take a business deduction for their services, and they will be exempt from Social Security and unemployment taxes. In the case of dependent children, they will also be taxed at much lower tax rates.

Both strategies are worth investigating with your tax advisor and, if you qualify, well suited to a home office.

3

The Market Economy Wants You to Work at Home

In 1983 American Telephone & Telegraph, sensing an emerging market opportunity, conducted a survey to determine how many people worked out of their homes. The findings showed that 7 percent of the total work force worked at home full-time. Six percent worked at home part-time. All told, AT&T estimated there were 11 million Americans working at home.

These home-based workers represent a wide range of economic levels and occupations. Some operate independent businesses that are their main sources of income; some are moonlighting. Some work a few days a week at home in addition to a few days at a traditional office. But they all have one thing in common: They are helping to stimulate the American economy. Working at home, as even big business is discovering, generates economic opportunity through high productivity and low overhead.

HIGHER PRODUCTIVITY

Several large corporations, include Control Data, American Express, and Blue Cross/Blue Shield, have experimented with work-at-home programs which allow employees to work at computer terminals or personal computers located in their homes rather than in a central office. They all noted a significant increase in worker productivity, with Control Data recording a 40 percent jump.

The reasons cited for this increase are numerous. Working at home eliminates much nonproductive time associated with a traditional office: No time is wasted on commuting to and from work; no time is lost to interruptions from coworkers; bad weather can't close the business down because commuters can't get into the office.

Another, perhaps more important reason has to do with worker morale and job satisfaction. The flexible work hours allow employees to work at their own personal "peak" hours and for as long as they choose. They can arrange their work schedule around family obligations, removing the need to chose between family and career. Being on their own gives them a greater sense of personal responsibility and control over their jobs and lives.

The higher productivity realized from work-at-home programs benefits both the employer, through an increase in business volume, and the employee, through higher wages based on increased value. The self-employed home-based worker, of course, reaps both business and personal income rewards.

LOWER OVERHEAD

For businesses located in traditional offices, rent is the second highest overhead expense (payroll is the highest). In some locations, such as New York City, rent can be *the* largest expense. Therefore, if an employer doesn't have to provide working space for an employee, the company's overhead decreases. This applies both to the primary floor space occupied by the employee's desk and to secondary space, such as that occupied by lunchrooms, restrooms, and parking space. It also reduces related service and utility costs, such as costs for security guards, janitorial services, heating, cooling, and electricity.

If the business engages the home-based worker as a subcontractor rather than hiring him or her as an employee, another important item of overhead can be reduced: fringe benefits. The combination of payroll taxes, health coverage, paid vacation and holidays, and other employee benefits adds between 25 percent and 50 percent to the employee's base salary.

Some of these expenses, including Social Security taxes, must be assumed by the subcontractor and thus are passed onto the employer in the form of a higher fee, but it still generally results in a lower overall cost to the business. This is because the subcontractor can design a package of discretionary benefits that most satisfies his or her particular needs, rather than getting stuck with a standardized employee package. For instance, the subcontractor may already be covered under a spouse's plan and not need health insurance.

In addition, whether engaged as a subcontractor or hired as an employee, the person working at home realizes other cost savings. No more daily commuting expenses; no more need for a full-time work wardrobe; no more daily lunches in restaurants. Parents of small children can eliminate or reduce child-care expenses. And, if it qualifies, the home office itself can provide significant income tax deductions. These cost savings give home-based workers room to negotiate a price that satisfies them and the companies that hire them.

OPPORTUNITY

The combination of higher productivity and lower overhead brought about by a home-based work force means increased business opportunity. Entrepreneurs can initiate home-based businesses without draining start-up capital for rent and related expenses. Small businesses can afford to grow because they don't have to spend money on "bricks" in order to house additional staff. Established businesses, by shifting away from costly on-site work forces, can lower or at least maintain their costs and thus stimulate demand for their products and services.

The option to work at home also opens up employment potential for people who otherwise would not be able to enter the work force. They include caretakers—parents who stay home to care for young children, adult children caring for infirm elderly parents, and people who care for the severely handicapped. They also include the home-bound disabled, people in isolated rural areas where there are no businesses, factories, or public transportation, and non-English-speaking individuals.

When these capable but previously unemployed people enter the work force as home-based workers, they do so in entry-level positions and, because of the cost savings generated by working at home, at lower labor costs to their employers. This in turn generates more jobs in this country by making the American labor force more competitive with foreign labor. It also means more wage earners buying more consumer goods and services.

DISSEMINATION OF TECHNOLOGY

Working at home has become a viable option for a wide range of professionals and business people due primarily to two technological advances: personal computers and telecommunications links. The powerful business software programs developed for personal computers mean that one or two people can administer a business operation without a large support staff. Telecommunications links mean that it really doesn't matter where an office is located; vast research resources, markets, and delivery services can be brought in over the telephone lines.

In turn, the proliferation of computerized, on-line home offices will spur further investment and development in telecommunications technology. Computer manufacturers, software publishers, long-distance phone services, information utilities—all will realize new market openings because of the dual consumer-business nature of the home office. Already items such as copiers and electronic typewriters, which several years ago were considered strictly business equipment, are making the jump into the home, and the home office is one of the major reasons.

4

Breaking Out on Your Own

Who hasn't at some time or another been stuck in traffic, pondering how the heck to get out of the nine-to-five office grind? Sure, working at home would solve the problem, along with making numerous tax advantages available and expanding career opportunities. But just how do you make the break?

There are two basic escape routes. One is to quit your job and go into business for yourself, maybe in the same field and maybe not. The other is to remain an employee but to join a work-at-home program. If your present employer doesn't have one, you can either try to get one started or find a company that does have one. Which route is right for you depends on the type of work you do and your ability (and desire) to deal with risk.

THE INDEPENDENT SUBCONTRACTOR

Going it alone in the business world sounds scary. Gone are regular paychecks, company fringe benefits, written job descriptions, and annual reviews. No more management consensus, corporate goals, or office give-and-take. Instead, lone entrepreneurs must determine their own goals, manage their own cash flow, produce their own results. It's not a life that everyone is cut out for.

But bright energetic professionals are discovering that the entrepreneurial option may not be as scary as the most recent demographic fallout from the postwar baby boom. It's a basic fact of corporate geometry that the higher up on the management pyramid one is, the fewer the opportunities for advancement. As the baby boom generation hits the professional juncture between middle and top management, legions will be halted in their march to the corporate suite. It won't matter how hard you study, or how hard you work, or how many years you've spent in a particular field or company—there simply isn't room at the top for everyone.

So what to do? Some casualties of the promotion ceiling give in and wait for early retirement; others jump back and forth between companies, pursuing elusive cracks in the door to opportunity; a few make midlife career changes, seeking rewards other than professional accolades.

Those with confidence in themselves and a strong desire for independence often try to start their own businesses. But instead of making a complete leap into the extremely risky, failure-prone world of the entrepreneur, they make a more conservative initial step by becoming independent subcontractors, providing their skills and knowledge under contract to previous employers, business contacts, and associates developed over the years. Essentially, they continue doing the same work they did as employees, and quite often for their former employers, but now they are their own bosses.

The advantages to converting from being an employee to being an independent subcontractor are numerous: The independent subcontractor has increased flexibility in work schedule, increased opportunities to pursue related or unrelated interests, increased financial reward derived from tax advantages, and in most cases higher productivity.

The client contracting the services cuts down on payroll taxes and lowers overhead. In addition, fluctuating workloads are better met by gearing up with outside help rather than by keeping workers on staff. Former employees operating as independent subcontractors are familiar with company procedures and well trained in job particulars.

Do You Have What It Takes?

We commonly think of writers, graphic artists, and photographers as freelancers, which is just another word for independent subcontractors. But this route to freedom isn't limited strictly to artistic fields. A lawyer, faced with the reality that she may never make partner, quits the firm and is called in on an hourly basis to consult on specific cases; a data processor leaves a salaried, nine-to-five position but continues to key information from a home terminal on a piecework basis; a corporate financial officer starts a consulting practice to aid companies looking for capital.

The major criteria for becoming a successful independent subcontractor are:

1. Your job basically is a one-person task. You may talk on the phone a lot or go to meetings, but when it comes right down to it, you can accomplish your job without the physical presence of coworkers, save perhaps some secretarial support. Obviously someone working on an automobile assembly line couldn't do the job alone; but most office work qualifies. In fact, most interaction in offices is basically nonessential and often nonproductive.

2. You like your work. Without a "boss" you will have to motivate yourself, and the best form of motivation is to find some enjoyment in your work and accomplishments.

3. You understand and are willing to accept the responsibilities of running a business. Suddenly, things that you might never have thought about will be very important, like keeping track of expenses, looking for business leads, filing reports with governmental agencies.

4. You find risk exciting. Put another way, when you wake up in the middle of the night in a cold sweat because a project isn't done or the bills are piling up and the income isn't, you jump out of bed and start working, rather than just lie there whimpering.

What Is an Independent Subcontractor?

There are three major differences between an employee and an independent subcontractor. First, the subcontractor is an independent business person, in business either as a sole proprietor, a member of a partnership, or an officer and sole stockholder in a corporation. But no matter how it is legally organized, the business will almost certainly have to register and file reports with federal, state, and local agencies. The independent subcontractor takes on the responsibility of generating business opportunities; estimating, billing, and collecting payments; paying expenses; keeping business records; and so forth.

On the other hand, an employee performs assigned duties to his or her employer's satisfaction—that is, he or she does a job. It's the employer's responsibility to make sure a job exists to be done.

Second, independent subcontractors usually work under written contracts that define *results*—that is, what tasks are to be performed for or delivered to the client by a certain deadline. The number of hours and cost of supplies it takes to fulfill the contract are the independent subcontractor's responsibility—and risk. If it takes less time to do the job than was estimated, the independent subcontractor should make a good profit; if it takes more, then there may be a loss.

In contrast, employees are usually paid on the basis of *time* spent on the job, regardless of what they accomplish during that time. If an employee is very productive, the employer benefits; if the employee is unproductive, the employer suffers the loss.

Third, and most importantly, an independent subcontractor is paid on the basis of a flat fee or rate. The client has no payroll tax liabilities for the payment. Independent subcontractors must report their own income and estimate and pay their own income taxes and self-employment taxes.

An employee doesn't have this responsibility; it is placed on the employer, who is bound by law to calculate, withhold, report and regularly deposit payroll taxes with the government—a not insignificant bookkeeping task. The employer must also pay employer contributions to FICA and federal and state unemployment funds, which can account for an additional 8 percent to 14 percent of the employee's gross salary.

Because of these tax ramifications, the IRS has several tests to determine whether someone claiming to be an independent subcontractor is actually a regular employee trying to avoid tax withholding. The primary test is the amount of work independence the independent subcontractor has from the client's direct supervision and control. If you contract to deliver certain results, and the timing, location, approach, and method you utilize to achieve these results are up to you, then you probably will qualify as a subcontractor. If, on the other hand, you are required to be at a certain location during certain hours each day, and each task is assigned, observed, and reviewed by a manager, you are going to be hard pressed to prove you're not an employee.

It follows then that work location is crucial, and of course, this is where the home office comes in. Start-up businesses, especially one-person operations, rarely can justify or afford to lease space in commercial office buildings. Such an overhead expense would place too great a burden on a business that is just beginning to build up clients and regular cash flow. The home office not only frees a new entrepreneur from the tyranny of monthly rent payments but, if it qualifies under IRS requirements, lends support to an independent subcontractor status.

To determine whether or not you are a valid independent subcontractor, the IRS will also consider the amount of investment you make in equipment and supplies, which indicates that you own your own "tools of the trade." The number of clients you service is also important. A one-person operation working for one client may mean trouble with the IRS, so it is imperative to try and find other clients, even if they provide work only now and then and don't represent very much income.

Further, try to bill on a project basis rather than on a time basis. Not only is this important to your tax status, but it will give you an opportunity to reap the rewards of a higher-than-normal productivity rate.

"Have I Got a Deal for You!"

The best way to convince your employer to hire you as an independent subcontractor is to show how cost-effective it will be. To do this, you must propose a price for your services that translates into a real cash savings for the employer and yet accounts for the fact that you will have to assume payment for lost fringe benefits, supplies, and equipment. The trick is to find an optimum price—one that saves the employer money and at the same time lets you walk away with more money than you presently earn on the payroll.

Using the worksheet in Figure 4-1, first enter estimates for the line items on the "Employee" side of the page. These represent typical cash outlays necessary to keep a worker on the payroll.

Gross wages. If you are a salaried employee, enter your current annual compensation. If you are paid on an hourly basis, enter what you earn during a typical work week times the weeks you work per year, including any overtime compensation. You can use your gross wages from last year's W-2 form, unless you recently experienced a significant raise or pay cut.

Employer FICA contribution. As an employee, you share the cost of FICA contributions equally with your employer. In 1985, the employer's share was 7.05 percent of employee gross wages up to $39,600 (any amount over this is not subject to FICA). Calculate this amount and add it in.

Employer contribution to state unemployment and disability funds. Again these costs are shared by the employer and employee and are based on a percentage of gross wages, up to a certain limit. The percentage varies from state to state and sometimes from business to business. Ask your employer's bookkeeper or payroll clerk what the *employer's* rate of contribution is (not what may be withheld from your wages).

Federal unemployment tax. This amount is paid entirely by the employer. Like state unemployment contributions, it is a percentage of gross wages up to a certain limit, and the *effective* rate varies depending on what your employer pays into the state unemployment fund. Ask the bookkeeper.

Figure 4-1 Employee/Subcontractor Worksheet

Employee			Independent Subcontractor		
1. Gross wages	$		1. Gross wages	$	
2. Employer FICA contributions	+$		2. Annual insurance premiums	+$	
3. Employer state unemployment contributions	+$		3. Other fringes	+$	
			4. Sum	$	
4. Federal unemployment contributions	+$		5. Estimated home-office deductions	−$	
5. Insurance premiums	+$		6. Estimated net income	$	
6. Pension/profit sharing	+$		7. Self-employment tax	+$	
7. Miscellaneous fringes	+$		8. Straight business expenses	+$	
Employer's cash outlay to keep you on the payroll	$		Gross annual income required by you	$	

Insurance premiums. If your employer provides health and/or life insurance coverage, ask what the cash equivalents of your monthly premiums are. If any part of the premium is considered taxable income, disregard it; it will be included in your gross wages.

Pension or profit-sharing plans. If your employer offers such plans, find out what the cash equivalent of the employer's contribution is, not what is withheld from your paycheck.

Miscellaneous benefits. Among these might be any *tax-free* day-care services, health club membership or exercise facilities, meals, lodgings, expense reimbursements, bonuses, stock options, etc. (If any of these benefits are taxable, disregard them, since they should show up on your W-2 form as gross wages.) Ask your employer what the cash equivalent for these various benefits would be, since it might be difficult for you to figure them out independently.

The sum of these estimates represents only part of an employer's cost of keeping you on the payroll. It does not include the office furniture, supplies, and equipment you require to do your job, secretarial support, office space, managerial oversight, and administrative costs associated with keeping track of all of this.

What it does represent is a benchmark in your negotiating range. If you offer to provide your services at approximately the same price as the sum of the items under "Employee" in Figure 4-1, your employer will perceive that he or she is still saving money.

The Contract Price

Now you must determine *your* bottom line contract price—what you will have to charge to maintain your present level of personal income and at the same time take into account the added expense and the tax advantages that will result when you work out of a home office. To do this go back to the worksheet in Figure 4-1, and fill in the estimates on the side of the worksheet headed "Independent Subcontractor."

Gross wages. This is the equivalent of your current base salary, minus any *taxable* benefits such as life insurance premiums, bonuses, day-care services, and other fringe benefits. Gross wages are essentially your starting point for calculating a price, because several of the other line items will be percentages of the figure you enter on this line. Initially, enter the base salary you now earn as an employee.

Health and life insurance premiums. This is the most common benefit lost by breaking out of the conventional work world, and you must find suitable alternative coverage for you and your family. Group rates are generally lower than rates for individual policies, so check out local HMOs and other group-oriented health-care providers and insurers. Almost all professional associations like the American Bar Association and the American Medical Association offer group coverage to members. Unless your business is incorporated and you are covered by a company plan that qualifies under IRS regulations, the cost of your health and life insurance premiums is not deductible. Add your estimated yearly premiums to gross wages.

Other lost fringe benefits. This might include pension and profit-sharing programs, health club memberships, day care, meals, lodgings, annual bonuses—whatever you used to calculate how much it cost your employer in fringe benefits to keep you on the payroll under the section headed "Employee." Only consider those that you actually will want to replace. For instance, if you don't use the company day-care facility, don't include it in your "Lost Fringes" calculation. Draw a sum on line 4.

Estimated home office-related deductions. After identifying the area of your home that will be put aside for regular and exclusive business use and which will otherwise qualify under the IRS requirements discussed in Chapter 2, estimate the percentage of square footage that the home office will occupy. Apply this percentage against what you are currently paying for utilities, real estate taxes, mortgage interest, or rent. This amount, plus any depreciation you may be able to claim, will become business expenses and thus deductible on Schedule C, Profit or Loss from a Business or Profession. *Subtract* this amount from the line above. The remainder is a rough estimate of your net income, used to calculate the next item.

Self-employment tax. As an independent subcontractor, you must assume the entire burden of FICA contributions, rather than sharing it with your employer. However, self-employment tax is calculated on the *net* profit from your business, not on *gross* wages, and at least until 1990 will not be as high as the combined employer-employee rates. (For example, in 1985 the combined FICA contributions for employees was 14.1 percent of gross wages. The self-employment tax was 11.8 percent of net profit.) Calculate your projected self-employment tax using your estimated net profit and the current tax rate.

Business operation expenses. In order to run your own office, you will have to pay for your own supplies, phone service, travel expenses, postage, copies, subscriptions to periodicals and information utilities, promotion costs, service contracts on equipment, business insurance, etc. These are expenses that are related entirely and directly to your business operation, ones that were previously assumed by an employer and now must be added into your cost of doing business. The remaining chapters of this book will provide information on the typical equipment needs, supplies, services, and other costs associated with the home office.

If you are wondering why these business operation expenses are added at this point and not before calculating your self-employment tax, the reason is that while they will be passed on to your client and thus be part of your gross income, they also are totally deductible and should net to zero when calculating net profit from your business.

The total of lines 6, 7, and 8 should represent approximately what you must earn each year as an independent subcontractor and maintain your present level of personal income. If you plan to charge on the basis of an hourly rate, divide this sum by the number of hours you plan to devote to the business each year *minus* those hours you think will be spent on marketing and generally administering your business operation. (For example, fifty 40-hour work weeks make a 2,000-hour work year. However, if you think one day a week will be spent developing new client leads and on general administrative tasks, you will only have 1,600 "billable" hours.)

If you plan to charge on a project basis, you multiply your hourly rate, as derived above, times the number of hours you estimate it will take to complete the project. Then add the cost of any special supplies and services the project will require you to purchase.

The totals under "Employee" and "Independent Subcontractor" will serve as your two basic benchmarks for negotiating contract prices with your present employer and other potential clients. On the one hand, you can't charge significantly more than the "Employee" column because this would wipe out any financial advantage to your clients; on the other hand, you can't charge less than your own bottom line unless you are willing to accept a drop in personal income.

Of course, there may be a slight decrease in your personal spending habits, because you will not have to dress up every day and commute to the office, eat out at restaurants, or pay for child care. And you could take advantage of some of the other tax-saving strategies discussed in Chapter 2, such as hiring your spouse or dependent children.

But also remember that there is no state unemployment or disability compensation safety net for the self-employed. And small businesses are vulnerable to cycles of feast and famine, so it always makes sense to put something aside when the times are good.

"And Consider This. . . ."

Many employers and managers, while tempted by your carefully considered financial presentation, will still be reluctant to relinquish the control they perceive they have over an on-site employee. There are three additional points you should make to persuade a tradition-bound employer.

"You know I can be trusted." Although you should have a written agreement describing what you are expected to produce, how does an employer know you can actually achieve those results? First, your employer should have a good idea of your work habits and performance levels. Good managers know exactly which employees are self-motivated and conscientious, and which aren't. If your past work performance can't be used to answer this concern, then maybe you shouldn't be considering working at home.

Second, you know the job, since you're doing it already. Hiring you as a subcontractor won't involve anywhere near the learning curve that would be associated with subcontracting to someone else or hiring a new employee.

"I can be more productive and work on flexible schedules that benefit the business." Quite often companies have peak load times that strain overtime budgets. By hiring you as a subcontractor, the employer solves this problem, since you have no fixed work hours, only the requirement to produce certain results by a certain date. Also, studies have shown that people who work at home *are* more productive. Thus, turnaround time is reduced, which will increase the employer's competitive position.

"Decreased accessibility can be a plus." As horrific as it may sound to intracompany communications experts, increased interaction among business

associates is not necessarily productive. Think about it; haven't you sometimes found it easier to query a coworker or boss about a problem rather than try to figure it out yourself? How long do you remember such relayed solutions? How productive is it for the other person to stop what he or she is doing and answer your questions?

By physically separating yourself from your employer and coworkers, you will have to concentrate more on solving your own problems. More importantly, *others* won't be bugging you with every little thing. When the need to consult with your client arises (and vice versa), communication will tend to be more precise for two reasons. First, time is money, and neither you nor your client will want to spend time "chatting" extensively about irrelevancies. Second, because you work under contract, written communications will have a legal importance. Work specifications, modifications, and deadline extensions should be in writing in order to protect both parties. And when people have to write down something, they usually think more carefully about what they are requesting.

Other Contractual Terms

Regardless of how you feel about lawyers and written contracts, you should consult an attorney to help you draw up a good written agreement to present to potential clients. In addition, an attorney can also give you advice on what federal, state, and local forms you may be required to file in connection with your home-based business, refer you to an accountant who is up-to-date on home-office tax laws, and generally advise you about potential legal problems related to your specific business.

The more specifically a business relationship is spelled out in a written contract, the less probability the contract will ever have to be tested. This is because all parties have a clear understanding of their responsibilities before agreeing to be bound. Figure 4-2 is a sample of a freelance artist's "Letter of Agreement" with a toy manufacturer, which contains sample clauses covering their business relationship.

Description of services. This should be as detailed as possible and reflect exactly the information you used to calculate your price. In the sample contract, the artist contracted to produce six black-and-white, quarter-page drawings to be used in advertisements. Of course, things might change: The toy manufacturer might decide it wants four half-page color drawings instead. As long as this change is reflected in the price and can be delivered by the deadline, everyone should be happy.

Delivery. This clause describes the material that the toy manufacturer must provide the artist, in this case a model of the toy being advertised, and the date

Figure 4-2 Sample Letter of Agreement with Client

GINNY LESLIE STUDIOS, INC.
608 Washington Avenue
Columbus, Ohio 34085

September 6, 1986

Mr. Jeff Bunyon
Pope Playthings, Inc.
14 Prince Street
Columbus, Ohio 34085

Dear Mr. Bunyon:

This letter when signed in the space provided below will constitute our agreement regarding my services for Pope Playthings, Inc.

Services to be provided and materials to be prepared by me shall include:

> Six B/W line drawings measuring 5 inches square of your new doll called "Sweet Sadie"

Upon your signing this letter you will provide me with all necessary models and specifications required for me to perform my services, including:

> A sample model of "Sweet Sadie"

I shall deliver my services and materials as follows:

> Rough sketches: by September 15, 1986, to be returned by you with written comments by September 20.
> Final art: by September 30, 1986.

As a fee for my services and to reimburse me for all my expenses connected herewith, you will pay me as follows:

> $300 upon delivery of rough sketches;
> $300 upon acceptance of final art. You agree to accept final art or to request specific changes in writing, not inconsistent with your written comments on the rough art, within three business days of final art delivery. Any changes to final art shall be made by me within three business days, and upon delivery of the revised final art, the $300 payment shall be paid to me.

I grant you all rights in and to the final art work, and any part thereof, throughout the world including the right to print, publish, sell, display them in all media and to otherwise deal with them in such manner as you deem appropriate.

We agree that I am an independent subcontractor. I shall not be entitled to any benefits of an employee. I shall be solely responsible for compliance with federal, state, and local laws and regulations relating to taxes and Social Security payments that may be required to be made by me in connection with payments made by you hereunder.

This agreement represents the entire agreement between you and me and shall not be subject to any waiver, modification, or discharge except in writing signed by us both. No representations or conditions are made by either of us except as

> expressly contained in this agreement. This agreement shall be interpreted in accordance with the laws of the State of Ohio.
>
> If the above terms are in accordance with our understanding and agreement, please sign where indicated below and return the original letter to me. You may keep the copy for your files.
>
> It is a pleasure to be working with you.
>
> Very truly yours,
>
> Ginny Leslie Studios, Inc.
>
> By: _____
>   President
>
> Agreed and Accepted:
>
> Pope Playthings, Inc.
>
> By: _____   Date: _____
>   Jeff Bunyon, President

for delivery of such. It also specifies the deadline for the artist to deliver rough sketches, the turnaround time the toy manufacturer has to approve such sketches, and the date for delivery of the final drawings.

If your services repeat over time, such as processing a certain number of forms per week, or monthly bookkeeping, or handling an annual advertising account, then the delivery clause would also spell out the term of the contract—that is, the date the services commence, how often they are to be performed, and the date the contract terminates. For example, an accountant doing monthly updates to a company's general ledger might insert the following language: "Commencing July 1, 1985, and ending June 30, 1986, you shall deliver to my office on the tenth of each month all records of income received and expenses paid during the previous month. By the fifteenth of each month covered by this agreement, I shall deliver to your office an updated general ledger reflecting cumulative financial activity to date for the year ending 6/30/86."

Payment. Besides containing the price agreed to for the drawings, this clause spells out when and how payment will be made. In the sample letter, the artist will be paid one half the price upon delivery of rough sketches and the other half upon the toy manufacturer's acceptance of the final drawings.

Payment for on-going services, such as those of the accountant just discussed, might be made on certain dates each month, much like a professional retainer. In addition, any expenses that are to be reimbursed by the client and not considered part of a flat fee must be specified in the agreement. For example, if you are required to make business trips on the behalf of and at the request of your client, such extraordinary expenses should either be paid for directly by the client or reimbursed upon presentation of a paid receipt.

Ownership of materials. Sometimes a subcontractor's services involve certain rights, such as the copyright to the artist's drawings in the sample contract. *Who* owns these rights must be defined in the agreement. In addition, if the client provides materials or equipment that you must use to perform your services, such as supplying you with a computer terminal, then the liability for these materials and equipment should be addressed. In this area especially, you should consult an attorney to make sure you don't give up your rights to your work unless that's part of the negotiated agreement with the client, and to help limit your liability for client's property that might be located in your office.

Independent subcontractor. This paragraph defines your status as an independent subcontractor not subject to employee withholdings, unemployment contributions, insurance, vacation, and other employee benefits. This is necessary to define and protect your status as an independent business and to limit your client's responsibilities.

Miscellaneous provision. These are simple boilerplate clauses covering such things as: under what terms either you or your client can assign the responsibilities described in the agreement; under what conditions the agreement can be modified; according to which state's laws it will be interpreted; and so on. Again, depending on the specific nature of your business, it's best to get an attorney's advice on these clauses.

There will of course be times when a client will want to insert additional clauses protecting his or her rights, such as a provision that you not discuss any of the company's business with competitors or provide your services to competitors. In some instances, your client will want you to sign their contract rather than agree to enter into yours. In any event, if you have any doubts about the concepts or language being proposed, consult an attorney.

WORK-AT-HOME EMPLOYEES

Not all types of occupations that could realistically be performed at home lend themselves to independent subcontractor status. Some don't involve enough independent work performance to qualify under IRS regulations. For example, a transcriber who calls a central tape bank, transcribes the recording, and sends the output back over the phone line to a central word-processing unit might be considered to be under the direct supervision and control of the central office. Therefore, the transcriber might be considered an employee for tax purposes.

Moreover, some workers are not willing or able to assume the financial risk associated with being in business on their own, or to shoulder the general administrative and marketing responsibilites that are involved. Or perhaps they would like to test the waters of working at home before making the jump to the world of the independent subcontractor. For them, a better route would be to remain an employee but to enroll in a work-at-home program.

These programs, whether formally organized or informally worked out between individual employees and supervisors, are more common than most people think. In early 1985, over 450 major corporations, including Blue Cross/Blue Shield, New York Telephone, Control Data, and American Express, had work-at-home programs involving over 100,000 workers. A large number work directly with computers as data processors, transcribers, catalog sales operators, computer programmers, and so forth. Others rely heavily on computers as tools in their work. And since most are linked to their central offices via phone lines and telecommunications equipment, they are often called *telecommuters*.

In addition, an untold number of people are involved in industrial homework—in crafts, electronic assembly, and the garment industries, to mention only a few. They take work assignments on a per-piece basis, with the materials and designs supplied by the employer.

Other types of salaried jobs that lend themselves to work-at-home programs are: insurance, booking and travel agents; researchers and analysts; telemarketing representatives; field representatives; and sales representatives.

Work-at-home employees retain the same tax status as employees who work in the central office. They have income and Social Security taxes withheld from their base pay and are entitled to the same employee benefits, review procedures, and unemployment compensation.

Whether they are entitled to home-office deductions for portions of utilities, real estate taxes, mortgage interest, or rent depends on the same factors discussed in Chapter 2: the home office must be used exclusively and regularly as their principal work site. In addition, the home office must be *at the convenience of the employer* and not the employee. Suppose a parent wanted to work at home for a year after the birth of a child. Even if the employer agreed to the arrangement, the employee would not be able to take a home-office deduction. On the other hand, if a typesetter hired employees to enter text on terminals in their homes because the company did not have the facilities at its work site, the at-home employees would be able to take the home-office deduction, assuming of course that they met the other tests.

Written Employment Contract

Employees working at home should have an employment contract with their employers that, in addition to describing the position and salary, clearly defines the following:

1. That the at-home employee is an employee and entitled to all the same benefits and protections that are extended to other employees, including employer's Social Security and unemployment compensation contributions.

Don't forget to include paid vacations and holidays, insurance coverage and pension plans, if included in the standard benefit package.

2. If applicable, that the employee must work at home as a condition of employment and as a convenience to the employer. The contract should directly state that the employer cannot and will not make adequate work space available at its business facilities. The employer should also state that there are no federal or state prohibitions against the employee working at home, and whether or not the employee is required to maintain any forms or handbooks under government regulations. (The Fair Standards Labor Act requires certain types of home-based workers to maintain homework handbooks showing hours worked and payment received, in order to enforce minimum-wage laws.)

3. Whether the employee is required to come to the employer's work site on a regular basis, and if so, when. The results of several work-at-home experiments show that employee morale benefits from regular weekly face-to-face contact with the employer. Thus some of the programs require the at-home employee to come into the central office one or two days a week.

4. What standards will be used to determine satisfactory job performance, who will be in charge of supervising and evaluating job performance, and performance review schedules. This should eliminate any confusion over production standards, lines of communications, and work hours (if standard hours are important to the employer). It should also keep the at-home employee from falling off the promotion ladder simply because he or she is not in front of the manager's eyes on a daily basis.

5. What expenses will be paid directly by the employer, what expenses will be reimbursed by the employer, and what expenses must be assumed by the employee. For instance, if a telephone line for data transmission must be installed in the home office, the employer should pay the expenses to the phone company directly. If the employee must use his or her own car on business trips, mileage should be reimbursed by the employer along with other travel and entertainment expenses. If the employee must furnish and equip the home office, then the equipment and furnishings belong to the employee and this also should be stated in the contract.

Important tax considerations to remember: reimbursements greater than the employee's qualified business expenses are treated as taxable income; unreimbursed expenses (i.e., those that the employee is expected to assume under the employment agreement, not those for which the employee simply fails to submit a request for reimbursement) can be deducted, but only on Schedule A (unless you qualify as an outside salesperson). All employee business expenses must be supported by detailed, contemporaneous logs and/or receipts.

Finding Work-at-Home Programs

Blue Cross/Blue Shield, Mountain Bell Telephone, American Express, Aetna Insurance, Infodyne, Honeywell, Reynolds and Reynolds, Digital Dispatch, AT&T, Bell Atlantic, Citibank, Equitable Life, General Motors, Hartford Insurance, IBM, Montgomery Ward, J.C. Penney, New York Telephone, and Xerox Corporation are only a small sampling of companies that either have or are considering work-at-home programs. However, some of the programs are limited to hiring the homebound disabled, and some are restricted to employees who would otherwise be on disability or childbirth leave.

By far the greatest number of formal work-at-home programs sponsored by large corporations are in the data processing and computer programming fields. Local computer science schools and training programs might be able to provide leads on employment possibilities or actually put you in touch with recruiters. Local classified ads and employment agencies might not be looking specifically for work-at-home employees, but they can provide good leads for who's hiring. It then will be up to you to convince potential employers that they will benefit by instituting a work-at-home program.

Small and very fast-growing businesses are also prime candidates to approach for work-at-home employment. These companies would perhaps like to expand their staffs but don't because they are reluctant to expand their facilities. And, of course, other home-based businesses will understand and appreciate the concept of hiring you as their home-based employee.

Persons who are homebound due to emotional or physical disabilities but who are otherwise capable of working can inquire through state vocational rehabilitation agencies, the Veterans Administration, and disability insurance carriers about work-at-home programs. Control Data, for instance, offers a 500-hour vocational training course in computer programming for the disabled called "Homework." Control Data installs a terminal in the trainee's home or rehabilitation center, provides computerized lessons, and then assists in finding employment. Disability benefits do not terminate until a program graduate is actually employed.

5

Creating Your Home Work Space

The office environment is a relatively new arena for human labor. Prior to the Industrial Revolution, few businesses were large enough to require workers who did nothing other than administer and manage. Prior to the 1890s, there were no telephones, typewriters, calculators, or copying machines. The "office" as we know it, didn't exist.

Today, over 50 percent of the working population works in an office. Large corporations hire highly trained and highly priced architects and interior designers to design and furnish their office buildings. Office-design concepts gave most of us our first encounters with "high tech" and even added a new word to our vocabulary: *ergonomics*. In tune with whatever is the latest management theory, office designers have either enclosed us in separate cubicles, or stranded us in a sea of openness, or placed us in flexible "work stations" defined by movable wall panels.

Unfortunately, little of what they have created has anything to do with the realities of a home office. Home-office workers generally have to make do with what they have: a home selected not on the basis that it would make a good office but on the basis that it would make a good home. Even if you are looking for a house or apartment with the idea of creating a home office, you will find few residences designed to meet this requirement.

WHAT MAKES THE "RIGHT" SPACE?

The space for a home office must be carefully carved out of what was previously living space; it must be made ready to accommodate furnishings, files, equipment, visitors, and perhaps employees; and most of all it must *function* as an office. Accomplishing this is a challenge requiring a great deal of ingenuity. And, frankly, that's part of the fun. The home office can be the ultimate in personalized work space and at the same time a cost-effective, comfortable, and efficient business location. Keep the following considerations in mind as you walk around your home looking for the best place to locate your office.

Tax Considerations

As discussed in Chapter 2, one of the requirements for qualifying for home-office deductions is that the space be used *exclusively* for business purposes. This means that there must be some way of defining where the personal part of the home ends and the office begins. It also means that there should be *no* personal-use items, such as beds or recreational electronics, located in the office area.

This is important because, as also discussed in Chapter 2, the burden of proof to show that the space is used only for business purposes is on the taxpayer; the IRS takes the position that a home is generally not a valid business location.

What does this mean to the office layout? It means that separate rooms, levels and structures make the best home offices, since there can be no doubt about their boundaries.

Sometimes utilizing such self-contained areas simply involves rethinking a traditional layout. A freelance graphic artist, for instance, who lives in a one-bedroom apartment wants to create a home studio. Initially, she considers converting part of her living/dining room into a studio; but since she does a good deal of entertaining, she decides it would be almost impossible to keep the studio exclusively for business use. So instead, she converts the bedroom into a studio and puts a convertible sofa bed and free-standing wardrobe in the living room. In addition to providing strong definition to the respective business and personal areas, this move also allows work in progress to remain undisturbed simply by closing the studio door.

If no distinctly separate room is available for the office, then you will have to create the dividing line between the work space and the rest of the home. Look for alcoves and other recessed spaces that, with the use of a screen or curtain, can become "separate." Consider large rooms that can be divided in two with a free-standing bookcase or furniture grouping. Just make sure that there is some sort of discernible boundary you can point to when you say "Here is my home office."

Another important tax consideration is to devote as much space to business use as possible. This will allow you to deduct a greater portion of your utilities, mortgage interest, real estate taxes, or rent as home-office expenses. The square footage doesn't have to be contiguous: Old files stored in the attic or garage, supplies kept in a linen closet, bookcases lining a hallway will all entitle you to include additional square footage in your home-office calculation, as long as the space in question is used exclusively for business purposes.

Privacy

The most classic privacy problem associated with a home office involves young children: It seems the temptation to wander into the office or pick up telephone extensions is almost too great to resist. The only ways to protect yourself against this type of invasion are closed doors, separate phone lines, and firm instructions that during working hours you are not to be disturbed except in case of an emergency. It's an instruction that will require repetition and, with a little more diplomacy, might even work with overly friendly neighbors.

Other adults living in the same home might be expected to be more sympathetic to the need for privacy but rarely are. Even though they generally exercise more self-discipline over directly demanding attention during working hours, they also tend to be more miffed when criticized for indirect interruptions, such as using the phone, running the vacuum cleaner, or asking if you know where yesterday's newspaper is. Feeling that, "By gum, it's my house too," they may feel the office is a serious intrusion on *their* freedom and privacy. The solution to these problems can be partially found through the proper layout of the office.

In general, direct interruptions can be reduced by separating the office as much as possible from the rest of the home and locating it away from heavy traffic routes. A room at the end of a hall will have less walk-by traffic than one located next to the kitchen, for instance. Have some way to signal "Do not disturb"—either a closed door, a drawn screen, or at very least, a turned back.

The telephone, which is the lifeline of a home office, also can be the source of nuisance calls. You can avoid personal calls during work hours by installing a separate business line and turning the ringer off on the residential line when you are busy. Or install a telephone answering machine that gives you the option to screen incoming calls before deciding whether you want to pick up the receiver or not.

Distracting sounds in the office environment are more insidious than people or telephone calls. In traditional offices there is a certain level of ambient or background noise that creates a sound barrier. The clatter of typewriters or printers, the ringing of telephones, the conversations in other offices, all blend together to keep any one sound from rising to discernible proportions. But in a home office the relative quiet makes almost all sounds discernible. Sudden conversations in the next room or even next door, or the neighbor's barking dogs, or the washing machine switching cycles, or trucks rolling down the street become very distracting.

One way to protect your office from intrusive noise is through soundproofing. Heavy drapes, carpets, and acoustic ceiling tiles will absorb noise, as will wall-mounted corkboards and bookcases. Another way is to select a location with a low level of white noise. Or create the background noise yourself with music or one of the commercially available white-noise recordings of rain or surf.

A warning at this point: Achieving ultimate privacy and a distractionless environment in a home office can be a hazard in itself. Imagine being locked alone in a soundproofed room with no windows and no communication with the outside world. The sense of isolation will soon grow into an overwhelming distraction. What's going on out there? What's everybody doing? What am I missing?

The home-office worker should create a space that affords some relief from this threat of isolation. Windows that look out over a landscape or cityscape are best. They allow a brief involvement with the outside world in a general, grand way—sort of the visual equivalent of white noise. Unfortunately, not all home offices have windows, much less interesting views out them. So substitutions must be found. One simple but visually intriguing solution is an illuminated tank of tropical fish. Whatever the solution, the point is that there is a fine line between privacy and isolation. A few minor interruptions are probably a blessing for the person working in a home office.

Image

If clients or customers never visit your home office, then you can allow your personal decorating eccentricities to run rampant without fear of ridicule. On the other hand, if you *ever* expect business-related visits, then how the office is furnished and decorated will greatly influence your business image.

It's important to realize first of all that home offices in general already fight an uphill battle trying to be taken seriously. The more "homey" the decor—overstuffed couches, fireplaces, wet bars, frilly drapes, plush rugs—the more difficulty others have in perceiving the home office as a place where a serious trade or business is conducted. While such furnishings might confer status in corporate boardrooms, in a home office they can defeat the business intent. They might place your tax deductions in question, too.

Does this mean that you must stick with a barren desk, a chair or two, a picture or two, and maybe a plant? Luckily, no. Professional office planners now realize that the memorabilia collected from an individual's professional and personal life can provoke creativity and provide a subliminal sense of security.

Offices are much more personal places than they were 20 years ago, when the clean-desk, strictly-business syndrome was the vogue.

What makes a "right" image depends on your profession. A lawyer might seem out of place, at least in some potential clients' minds, practicing out of an office that looks like a cluttered Victorian living room complete with lace curtains; while a child psychologist may intimidate young patients by conducting sessions in a sleek, ultramodern, minimal office. Not that either style is wrong; it's just that the images might be inappropriate to the respective professions.

Flexibility

In the same way a home office is carved out of living space, it may someday be converted back. Thus, any alterations which would preclude its return to personal use will ultimately reduce the value of your property, not only for you but for prospective buyers or renters. This would include alterations such as built-in fluorescent lighting and store fronts.

In addition, if the office area is visible from the personal area, then it should be decorated in a manner that allows it to blend in with or complement the general decor of the home. There also should be some way to conceal work in process. Office furniture stores offer numerous variations on the old rolltop desks. One has a second work surface that flips down over the desktop, effectively and esthetically covering paper work. Another closes up like a steamer trunk.

Two-drawer filing cabinets come in woodgrain and formica finishes that blend into home decor and can be used as end tables. The home office can also be housed in a massive wall system that can be completely closed up at the end of the day, leaving no visual remnants of the business activity.

Access

How will clients or customers get to the home office? Will they have to get past a security lock on an apartment building door? Will they have to enter through the garage and traipse through the kitchen? Will they have to walk through the back yard where the dog is penned?

The access route is as important to the home-office image as the office itself. It's also a security factor: You may not want business visitors or repair persons to have access to the private areas of your residence as they come and go. Also remember that some delivery services charge extra for carrying cartons upstairs.

Utility Links

If you plan to use any of the myriad of electrically powered equipment common to most offices, check your home-office electrical circuit. The typical 15-amp household circuit can safely handle about 1,400 watts, or fourteen 100-watt light bulbs. Compare this with the electricity demands of a typewriter, computer, printer, copier, air conditioner, space heater, humidifier, pencil sharpener, answering machine, and/or dictating/transcribing machine, and you can start to understand the problem. The typical household circuit may not be able to carry the amperage necessary to run all this equipment. Overloading the circuit can not only cause repeated circuit breaks but could also present a serious fire hazard.

Also, beware of operating a computer on the same circuit as a refrigerator, washing machine, air conditioner, or other heavy household appliance. As they switch on and off, the appliances can create power fluctuations on the circuit and wreak havoc on the computer equipment and software.

Electrical wiring is not something to play around with, so unless you know what you're doing, the best advice is to call in an electrician to check out the electrical demands on your household system. If you have to do extensive rewiring to accommodate the home office, then consider having a separate meter installed so you can deduct the actual cost of office-related electrical usage.

Almost every home office also requires phone service. Many times the room or area which is to be converted to an office already has a phone. This phone can either be used as is or, through a relatively simple switch, converted to another, separate number. If you are considering installing a multiline phone for the business, any single-line phone cable that is currently in place will have to be removed and replaced with multiline cable. Depending on the construction of your home, this could become a very complex and expensive operation.

Task-Oriented Office Design

Who ever saw a clean desk in any office where real work was being generated? In a busy office, paper—the physical evidence of office work—is usually stacked on the desk and spilling onto chairs, bookshelves, credenzas, even the floor. This allows the worker to have ongoing access to projects that typically take days, weeks, or sometimes months to complete. And in the home office particularly, the worker juggles multiple tasks at once, requiring the paper work associated with each to be kept close at hand.

The prescribed method of handling the confusion that can result from multiple ongoing projects is multiple, task-oriented work areas. Each area is devoted to a category of task or a step in the work process. For example, you may create a "financial" area where you keep all financial and bookkeeping records, including the checkbook, ledgers, bills, and receipts. Or you may group the copier, postage meter, and stamps together, because everything that goes out of the office must be copied and packaged. A task-oriented work area doesn't necessarily require a separate desk or a lot of space; it could simply be a pull-out shelf in a bookcase.

Another benefit of multiple work areas is that they require you to get up and move around. Ideally, at least one area should require you to stand up, since this will help relieve the physical fatigue and back problems that often accompany prolonged desk work.

Storage

Eventually—hopefully—work gets completed, and the related materials must be filed. There are also office supplies, reference materials, financial records, and correspondence copies that must be put away somewhere. It's evident that storage space is a necessity for any office.

When the business is first starting out, desk drawers and two-drawer filing cabinets can usually accommodate the office's storage requirements. Four-drawer filing cabinets, the almost universal storage furniture, should be avoided if space in the home office is tight. They monopolize floor space without providing any additional function besides storage. A pair of two-drawer or three-drawer cabinets, on the other hand, can support a work surface while storing the same amount of records. Never let storage space squeeze out precious work space.

As the business grows and needs more room for storage, look for small areas *outside* the home office to devote to business-related storage, such as in hall closets, or along the wall in a bedroom, or in the garage. (Be careful about the storage of office supplies, however. High humidity and heat can render an investment in stationery, paper products, diskettes, and carbon ribbons worthless.) As long as these spaces are used exclusively and regularly in connection with your business (and, as already noted, there's not much else you can do with a space if a four-drawer filing cabinet is sitting there), then they should be counted in your square-foot calculations in allocating home-office deductions.

As is the case with personal papers, extremely important legal documents should be stored in a bank safety-deposit box. These might include contracts, important financial documents, and any proprietary information that is essential to your business.

Restrooms

If your home office is open to the public, you may be required under local law to provide restroom facilities. Even if you aren't open to the public, you must consider the needs of any business visitors or employees.

Since few of us would relish sharing our personal bathroom with relative strangers, the ideal situation would be for the home office to have its own, separate lavatory. This would also allow you to deduct the cost of restroom-related supplies.

If separate facilities aren't available, then your personal bathroom will have to double, in which case it's important that it be kept clean and that you remove any items of personal hygiene that you would not want to share with visitors or employees. Of course, if you never have business visitors or even temporary help, then you don't have to concern yourself with this issue.

Ergonomics

Ergonomics is a relatively new study of how individual workers physically fit into their work areas and work processes. It has become an important issue because of the widespread introduction of computers in offices. Office and equipment designers study lighting, seating height, back and arm rests, viewing distance, keyboard placement, document-holder position, and a myriad of other factors that physically affect the productivity of workers who spend long hours at computer terminals.

The results have been specially designed "ergonomically correct" computer workstations and accessories that can be bought at an office furniture store or ordered through the mail. Or by applying some of the principles discussed in this chapter, you can adapt more traditional office and home furniture. Whatever you do, just keep in mind that any work posture and environment has to maximize your physical comfort or you will find your productivity suffering.

Budget Savers

Before locating the space and furnishing a home office, you should carefully analyze the tasks you expect to accomplish there. This is the only way you can realistically evaluate your needs. For example, will you meet with visitors? Then you will need an extra chair in the office and perhaps a conference area. Will you have an employee or temporary help? This will require a separate work surface and chair.

Will you be using a computer, printer, monitor, and modem? If you're not sure about the answer to this question, then plan room for expansion when and if the need arises. Do you expect to put your computer on-line with an information utility or other telecommunications service? Perhaps you should plan to run two phone lines into the office, one for you and one for the computer.

Will you require library space for reference and resource material? Will you be storing extensive files or inventory? Will you be regularly generating correspondence and other paper work that will need copies? Will you do any bulk mailings?

Will you be using any especially heavy equipment that requires additional floor support? Any chemicals that require exhaust venting and special storage environments? Any materials that are ultrasensitive to dust and temperature changes?

Once you determine what work tasks will take place in your home office, you can assess how much space and what types of utility lines, furnishings, and equipment you will require. This should help you avoid two of the biggest wastes of resources: first, buying things you don't really need and won't use; and second, *not* buying the things you really do need, or not allowing enough space to effectively use them. If after setting aside a part of your home for an office, and furnishing and equipping it, you can't function effectively in it, then your efforts will be futile and the resources squandered.

Recycled household furnishings. After determining your needs, it's time to scavenge through castoff household furnishings to find those that can be used in the office. Prime candidates are: armchairs, couches, and coffee tables for conference areas; pictures, lamps, bookcases, wastebaskets, clocks, coat racks, drapes, window shades, and rugs; dining room sideboards that can store supplies and provide stand-up work surfaces; kitchen stools; card tables to serve as temporary work surfaces; kitchen wall cabinets to take advantage of vertical space. The only limitation on finding new uses for old household furnishings is your own imagination.

Second-hand office furniture. Due to tax considerations, businesses quite often decide to replace office furniture prior to the end of its useful life. Since the businesses aren't trying to make any money on these used items, you can find some great bargains at used office furniture sales.

Some commercial office furniture stores specialize in used furniture or periodically hold auctions. So do government agencies. Ask them to put your name on their mailing lists so you will get announcements of upcoming auctions.

But the best bet by far is to follow local classified ads and find businesses that are trying to unload items themselves. If you find an ad that seems interesting, call and ask for a complete description of the item, including any extra options; how old it is; how much use it's gotten; why they are selling; whether any manufacturer's warranty or service agreement still applies; who is responsible for transporting the item to your office if you buy it; what their bottom-line price is.

In general, used furniture is a better buy than used equipment. With furniture, you can see the actual condition and any need for repairs. It's an easy task to put on a new coat of paint, replace an electrical cord, or sand down a sticking drawer. But unless you're an experienced repair person, the actual condition of used equipment sometimes may not be evident. Also, manufacturer's warranties sometimes apply only to the original owner, and a servicer often will not offer service contracts on used equipment.

Do-it-yourself projects. Many of the office layouts that are discussed in the following section ("Six Sites for the Home Office") can be built by anyone with even a passing acquaintance with a hammer and saw. Essentially, these layouts are combinations of built-in bookcases, desks, cabinets, and closets. With the right tools, mechanical ability, and a little time, a homeowner can create the basic construction of the office. Electrical and plumbing installations are probably best left to professionals.

Even if you aren't up to built-in construction, there are simple ways to build your own office furniture. A piece of particle board laid across a pair of two-drawer filing cabinets, for example, creates a functional desk. Stacked and secured wooden wine crates make great bookcases.

Detailed plans for constructing office furniture and built-in work spaces are available in do-it-yourself, home improvement magazines such as *The Family Handyman* and *Mechanix Illustrated*. Visit the library to find back issues, or write the publishers for the plans.

SIX SITES FOR THE HOME OFFICE

Often the perfect space for the home office is as evident as the nose on your face and just as difficult for you to see. The eye tends to define space in the way it is accustomed to seeing it used: The front hall is for greeting visitors even though everybody comes in the back door; a closet is for hanging clothes even though they are rarely worn; a dining room is for meals even though the family always eats in the TV room. Each of these spaces can, with a little rethinking and refurbishing, be converted into a functional home office without sacrificing important living space.

Spare Room

As was discussed in Chapter 2, locating the home office in a separate room (or group of rooms) helps support the claim that it is used exclusively for business purposes. Thus, if possible, the spare room is the most desirable place for the home office and should be the first type of space sought.

Older homes quite often have extra rooms available, since they were built when the average family was larger than it is today; also, as children get older and leave home, their bedrooms can be converted to other uses. Basements, enclosed porches, attics and utility rooms offer unfinished square footage out of which a room can be built.

Homes with very high or two-story ceilings are good candidates for lofts. Lofts create additional square footage by dividing space horizontally. How the two areas created can be used depends on the amount of headroom. For example, if your ceiling is 12 feet high, you can create a sleeping loft with 4 feet of clearance and a space underneath the loft with 7 feet of headroom, enough for most people to feel comfortable standing. Anything less than 7 feet can be used for sitting areas, perhaps for dining or working at a desk. Designing and building a loft is not a matter for the amateur since the load-bearing capabilities of the floor and walls and how the supports are placed are essential construction elements.

A home office can also be created out of an underused room, such as a formal dining room or a guest room. Transfer the dining function to the living room by the addition of banquettes and a foldout table top. Let the family room double as a guest room by adding a convertible sofa bed. The room that is freed up then becomes the home office. (An added benefit is that formal dining rooms and guest rooms are usually off the heavy traffic routes in the house and have a high degree of privacy.)

Spare Closet

It's time to bring closets out of the closet! Although most people bemoan their lack of closet space, the fact is that most people don't make good use of their closets. Too often, we hold on to clothes that should be thrown or given away, or we take closet space that is highly accessible and use it to store things that we don't really need access to. It would be wiser to package these "treasures" and slide them under the bed or stack them in the garage.

If locating a home office in a closet sounds claustrophobic, don't worry—only the desk and bookshelves go in the closet. The worker sits in the room facing the closet opening. All that's needed is a closet that is at least 2 feet deep for leg clearance (a standard office desk is 2½ feet deep). Ideally, the closet should be wider than it is deep, and the closet opening should run the entire length. The closet door can either be left on the opening, or replaced with a sliding screen, aluminum blinds, or bamboo shades. If the door is removed and the opening left permanently exposed, remove the door molding also so the recessed space seems more like part of the room.

Closet offices are essentially built-in affairs. Before starting any carpentry, however, have an electrician and a representative from the phone company in to determine how to run electricity and telephone service into the closet. Even if there's already a light in the closet, it will have to be moved from the ceiling.

The upper half of the closet will contain shelves or cabinets, with lighting fixtures suspended under the surface immediately above the desktop. Standard desktop height is 29 inches, unless there will be a lot of typing done there, in which case the desktop should be 3 inches lower. Desk drawers are nice but not necessary. Use tin cans to store pens and pencils, and small boxes or dishes for paper clips, rubber bands, loose change, stamps, keys, and the other odds and ends that tend to accumulate on desktops. If the closet opening is wide enough, a hinged board that folds down to form an L-shaped desk can be attached to expand the work surface.

Under the work surface leave an opening of at least 2 feet across for leg room, more if a trashcan is going to slide in. Two-drawer filing cabinets can either be built in or slid under the desktop.

If you like to stand when working, build the work surface at your waist height or whatever feels comfortable. A 29-inch-high table or desk can then be put on castors and kept under the stand-up surface, to be rolled out when needed. Or the space under the stand-up work surface can be completely closed in and used for storage.

Line the exposed portion of the back wall of the closet with corkboard so calendars, notes, and schedules can be prominently displayed. Keep the colors as light as possible or use reflective surfaces to avoid a closed-in feeling.

Recessed Spaces

A closet is enclosed recessed space. Open recessed space, the little nooks and crannies that are present in most homes, also make good home offices. Sometimes the recessed area is obvious: a breakfast nook, a bay window, a dressing table alcove, the end of an enclosed porch. Other times it takes a little imagination to see the recessed space available under stairs, in an unused foyer, or on landings.

Recessed areas can be created by building permanent partitions or closets on each end of a wall and using the space in between for the home office. The open recessed area needn't be more than 2½ feet deep to provide a functional work area, much less than would be necessary for a completely enclosed office. Close off the opening to the alcove with louvered doors, drapes, or fabric panels whenever you prefer your work in process not to be visible.

Free-standing or floor-mounted screens, draperies, shades, blinds, and folding doors can also be used to create an alcove, but they are not substantial enough to mount shelves, cabinets, or lighting. They can be used effectively, however, to screen off a home office located in the corner of a room.

The Bunker Office

Essentially "space within a space," bunker offices are effective in large rooms where it is more desirable to suggest the division between the office and the rest of the room rather than to create ceiling-to-floor partitions. In a large living room, for instance, the sofa and chairs can be grouped into a comfortable conversation area in one part of the room and the other part used for a home office. The free-standing "walls" of the office can be created with high, open shelves partially filled with books; low cabinets or shelves combined with hanging lamps or large plants; or simply by facing the office desks, tables, bookcases, and filing cabinets toward one another and away from the rest of the room.

The change in level created by a low platform also marks an effective division for the bunker-style home office without eliminating the spacious feeling of the room as a whole. Depending on how high the platform is, the space below can be used for storage, and the edge can provide additional seating.

The sense of division should be augmented with separate lighting. When you are entertaining at night, the office area can then remain obscured in relative darkness. Changes in carpeting, wall covering, and color schemes also delineate the division. However, the difference in decor shouldn't be so great that the two parts of the room clash.

One large drawback of the bunker office, and of closets and recessed spaces as well, is that they do not afford much privacy. They are most appropriate for people who live alone or for rooms that are not used by other household members during work hours.

Recycled Structures

Rural and suburban homes frequently have unattached garages, tool sheds, greenhouses, pool houses, stables, and other types of outbuildings that can house the home office. Even house trailers and boats can serve as home offices and still qualify for the home-office deductions under IRS regulations.

The major advantage to a separate structure is that the home office does not have to meet either the principal-place-of-business or meeting-and-dealing test. It can simply be a secondary work location. A separate structure also offers maximum privacy from other members of the household, and the short "commute" to and from the office provides a clear start and finish to the workday.

Obviously, before moving in files and electronic equipment, the structure must be sealed against the weather, ventilated, heated and/or air conditioned, secured, wired with electricity and phone connections, and furnished. Depending on how far away the main house is, a restroom might prove convenient.

Making a previously uninhabitable structure inhabitable could run you afoul of municipal zoning regulations, especially if the renovation includes building a bathroom or kitchen area. And in municipalities that regulate construction, almost any electrical, plumbing, and enclosing carpentry work will require a building permit.

Additions

If you have the time, the money, and the land, you might consider building an addition onto the house or erecting a separate outbuilding. This route also might be best for doctors, dentists, veterinarians, and other medical professionals who want to set up home-based clinics. A specially designed addition to the house could provide the numerous rooms needed to handle patients and have the structural ability to accommodate heavy equipment such as x-ray machines. Similarly, architects and construction professionals may want to design and build a home-office addition in order to display their talent and ability.

Unfortunately, zoning laws may preclude adding on to your home's square footage or erecting a separate structure, so the first step is to check with local officials. Find out what the laws are and the possibility of getting a variance. For instance, does enclosing an open porch fall under the classification of an addition? What if a separate structure is connected to the main house by a portico? Is the intended use a factor?

Erecting a separate structure could be as simple as buying a small trailer and parking it in your driveway. Or you could purchase a small, prefabricated building—similar to those used on construction sites—and assemble it in the backyard. Neither are necessarily permanent, which may be an advantage or disadvantage.

If the new structure is to be permanent, it too should have flexibility of design so that it can later be used as a guest house, garage, or other nonbusiness structure. Zoning regulations allowing, a home office that can also be transformed into a fully contained apartment would greatly increase your property's value.

HOME-OFFICE FURNISHINGS

The home office can be furnished with a card table and chair, or with a five-piece, solid walnut office suite complete with Persian rugs and Picasso prints—it just depends on how much space and money are available. The following furnishings are typical in offices, but certainly not required.

Desks

Aunt Martha's antique cherry secretary may be fine for writing thank-you notes and addressing Christmas cards, but it will fare poorly as a functional, home-office desk. Not only is it not designed for business tasks and modern office equipment, but it will also be subjected to spills, scratches, dents, and nicks—not a good idea for an appreciating antique. A work surface that is especially designed for office use is a far wiser investment.

The standard commercial desk is 60 inches wide, 30 inches deep, and 29 inches high. A "conference" desk has an overhang of 6 inches on each side and 10 inches along the back, to allow leg room for seating others. A "space saver" desk that measures 48 inches wide by 30 inches deep is also manufactured.

Most office desks have at least one file-sized drawer and one shallow supply drawer. A secretarial desk has an attachable extension called a *return* that forms an L-shape and is 3 inches lower to accommodate a typewriter (keyboard height should allow the typist to type without bending the wrists while holding the forearms at approximately a 90-degree angle). Returns can be either on the left or right side of the desk.

The design of the standard office desk is derived from the table, and so the desk is traditionally placed in the middle of the room, usually facing the door. (A holdover from prehistoric days when it was dangerous to turn your back on the cave entrance, no doubt.) However, placing the desk in the middle of the office is not a particularly effective use of the vertical space above and below the desktop.

If space is tight in the home office, a more efficient approach is a narrower, 24-inch-deep table placed against the wall with shelves and/or cabinets mounted above. If the surface of the table is soft or easily scratched, cover it with a sheet of plexiglass or other protective covering.

Even if floor space is not tight, it still is more efficient to have several small desks or work stations rather than one mammoth executive desk. Multiple work areas help keep various tasks organized and provide changes in posture and changes in pace, good for the psyche and physique alike.

Stands

Stands are designed primarily to hold specific pieces of equipment. Standard typewriter stands are typewriter height (26 inches) and may have a slide-open shelf on the side for documents and a storage shelf underneath for stationery. Printer stands usually have a slot at the back to allow continuous-form paper to feed through.

Typewriter and printer stands should be extra sturdy because of the vibration the equipment produces. They also should be on castors for mobility.

Chairs

Winston Churchill wrote *A History of the English-Speaking Peoples* at a stand-up desk. Ernest Hemingway and Oscar Hammerstein also wrote standing up. For them, an office chair was of little consequence. For you, it may be the most important piece of furniture in the office.

The ergonomically correct chair will be designed so that the entire sole of the user's foot rests on the floor or a footrest; the user's leg is approximately an inch away from the front edge of the seat; the user's back is supported in any of various positions; and the user can easily roll and swivel the chair. Whether it has armrests depends on whether they would tend to get in the user's way or keep the chair from fitting under the front of the desk.

Conference Furniture

Unless you intend to hold numerous meetings of long duration, the rule is to keep conference furniture light, movable, and flexible. The table should be large enough to put coffee cups on but small enough to move to the side when not in use. Conference chairs should be lightweight and movable so visitors can sit side by side, across from one another, or clustered in a group, depending on the nature of the meeting. If plans or sketches must be worked on by numerous people, use a stand-up work surface rather than bringing in a large conference table.

Display

Visual recall is an extremely strong organizational tool. Instead of filing away your work in progress and having to rely solely on a "To-Do" list, use the work itself—displayed in an organized, compact way—to help trigger the day's priorities.

Display furnishings take many forms: a bulletin board for posting notes; desktop In and Out baskets; vertical file holders; stackable wire-mesh baskets.

Wall-mounted pockets are less flexible than desktop display furnishings, but they don't take up work surfaces. Slanted magazine shelves, such as those the library uses to display periodicals, combined with color-coded file folders, also take good advantage of vertical space. Bankers' box organizers, which contain stacked, letter-sized or legal-sized pigeonholes, are an effective way to organize a large number of projects and yet keep the paper work close at hand.

Display furnishings are most effective when their location is coordinated with the work process. For example, wall-mounted pockets are convenient outgoing mail drops. They should be mounted at the office door or near the typewriter or printer. Throughout the day, place finished correspondence and other outgoing mail in the pocket. That way you won't forget to take everything to the post office or mailbox at the end of the day. There's nothing quite so frustrating as forgetting to mail a letter because it got lost in the shuffle on your desk.

Shelves

Convenient for displaying work in progress, shelves are also essential to store books, magazines, phone directories, office supplies, stationery, diskettes and cassettes, computer manuals, art supplies, checkbooks and ledgers, and anything else that needs accessibility.

Large, free-standing bookshelves are unnecessary unless you have large, multivolume reference books such as those in a law library. Otherwise, several sets of wall-mounted shelves or cabinets, or smaller bookshelves that can be placed on desks will make better use of vertical space and keep books and materials close to the area where they are actually used: dictionaries near the typewriter or computer; phone directories near the phone; and so forth.

Storage

A typical office has two types of storage requirements: supplies and business records. A limited amount of office supplies can be kept at the work area where they are used. Larger supply inventories should be stored in closets, supply cabinets, and boxes where they do not take up work space.

Care must be taken to protect paper supplies from high humidity, to keep aerosol cans away from high temperatures, and so forth. Most supplies also have a limited shelf life, so while there may be some money saved by buying in bulk, it could be lost if the supplies are stored past their period of usefulness.

The same tenets as for storing supplies—keep them out of the way, protected, and limited—hold true for business records, The need for storing records grows with the age of the business and necessitates the gradual addition of storage furniture.

Standard free-standing file cabinets come with two, three, four, or five drawers; in letter, legal, or computer-printout widths; with or without locks; fireproof or not; made out of metal, wood, or paper; with drawers that allow access to files from the front or drawers that access from the side; and in numerous colors. The quality and price of filing cabinets also vary widely. Generally the more expense, name-brand cabinets are sturdier and their drawers don't get jammed, warped, or jump the track as frequently as less expensive "bargain" cabinets. One final note: *Always* fill a free-standing file cabinet from the bottom drawer up; otherwise it will get top-heavy and topple over when the top drawer is pulled out.

Computer diskettes or cassettes can be filed in boxes and notebooks that are specially designed as computer "libraries." They should never be placed near any sort of electrical motor—like the computer itself or the telephone—since the magnetic field could erase the data. A convenient way to store 11-inch by 14⅞-inch computer printouts is to make reduced, letter-sized photocopies and file them in regular file cabinets.

Any files or records that are needed only rarely or that are kept only for legal or tax reasons should be removed from file cabinets, boxed, and stored in attics, basements, the backs of closets, or over the rafters in the garage.

Lamps

Lighting, like a good chair, is a critical area that warrants investing in proper equipment rather than limping along with household hand-me-downs, especially where computer monitors are involved.

Several adjustable lamps positioned to focus light on individual work surfaces are preferable to one overhead room light. Dimmer switches increase lighting flexibility, match the level of light to the specific task, and also save on electricity.

Don't position a bright light immediately behind a computer monitor screen, as it will create too great a contrast between the background and the screen. Lighting and windows positioned behind the computer user will produce a glare on the screen that will cause eyestrain. Ideally, the light source should be from the side, and the screen should face a relatively dark part of the room.

Fluorescent lamps burn less electricity and are cooler than incandescent bulbs but produce a hum and bluish "gas-station" light that some people find undesirable; fluorescent bulbs are also more expensive than incandescent bulbs to replace.

If the home office doesn't have any windows, the lack of exposure to sunlight can, in certain people, lead to a mild form of depression. Halogen lamps, which produce a very bright light with a wide color spectrum, similar to sunlight, have been proven to ease this light-related depression and increase productivity.

Lamps can be mounted on the ceiling, under shelves, on walls, or clamped on the edge of the desktop to conserve space. Artist lamps, which have long adjustable necks, can double between two ajoining work spaces.

Carpeting

Although carpeting is effective for absorbing noises and adds a more "furnished" feel to the office, it can also create problems. Office chairs and equipment stands do not roll well on deep pile carpeting. The constant in-and-out motion of a desk chair can quickly wear bare spots in the rug. And deep-pile carpeting hides paperclips, staples, and pushpins—until you step down, that is.

Deep-pile wool and nylon carpeting also generates a high level of static electricity during low-humidity months, which if conducted to an operating computer will result in the electronic equivalent of a dropped jigsaw puzzle.

The wise course is to select industrial- or commercial-quality carpeting for the office. If the office is already furnished with deep-pile carpeting, use clear vinyl mats under desk chairs. Antistatic mats and sprays will help solve problems with static electricity.

Windows and Walls

Windows need some sort of shade, drape, or blind to allow a reduction in bright light, especially important in offices with computer monitors. Other than that, windows are big psychological pluses in a home office because they offer visual breaks from work, decrease the sense of isolation, and provide exposure to sunlight. If the view *outside* the window isn't particularly attractive, a flower box or pots on the outside ledge can help in the summer, and a birdfeeding station in the winter provides an interesting visual diversion. You can also dress up the view by putting flowering house plants on glass shelves mounted on the inside window molding.

The color of the walls depends on personal preference and the general decor of the room; however, as a general rule dark colors will make a room seem smaller and light colors will make it seem larger. A bright white wall behind a computer monitor will create too much contrast between the screen and the wall and result in eyestrain.

Lining the walls with carpeting or corkboard not only reduces noise but provides space for posting notes and schedules with pushpins. Paintings, prints, posters, and photographs, especially if they have some personal meaning, will help transform walls from mere enclosures into expressive, creative displays.

Miscellaneous

Other types of furnishings recommended for a typical home office are: a circular file (like a Rolodex) or index card box for telephone numbers and addresses; wastepaper baskets near each work station; ashtrays; a coat rack; bookends; a petty-cash box or safe if retail sales are involved; a pencil sharpener; a clock; a postage scale; and a fire extinguisher. If you hire employees who work in your home office, or regularly entertain clients or customers, consider a small refrigerator, coffee maker, mugs, and flatware.

6

Equipping the Home Office

The development and dissemination of sophisticated electronic equipment is one of the major reasons that home offices have become practical for more people. Whereas the traditional office depends on physical proximity for intraoffice communication and on support staffs for completing administrative tasks, home-office workers rely on advanced telecommunications and multiprogrammable personal computers. Without such electronic advances, operating a one-person shop removed from the business district would be a much more difficult and perhaps unfeasible undertaking.

As is the case with office furnishings, what types of electronic equipment are appropriate for your home office depends on the type and size of the business operation—and your financial resources. First, realistically evaluate your business needs. For example, to determine how many telephone sets you need, you must ask yourself how many people will be using them and how far apart your work areas are; whether you should get a word processor depends on the amount and length of your written documents; whether you should buy a computer

Equipping the Home Office

depends on your need for financial analysis and data bank management; whether to lease or buy a copier depends on the volume and type of copies you require each month.

Once you determine your current needs, consider future growth. The general rule is to think of business equipment purchases as two-year investments. Where does your business plan put you in two years? You should select equipment that will take you there but not necessarily beyond since at that point you may want to upgrade and take advantage of new technology.

You must also decide whether to buy or lease. Each route has advantages and disadvantages. Advantages to outright purchase are: immediate business-expense tax deduction for the cost up to $5,000, $7,500, or $10,000 depending on the year of purchase; depreciation deductions for larger amounts; business-owned assets that can be readily relocated or transferred; no long-term, ongoing monthly rental commitment; and a greater number of brands and models to choose from on the consumer market.

On the other hand, advantages to leasing are: service and regular maintenance costs included in monthly rental charges; no installation charges; no worry about being left with an "orphaned" piece of equipment if the manufacturer goes out of business; and ease of upgrading if business need increases or new technology becomes available. In addition, if the business income is low (as is often the case with start-up ventures), there may not be any immediate tax benefit to be derived from taking a large expense deduction on the outright purchase of business equipment.

Leasing also allows a new business a chance to prove its viability, project cash flow, and experiment with different models before making a major investment in equipment.

Telephone equipment can be leased from AT&T on a month-to-month agreement. When you decide you don't want it any more, you just call the company, and they come out and take it away.

Some multiline key systems, copiers, and computer hardware are available under lease/purchase agreements which apply a part of each month's rent against the purchase price of the equipment. You will be required to sign an agreement that commits you to making payments for a certain period of time, usually three years. The lessor can generally switch built-up equity in one piece of equipment to a higher-priced model, but will forfeit all equity if the lease agreement is cancelled or defaulted.

Whether purchasing or leasing, always investigate the business stability of the manufacturer or supplier, since warranties and service contracts are meaningless if the company is fly-by-night. And if a lease agreement must be signed, have it made out in the name of your business rather than your own name. Have an attorney look it over and explain exactly what is being agreed to. If you don't like some term of the agreement, try to negotiate before signing.

Another way to hold down equipment expenses is by purchasing secondhand or reconditioned equipment. Secondhand equipment can be found through government auctions, office equipment suppliers, and the classified ads. In general, used equipment is a risky investment since there's no sure way to determine how much or how well it has been used. Also, sometimes manufacturer's warranties and service contracts will not transfer from the original owners. However, if the price is low enough, secondhand equipment can be a good buy, especially if it is used as a standby back-up in case other equipment breaks down.

Reconditioned equipment is used equipment that the manufacturer has taken back for some reason—in a trade-in or defaulted lease/purchase agreement, for instance—and is now reselling. The equipment should have been completely cleaned, repaired, and upgraded. It should have the same warranty coverage as brand-new equipment. After the warranty expires, always get a service contract, since reconditioned equipment will have more mechanical problems than new equipment; and realize that reconditioned equipment will have a shorter useful life.

TELEPHONES

In the home office the telephone is *the* major link with the rest of the workaday world. It is the medium through which customers and clients are contacted; new business located; supplies ordered; deals closed; orders taken; repairs arranged; computer data received and transmitted; money collected and money spent. It is also the source of annoying solicitations, distractions, and significant expense.

With the wide range of telephone models and options now on the market, decisions about what type of equipment to install and whether to buy or lease require a great deal of consumer sophistication and investigation. First, phones must be compatible with the local phone company's operating system, which will utilize either pulse-generated or tone-generated signals. Don't assume that just because the local system can accommodate push-button phones that it is a tone-generated system; the "beeps" produced through a push-button phone may not be true tones.

In addition, access to many discount long-distance services (such as MCI and Sprint) and information utilities can only be achieved with tone-generating equipment. That's why some telephone equipment has both pulse and tone capabilities: The first is used to link up with the local phone system, the second to tie into computer-access services.

Multiline and Single-Line Phones

There are two basic models of telephone equipment: single-line and multiline. Most residential telephones are single-line sets; they receive and conduct calls on

77 *Equipping the Home Office*

only one phone number. If a second line is installed, it must have its own separate telephone. Simple single-line phones are very inexpensive and are available through a wide range of retail outlets and mail-order companies. They are even given away free sometimes as bonuses for subscribing to magazines or opening bank accounts.

On the other hand, typical business phones are multiline sets and can accommodate two or more different phone numbers, each represented by a separate button along the bottom or side of the phone. Multiline sets also commonly have a "hold" button, which allows the user to hang up the receiver or use another line without disconnecting the caller on the first line, and an intercom line, which connects different telephone sets on the same lines to each other. Multiline phones are more expensive both to rent and buy than single-line sets. However, multiline phones are beginning to appear on the general consumer market and prices can be expected to fall. In addition, you can buy an inexpensive, two-button switch to install on a multiline telephone cable that allows you to use single-line equipment. To change from one line to the other, you simply push a button on the cable attachment.

Sophisticated office "key" systems are groups of multiline phones and interfacing equipment designed for offices with more than two lines and at least four phones. They include security features that keep one extension from breaking in on another's call, individual intercom lines, automatic button restoration, multiline conferences, and more. Key systems, are *much* more expensive than individual multiline phones, partially because of the significant installation charge. They have more capability than the typical home office can utilize and are not recommended unless you have numerous people working out of your home office or unless your business lines run throughout the entire house.

Whether to get single- or multiline equipment for the home office depends on what type of phone service you have and how many lines will be running into the office and/or other parts of the residence. If the phone is not a very important part of your business, then the residential line can be used for both business and personal purposes, and a simple, single-line extension installed in the office. The business usage of a residential phone is tax deductible. However, if the home office is the principal place of business, running residential service into it may be against phone company tariff restrictions, as further discussed in Chapter 8.

If the business has its own separate line and it is the *only* line that runs into the home office, then again a single-line set is appropriate. However, if the business has two or more lines, which is especially necessary when more than one person works in the home office or when the business is based in sales or uses computer telecommunication links, a multiline system is advisable. Not only will one multiline set take up less desk space than two single-line sets, but it can automatically relay incoming calls from a busy line to an open one.

Multiline phones can also be used elsewhere in the residence to combine the business and residential lines in one phone set. This is a convenient way to avoid having to run to the office to anwer every business call. The tax deduction for the cost of multiline equipment located in the residence is based on the percentage of business use.

Telephone Options

The options available on telephones range from the very useful to the ridiculous. Some that are recommended for home-office phones are:

Automatic redial. In its simplest form, at the push of a button the phone redials the last number tried; in its more advanced forms, the phone dials and redials a number on its own at regular intervals until it gets through. Then it either goes ahead and makes the connection (which can be a problem if the user has forgotten the call and left the room) or signals with a "success" light that the line is now open. Automatic redial is a built-in feature on some phones; it can be added to existing phones with an attachment.

Programmable memory. This feature allows phone numbers to be stored and called by pushing a single button or entering a code. The major variations involve the number of phone numbers that can be stored and how long they are. Length of number is very important if you use a discount long-distance service or information utility that requires a seven- or eleven-digit access number, in addition to the phone number and the account number. Some models will wait to "hear" a second dial tone after getting access to the long-distance lines, while others will simply wait a set interval of time before dialing the rest of the number. Like automatic redial, the memory feature can either be built into the phone or added with an attachment.

Cordless phone. The remote unit, which looks either like a traditional handset or like a Walkman headset, transmits on FM frequencies to a base unit that is plugged into the telephone wall jack and an electrical outlet. You can either receive or make calls without returning to the base unit; however, the remote unit must be electrically recharged every six to eight hours. The major difference between cordless models lies in their ranges, which vary between 500 and 1,500 feet, depending on terrain.

There are two important things to know about cordless phones. First, the remote units operate on pulses. If the cordless phone is to be used for tone-only access services, such as MCI, make sure the base unit can make the switch to tone operation. Second, cordless phones "broadcast" on open FM frequencies. There is always the possibility that someone else in the neighborhood could gain access to your frequency and make costly, unauthorized long-distance calls on your phone number. Models are available that have security features to safeguard access to the base unit.

Speaker phones. One-way speaker phones let you hear what the person on the other end of the line is saying but won't let you talk back without using the handset. They are convenient in combination with the automatic redial feature that makes a connection once the line is clear, since otherwise you would have to continue holding the handset.

Two-way speaker phones allow you to carry on a complete conversation without a handset. They are useful if several people in the same office have to participate in the same telephone conversation or if the user likes to have his or her hands free while talking.

Cellular Phones

A phone in your car used to be a sign that you had really hit the top of the success ladder. Now they are much more common, although they are still relatively expensive, at least compared with other types of phone equipment. A cellular phone operates on a broadcast signal and involves the installation of a receiver/broadcaster in the trunk of your car. Signals are transmitted to and received from your car through local telephone company antennas, which are clustered primarily in major urban areas. The signal is only effective within a certain radius of the antennas, usually under 12 miles. You can make or receive calls on your car phone, although you may be limited by the phone company on the amount of "prime" time (9 A.M. to 5 P.M.) you can use on the phone each month.

If you spend a great deal of time in your car traveling around a major metropolitan area, a cellular phone might be a good way to stay in touch with your office or clients and customers. If you travel between metropolitan areas, you should check to see if your system operates in those particular cities. If you live out in the countryside or spend most of your driving time on lonely stretches of interstate highway, forget getting a cellular phone, because it won't operate outside its broadcast radius.

TELEPHONE ANSWERING MACHINES

Gone are the days of surprise and confusion upon being asked to leave a concise message at the sound of the beep. Tape-recorder answering machines have become almost as ubiquitous as the telephones they serve, and almost everyone has grown accustomed to talking to a machine. In fact, it's gotten to the point that it's annoying when someone *doesn't* have an answering machine and must be called and recalled until finally reached.

For the home office, the convenience afforded by telephone answering machines is two-fold. First, they take telephone messages when the office is vacant; and second, they allow screening of incoming calls, thus allow you to avoid all calls or someone in particular.

Types of Answering Machines

An answering machine consists of two tapes: a short, recycling tape with an outgoing announcement informing the caller that you are not available; and a regular cassette that records the messages that callers leave. The basic difference in models centers on how long the caller's message can be. Some models simply record messages for a set interval, such as 30 seconds. Others are voice-activated and will continue recording as long as the caller is talking and there's still room on the cassette.

If you are out of the office often, you can get a remote control answering machine that lets you call your office and signal the machine to rewind and replay your messages. There are some remote models that will also allow you to re-record the outgoing announcement over the phone.

Answering Machine Options

An option available on basic answering machines that adds to their convenience is two-way dictation, which allows the machine to record regular telephone calls on the line and is commonly used for taking dictation. Since it's illegal to surreptitiously record telephone conversations, any two-way record feature will automatically beep every 10 seconds or so.

Some remote models have ringer adjustments that won't answer when you call if there are no new messages recorded, thus saving long-distance toll charges. You can also buy a machine with a synthesized voice that records the time and day along with each caller's message.

Installing an Answering Machine

Answering machines either plug directly into a wall jack and take the place of a separate telephone or plug into an adaptor (available at most consumer electronics outlets) that connects the wall jack and the telephone cord, allowing both the answering machine and the separate telephone to operate off one jack. You can buy combination telephone/answering machine equipment, which may feature other telephone options such as automatic redial and programmable memory. Almost all answering machines must also be plugged into an electrical outlet.

If your office has a modular telephone wall jack, installing the answering machine is a simple do-it-yourself affair. You unplug the phone and plug in the answering machine or the adaptor. However, you must register the fact that you have installed an answering machine with the phone company, which is a simple matter of calling and giving them the machine's model number.

Just what your answering machine should announce to callers depends on how long the announcement tape (which can be easily replaced) is and your type of business image and personality. A musician, for instance, might record a message in song; a computer programmer might use a synthesized voice. But in general, cuteness and bizarre approaches should be avoided. You never know who will be calling or whether they will find your newest ditty or limerick as amusing as you do.

Also, it's not necessary to announce that the office is empty, since this could precipitate an unwelcome, larcenous visit. The very fact that the machine has answered the phone is enough of an indication that—for whatever reason—you are not available. A typical message might go: "Hello, you have reached Dogtrot Pet Sitters. If you will leave your name, phone number, and a brief message, we will get back to you as soon as possible. Please wait until you hear the tone. Thank you."

TYPEWRITERS

Any home office that produces daily correspondence will require a typewriter, even if it has a computer and printer. Addressing single envelopes, filling out forms, and typing short letters just don't warrant gearing up sophisticated equipment when they can be banged out quicker and easier on a typewriter. Besides, the computer might be busy on another, more complicated job or (horrors) broken, in which case the lowly typewriter will have to fill the breach.

Types of Typewriters

There are three basic types of typewriters. *Manual* models rely on mechanical works powered by physical pressure on keys. They are limited to one style and size of type, since each key connects directly to a bar with a raised letter on the end. *Electric* typewriters again use mechanical works, but the key pressure is electrically augmented. The raised letter can either be on a bar or on a changeable round ball, called a *type element*.

The newest type equipment is the *electronic* typewriter, in which much of the mechanical machinery has been replaced with circuit boards containing semiconductor chips. Electronic typewriters don't break down as often as electric ones because they have fewer moving parts. The semiconductor chips provide advance features such as memory capacity and in some instances can be utilized as computer printers. Additionally, they are much faster and quieter than electric or manual typewriters.

Electronic typewriters use either interchangeable, ball-shaped type elements, "daisy wheels" (the raised letters are at the end of open spokes radiating from a central hub), or some form of "dot-matrix" print head with tiny metal rods that are extended in different combinations to form specific letters. Depending on the density of the rods, dot-matrix typewriters may or may not be suitable for formal business correspondence. On the other hand, ball-shaped elements and daisy wheels can't produce the professional-looking charts, graphs, and other graphics that dot-matrix equipment can.

Options

Electric and electronic typewriter models feature a wide range of options. Several that are particularly suitable for home-office use are:

Self-correcting. The typewriter uses two special ribbon cartridges. The one that makes the impression is black or colored carbon; the second lifts off the impression left by the first when the same key is struck over. Electric typewriters require that each character be erased individually, whereas electronic typewriters can "remember" a string of just-typed characters and erase them all with one strike of the correcting key.

Adjustable pitch control. Pitch is the spacing between typed characters. The two most common spacings are 10 characters per inch, which corresponds to pica-sized type, and 12 characters per inch, which corresponds to the smaller elite type. Using 12-character pitch and elite type allows more written information to be produced in a smaller space, useful especially when filling out printed forms. Pica type and 10-character pitch is easier to read and standard for general correspondence and documents. Dot-matrix typewriters often offer a wider range of type sizes and pitches than typical type-element and daisy-wheel typewriters, since the individual letters are crafted out of a combination of tiny points.

Portability. It makes no sense to leave an idle typewriter back in the office when it could be useful on business trips or vacations. The new electronic typewriters, with their lightweight circuitry, are considerably more portable and compact than their electric cousins. Some models can operate on batteries, so they can be used on the train or while waiting for the dentist.

Display screen. Some electronic typewriters come equipped with memory capability and LCD (Liquid Crystal Display, which is what is used in digital watches). The displays show the characters typed before they are printed. This allows you to check spelling and wording, and make corrections before the text is committed to paper. Models vary depending on how many characters the screen displays, with 15 characters being the minimum.

Electronic typewriters may also feature automatic carrier return when the typist reaches the right margin; automatic underlining, centering, and double strikes for boldness; and justification of both left and right margins for a typeset appearance. At the very top of the line, electronic typewriters are equipped with multiline display screens, internal and external memory storage, spelling checkers, and many other features that closely resemble those of a word processor. In fact, in the not-too-distant future, technology will blur the traditional boundaries between typewriters and word processors and computers.

DICTATING AND TRANSCRIBING EQUIPMENT

For those who don't type and have neither the patience nor penmanship to write in longhand, and for those who like to dictate while driving, a cassette recorder/transcriber is essential. Dictating into a recorder is also preferable to dictating to a stenographer, since it only takes up one person's time and not two.

Basic Equipment

Dictation recorders come in small, hand-held models with built-in microphones or in larger, combination dictating/transcribing desktop models that have attached microphones with control switches. They record on either regular, macro-, or micro-cassettes, depending on the model. The recording function is activated through a thumb switch or by a sound sensor which begins recording whenever the user starts talking. Like most cassette recorders, they have volume control and playback, rewind, and fast-forward functions.

Transcribing equipment is different from regular recording equipment in that it has a foot pedal for controlling the playback, fast-forward, and rewind functions. Some equipment will automatically rewind briefly whenever the foot pedal is released, so that the last few words are repeated the next time the playback pedal is depressed. Most transcribing machines also have headspeakers, erase functions, and adjustable playback speed and tone. Top-of-the-line models might include auto scan, which will search for special tones recorded between dictated letters or documents.

PHOTOCOPIERS

While all businesses at some point need copies of documents and correspondence, not every business needs a photocopier. For infrequent and few copies, the copiers found in most Post Offices, commercial duplicating centers, and office supply stores will do the trick at a reasonable cost. It is also possible to make a deal with a local business, professional office, or real estate agency to use their copier at a per-copy cost billed monthly. They will usually be only too happy to have someone else share the cost of their equipment.

At some point the need for copies may become too frequent and the volume too great for such an arrangement to continue being cost-effective. Or the hours the other equipment is available may not coincide with the time you need copies—say, on Sunday or very early in the morning before a trip. Then it's time to consider purchasing or leasing photocopying equipment for the home office.

Luckily, the selection of small, relatively inexpensive "personal copiers" is much larger today than it was several years ago. Photocopier manufacturers are starting to pursue the small business, consumer, and home-office markets by developing low-volume, high-quality equipment that is compact; easy to use, maintain and repair; energy efficient; and doesn't require expensive chemicals and paper supplies. They are available through mail-order catalogs, and in camera stores, discount outlets, and some mass-market retail stores, in addition to traditional office equipment stores. And prospects are good that prices will drop further and more sophisticated features will appear as consumer-market competition heats up.

How to Choose a Copier

Selecting the best photocopier equipment for a home office depends on your needs and the following features:

Volume. Because different models of personal copiers are designed for different monthly volume demands, the first question a sales representative will ask is how many copies you will want to make a month. The inability to realistically gauge the number of copies the newly established home office will make each month is probably the best argument for not buying or leasing equipment initially but instead using someone else's. (Of course, when the copier is in place in the home office, usage will tend to increase because the equipment is more convenient.)

Types and sizes of copies. Generally, copies are needed for either convenience or distribution. Convenience copies are for business records, reference, and operating needs. File copies of your outgoing correspondence are convenience copies. They do not require a high quality of reproduction or more than two or three copies of each original. Distribution copies are intended for use outside the office, such as a press release or financial report. They require a higher degree of reproduction quality and often involve multiple, collated copies of each original for broad dissemination.

The types of copies also depends on the size of the original documents and whether reduction or enlargement is needed. For example, a law office might need distribution copies of legal-sized (8½-inch by 14-inch) papers. A graphic layout artist might need convenience copies of magazine spreads measuring 11 by 14 inches. An accountant may want to reduce oversized computer printouts to 8-by-11-inch distribution copies. If copies from books and magazines will be needed, this too will affect the decision on the best type of equipment, since not all models have the flat copy window necessary to accommodate bound material.

Per-copy cost. Comparing prices between different types of photocopiers must be based on their relative cost per copy. If the copier is going to be purchased outright, multiply the estimated volume per month times expected lifetime (for example, 24 months or two years), then divide this figure into the purchase price. Add the estimated per-copy paper, toner, developer, and other fixed supply costs. And since some sort of service contract is almost always necessary with copiers, divide monthly service contract charges by estimated monthly volume, and add this figure too.

If you are going to lease a copier, calculate the monthly per-copy cost by dividing monthly rent by estimated usage. Most leasing agreements also include a per-copy usage charge over a certain minimum number of copies, so add that along with fixed supply costs. Add service costs only if service calls and parts are not covered under the leasing agreement.

Per-copy cost is the only effective way to compare different copiers. Whereas one model may have a low equipment cost, the cost of supplies might offset this advantage. A more expensive model could end up costing less in the long run.

Basic Types of Copiers and Options

Photocopiers fall into two broad categories. The first and generally less expensive type of equipment uses a special coated paper. In some coated-paper models the copying process is entirely internal; others use a transfer process which requires two sheets of special paper for every copy.

Two-sheet coated paper copiers are designed for offices with very low volume, perhaps a few copies a day, since the process is slow and the cost of paper supplies high. Coated-paper copies do not have a high reproduction quality and thus are not particularly suitable for distribution. The surface texture of the copies is noticeably different from that of plain bond paper and can absorb and fade pen markings.

The second type of copier uses plain bond paper. Essentially, they can use any brand of paper; however, most manufacturers recommend their own brand of paper and sometimes will not be responsible for warranty and service agreements if other, discount brands are used. Some plain bond paper copiers use liquid toners and developers, others use dry chemicals. Dry-process copiers are best for high-quality copying onto letterhead with a high rag content, adhesive labels, and clear acetate and other novelty papers.

Common options available on copiers include reduction (usually to 74 percent and 64 percent of original) and enlargement (115 percent of original). Both are practical for filing computer printouts and for any sort of graphic arts work. Copiers also offer interchangeable toner cassettes for copying in different colors; collators for sorting multiple copies; and document feeders that automatically feed in multipage original documents.

The Copier in the Home Office

The proper placement and use of the copier can greatly increase its cost-effectiveness and the office's general operation. First, business copiers are heavy pieces of equipment and not meant to be frequently moved around. They should be placed on a sturdy stand that puts the copying surface at countertop height. Copier manufacturers sell rolling stands for their equipment which also include storage space underneath for paper and chemical supplies.

Copiers and their paper supplies are very susceptible to high humidity. If the home office is in the basement or otherwise prone to dampness, ask the manufacturer's representative about possible equipment damage from moisture. Some models can have damp-chasers installed similar to those put in pianos. Never open more than one package of paper at a time, and place unused paper in a watertight bag over weekends or other periods when the copier is not in use.

Don't ever try to copy onto novelty paper like acetate if there's any question about whether or not the copier can take it. Acetate can stick to the drum, causing a very expensive repair which will not be covered under any service contract. Also, don't leave art work or photographs with rubber cement on them on the copy window, since the heat will melt the rubber cement along with the ink or photographic image.

Keep three shallow baskets on a shelf next to the copier. The first is for copies for the chronological correspondence file and is emptied at the end of each month; the second is for file copies that get filed whenever convenient; the third is for bad copies that can't be used. Rather than throwing these mistakes away, use the other side as scrap paper for typing drafts or taking notes.

POSTAGE METERS

Essentially, a postage meter is a machine for dispensing prepaid, precanceled postage. You take the meter to the Post Office, pay for a certain amount of postage (say, $150), and the Post Office employee will set the meter so that it will stamp letters in any amount until it reaches $150 total.

Equipping the Home Office

Each time you mail a letter or package, you set the meter for the proper amount of postage and the day's date, and run the envelope or adhesive label through the meter's slot, which stamps a precanceled ink impression on it. If you make a mistake, you can take the unmailed envelope or label back to the Post Office for credit (since it also shows your meter's unique registration number).

Postage meters cannot be bought; they can only be leased and are not inexpensive. Advantages to a postage meter are: Because the mail is precanceled, it bypasses this step in the Post Office, which may result in faster handling; and if you do a great quantity of mailing, the meter is much faster and easier than putting stamps on hundreds of letters or cards. The disadvantages are the cost of renting the meter and the inconvenience of keeping the daily postage logs required by the Post Office.

7

The Home Office Computer

The Question: Do you really need a personal computer in your home office? The Answer: Yes!

A personal computer is essential for one-person operations. It will enable you to manage the multiple tasks involved with running the business: accounts, correspondence, financial information, addresses, telephone numbers. It also can file and retrieve large amounts of marketing statistics, reference information, and resource listings.

A personal computer can put you on-line with huge data banks all across the nation; it can link you electronically with your clients and customers; it can provide access to "electronic" malls of consumer and business goods; it can even provide an advertising outlet for your products or services.

If you are in the "information" business—consulting, advising, producing written documents and financial data—a computer is crucial to your achieving your work in a precise, effective manner. It is the ultimate tool for gathering, storing, retrieving, changing, and disseminating information.

Finally, like it or not, personal computers are the future. Not being able to transmit or receive data with a computer will hamstring your home office and could knock you entirely out of the business competition.

Now that you know all the reasons why you need a computer, how do you know which one? A common mistake first-time buyers make when trying to select a computer is to jump immediately into the fracas of RAM versus ROM, hard versus floppy, parallel versus serial, DOS versus CP/M, bits versus bytes. All this technical jargon is intimidating and probably accounts for the thousands of otherwise savvy business people who eschew computerizing their operations.

Actually, you can ignore thinking about different types of computer equipment altogether until you answer the following question: "What types of business tasks do I want the computer to do?" Put another way: You must first determine what types of software you will need before you can select the right kind of computer.

SOFTWARE: THE ELECTRONIC INTELLECT

A personal computer is little more than electronic circuitry and mechanical drives wired together in a plastic box. By itself, it's fairly mindless. What really makes a computer function is software—the programs that provide it instructions about how to interpret and process the information that you enter.

Video games are types of software, as are word processors. Each are simple computers with built-in software, either game or word-processing programs. They cannot run any other type of software.

Personal computers, on the other hand, can run all types of programs, including games, educational programs, utility programs, word processing, spreadsheets, graphs, and more. New software is being developed constantly to do everything imaginable, from watering houseplants to projecting stock performance.

While it is possible to design your own software, this requires knowledge of computer programming and a great deal of time, something that entrepreneurs and professionals usually don't have in great abundance. On the other hand, you can buy or acquire hundreds of off-the-shelf software packages that are specifically designed for small businesses and include the following basic applications.

Word-Processing Software

Word-processing programs are designed for drafting and editing text for letters, memoranda, reports, briefs, articles, books, contracts, and any other sort of written document. You type in your text and then delete, add to, move, and/or correct it prior to printing it.

The biggest advantage of word-processing programs is that when you make a revision to a letter or document, you don't have to retype the entire thing. You simply make the specific change to the word or sentence and then reprint the document. This greatly reduces the probability of making additional typing errors. Word processing also facilitates the creation of form letters in which only an address or incidental portion of the text changes.

Different types of word processing programs vary based on the following factors:

Complexity. How complex are the various editing functions to execute? For example, in one program deleting a word may require pushing two or three keys, while another program requires pushing only one. Also, one program may require that you memorize entire strings of commands, while another has screen prompts or dedicated keys.

Front-end features. These are features that make creating and editing a document easier and faster. Front-end features include such things as search and replace functions, which allow you to replace a word or string of words with another word or string of words by pressing two or three keys. Or the program might have split screens, or "windows," which allow you to compare two or more documents on the screen simultaneously. Other front-end features are copying and moving text between documents; inserting boilerplate text from separate files; and a built-in thesaurus for expanding vocabulary.

Back-end features. These are features that affect how the printed document will look. Typical features are the ability to underline, create boldface type, justify margins, center text, create proportional letter spacing and nonbreak spacing, and leave blank lines. Other back-end features include format functions that automatically number pages, chapters, sections, or paragraphs; insert running heads at the top of each page; stop printing for text to be entered from the keyboard; print footnotes; and so forth. (The ability to integrate with other types of programs is also an important back-end feature and is discussed under the section on integrated software that follows on page 97.)

A common and very useful back-end function is a spelling checker. Depending on the program, a spelling check will identify, query, and perhaps suggest substitutions for words it does not recognize, meaning words that are not included in its built-in dictionary. Most programs will not recognize bad word usage; for example, they will not know that "to" should be "too" based on the way the word is used in a sentence. Some programs do feature basic grammar rules and can in an elementary way check word usage. But since they must use general rules (for example, rules for adding prefixes and suffixes), they often overlook combinations that—to the human eye—are clearly not correct.

Spelling checkers also let you customize the dictionary to include proper names, technical jargon, and abbreviations that are prevalent in your documents.

However, spelling and grammar checkers will never replace your own careful proofreading. They are only meant to be supplementary tools, and when used that way they are immensely helpful.

Length of document. The length of a document is limited in some word-processing programs by the internal memory of the computer. Other programs build "swap" files that temporarily store portions of the document on the disk and clear the internal memory for additional text. By automatically exchanging data between the internal memory and the disk, the length of document can be much longer than what the computer's memory can accommodate at one time.

How the files are saved to disk. There are two methods: standard ASCII codes or binary-encoded files. The major difference you need to consider is that only files saved in ASCII codes can be sent over telephone lines. So if telecommunications capabilities are important to you, for electronic mail or subscribing to an information utility, the word-processing software must be ASCII-based or provide some way to translate the files to ASCII codes.

Spreadsheet Software

These powerful number crunchers are the darlings of financial planners and managers. The spreadsheet starts with a blank electronic matrix. You then enter numbers, equations, and identifying labels in the squares.

Equations can call for an arithmetic function (such as add, subtract, multiply, divide, compute a logarithm, compute a square root, find an average), a trigonometric function (such as computing arc tangents, cosines, and sines), or a logical function (such as "if x, then y; if not x, then z"). The column widths are adjustable, as are the positions (center, flush left, flush right) of the data and type of notation (scientific, dollar amounts, decimals).

Once a spreadsheet has been set up, "what if" projections can be calculated by substituting different numerical values and having the program recompute based on the new numbers. Complex cash-flow projections that would take days to recalculate if done by hand can be computed in minutes by a spreadsheet program.

The two major differences between different spreadsheet software programs are size and ease of entering data. Some spreadsheets have hundreds of columns and thousands of rows, although of course you can only view a small section at a time on the screen. But of greater import than the physical size of the spreadsheet is how much data it can process. Storing identifying labels and equations takes up space in the memory, as does the program itself. Unless the software can automatically swap information with a disk, it is severely limited in how many numbers it can actually crunch, the whole point of the program anyway.

Ease of entering data depends on how the squares in the matrix are identified (by column letter and row number, or by their identifying labels) and by the ability to enter formulas that automatically vary references according to the position on the matrix. For example, if one column is a cumulative total based on a changing number in the preceding column, each formula in the cumulative column must have different references; that is, B1 + A2 = B2, B2 + A3 = B3, and so forth. It would be tedious to have to enter each equation. A program that makes variable reference changes automatically is easier to work with.

Data-Base Management Software

This is a fancy name for a fancy filing program—and one of the most valuable pieces of software a small business can have. There are two major types of data-base management software: *fixed-record* and *universal-record*.

Fixed-record programs. With a fixed-record format, you design specific data fields that can contain names, titles, organizations, addresses, telephone numbers, dates, Social Security numbers, dollar amounts, quantities, file numbers, comments—whatever you wish. Once you construct the general format, then you enter the information for each particular record.

The program is capable of sorting through all the individual records and selecting subsets, again defined by you. For example, if the data base contains records of customer names, addresses, phone numbers, and monthly purchases by item and amounts, the data-base management program can select out: all customers in certain ZIP code areas, or all customers who purchased over a certain dollar amount in the last two months, or all customers who bought a certain product. These subsets can also be sorted, such as a listing of customers who bought a certain product, with the biggest dollar-amount purchaser first and the least last.

Most fixed-record data-base management software has a simple word-processing function or can be used in connection with integrated word-processing software. This means you can address envelopes and labels and print customized form letters, file cards, invoices, and so forth, using the data records in the data base.

Fixed-record data-base management programs, like word processing and spreadsheets, vary according to the amount of information they can process. Size limits apply to the number of fields a record can have, how many characters in each record, and the number of records that can be read and sorted at once. Programs also differ based on how the subsets are defined, whether with absolute values (e.g., all addresses in the 10003 ZIP code), relative values (all ZIPs between 59999 and 69999), or logical commands (the ability to search for a piece of information in any one of several different fields during one sort).

All fixed-record data-base management programs share one thing. They are only as effective as the basic record format designed by the user. Before creating the basic record, you should sit down and list all the information the filing program should contain and how that information will be used. Working with a grid sheet that reflects the height and width of the computer screen, which also reflects the physical setup of the basic record format, will save time when you actually try to enter the format on the computer.

Universal-record programs. The second type of data-base management software doesn't have fixed fields for entering data in each record. Instead, you can enter just about anything you want: single words, sentences, paragraphs, listings, numbers, references, and so on. The program can search anywhere in the record for any key word or string of words that you instruct it to. And, like fixed-record programs, it can sort and organize that information any way you wish.

The universal-record data-base management programs are designed to manage large amounts of textual information, whereas the fixed-record programs are more suited to keeping track of mailing lists and client records. For instance, a law firm paralegal enters in a universal-record data-base program abstracts of all legal articles appearing in university law reviews and professional journals. Then, by instructing the program to search for all instance where the words *libel* and *magazine* appear within 10 words of each other, the research assistant easily locates references to all current articles on magazine-related libel law and cases.

Universal-record programs are also used to organize eclectic groupings of information into a logical structure, in the same way an outline structures a report of article. You enter information as you run across it and concepts as they occur to you. The program can then group and retrieve records according to key words that form headings, subheadings, and so on. The ease of manipulating the key words and recalling the records means information and concepts can be woven into a cohesive argument. For this reason, these software programs are sometimes called "idea-management" programs.

Accounting Software

Accounting software is a godsend for small businesses and independent professionals. Done manually, bookkeeping tasks are tedious and time-consuming. Too often the crush of other work results in a haphazard stack of unpaid invoices, late billings, and boxes full of receipts that take days to sort out at tax time.

Accounts payable software. This is basically a data-base management program with the ability to calculate. You set up individual vendor files and enter invoices by date, amount, date due, discounts (if any), and type of expense. The program keeps track of unpaid invoices by vendor and by age. Some payables software can automatically post recurring monthly expenses such as equipment rental and can print checks. The check-writing program requires special, continuous-form checks that are designed to match the software.

Accounts receivable software. This operates essentially the same way, except the records reflect your business billings and the amounts paid by your customers or clients. One important thing to remember when purchasing a receivable program: Make sure it conforms to your type of business. For example, don't purchase software designed for a retailer who sells products when your business is service-oriented. Product-based billing records will contain such items as quantity and type of merchandise and shipping costs, which will have no relevance to a service-based operation.

Payroll software. Payroll software automatically calculates and deducts employee withholdings for income taxes, FICA, unemployment taxes, and any other benefits, such as life insurance premiums. It also calculates employer contributions to FICA and unemployment taxes. The program writes payroll checks and prepares government payroll filings.

General-ledger software. This records financial transactions for the accounting period and year to date, and generates *accurate* balance sheets and income statements. Some programs can compare the current financial position with that of a year or two ago. If the general-ledger program is used with compatible accounts payable, accounts receivable, and payroll programs, their expense and income postings can be transferred electronically to the general ledger.

Graphics Software

Graphics can give added impact to statistical and numerical comparisons. Standard graphic packages include the ability to create bar charts, line graphs, area charts, and pie charts. All you have to do is enter the relevant numerical values and identifying labels. Some graphics software can electronically read data from compatible spreadsheet programs.

Of course, the impact of a graphics program is heavily dependent on the two forms of visual output: the monitor screen and the hard copy generated by a dot-matrix printer (daisy-wheel printers are not suitable for graphics). High-resolution color in the monitor and multicolor capabilities in the printer are necessary if professional-looking graphics are to be a common and important part of your presentations.

Features to look for in the graphics software itself are: the ability to fill in areas with color of shading; a choice of thin or thick lines to outline the images;

the option to place labels and legends wherever you desire rather than in fixed positions; enlarging and reducing functions; different type styles; and so forth.

Communications Software

Communications software is required for personal computers to talk to one another over telephone lines. It is what turns a "dumb" terminal into a "smart" one. (See page 147 for more information on computer-to-computer telephone links.)

Fairly basic types of communications programs will let you store data received over telephone lines, edit messages before they are transmitted, and operate options on your modem such as auto answer and auto dial. More advanced software will let you program *micros*, which are one or two keystroke combinations that replace longer, frequently used strings of text or commands. Micros are important because they save time on phone connections.

The most powerful versions of communications software make your personal computer accessible over the phone lines to other people (or to you when you're away from the office). The computer will answer incoming calls, log the caller onto your computer system (requesting a password if necessary), and run programs and display data files. The callers can even leave messages or update your data files.

You can purchase communications software separately, or as part of package when you buy a modem or subscribe to on-line information utility. While it is not absolutely necessary that two computers exchanging information over the phone lines have the same software package, it is simpler. Otherwise you will have to learn the command structure of the software operating the computer at the other end of your telephone connection.

Integrated Software

One of the major problems with software developed right after personal computers first became popular was that only one program could be run at a time. Whenever you wanted to switch from word processing to a spreadsheet program, for instance, you had no option but to shut down the word-processing program, change the disk, and load the spreadsheet program.

Integrated software solves this problem by combining word processing, data-base management, spreadsheets, graphs, and telecommunications (or some combination thereof) on one disk.

With a fully integrated system a report can be drafted and edited, financial information and graphs inserted, and the final version transmitted by electronic mail to a mailing list of 50 different clients—all without changing the disk or quitting and loading different programs. Integrated software typically features "windows" which allow you to view and work with the various programs on the screen at one time.

If in a typical workday you plan to run numerous types of programs—spreadsheets, word processing, data management—then you should consider buying integrated software. For one thing, an integrated package can be less expensive than five separate, top-quality programs. Secondly, data needs to be entered only once in an integrated system, whereas with stand-alone packages the same piece of information has to be entered for each type of program.

On the other hand, if you need only one or two types of software, say word processing and telecommuting, buying a package that includes high-powered spreadsheet and data-base management capabilities is a waste of money. A better idea would be to buy a top-quality word processing program with built-in communications capabilities, and then pick up more moderately priced spreadsheet and data-base programs as needed. Also, loading an integrated software package into your computer eats up huge blocks of the computer's internal memory. If your computer only has a 64 or 128 kilobyte memory, an integrated package won't leave much room for you to enter the data you will actually want to process.

Three More Things You Should Know About Software

Software versions. Buying computer software is like buying an almanac or a new car: By the next year a newer, better version will be put out, and you will be left with an outdated product. The problem is compounded when the software manuals, which generally aren't updated as often as the programs themselves, don't jibe with the way the program actually runs. Trying to run the 1.25 version of a word-processing program while consulting a manual that was written for the 1.0 version can result in computer mayhem.

When you buy software from computer stores or through the mail, always specify the most current version. And remember, if you run across a popular software package that is heavily discounted or "thrown in for free" as part of a hardware package, it's probably because the software is an older version. It still might be a good deal, but don't confuse its capabilities with what you might have just read about the program in a current computer magazine.

Software support. The degree of assistance a software publisher provides a user who purchases its product can make the difference between a well-loved, well-utilized software tool and a software package that sits idle on the shelf. Good support includes well-written manuals describing how to install, operate, and diagnose problems in the program; tutorial lessons on the program disk itself so that you learn as you run the program; a toll-free telephone number that puts you promptly in touch with a helpful customer service representative; periodic free program updates, both in written and disk form; and referrals to user groups in local areas. Bad support includes manuals that are incomprehensible; no telephone assistance; and no concern about mistakes in program operation.

The bigger and more established the software publisher, the better the support should be. New, small publishers may not be around very long, abandoning you and your software.

Cost. No doubt about it, software is EXPENSIVE. And there are no money-back guarantees if you are not completely satisfied, either. That's why you should never buy any program that you can't or won't use, either because it's not compatible with your hardware or too complex.

In addition, don't buy more powerful—and more expensive—software than you need. If all you really need is a spreadsheet to calculate next year's cash flow, it doesn't make sense to buy a program that can project the Gross National Product into the year 1999. And don't forget that there are plenty of software programs that are in the public domain, meaning that you can copy and use them free of charge. The electronic bulletin boards on many information utilities feature public domain software that can be "downloaded" into personal computers. Several book publishers are also finding out that a lot of computer users are willing to pay $19.95 for a book full of public domain programs, even if they do have to enter the programs themselves.

THE COMPUTER SHOPPING LIST

Now that you are thoroughly familiar with the different types of software applications and what sets one particular program apart from another, you are ready to make up your "Computer Shopping List."

Following the form in Figure 7-1, consider the business applications you want to run on your computer: word processing, spreadsheets, data-base management, accounting, graphics, and/or communications. Then, in the columns provided enter your best estimates of how much information you want your computer to handle and in what form you will need it.

For instance, if you decide you want to use your computer for word processing, estimate how long your documents will be (single-page letters or book manuscripts) and how the documents must look (letter perfect or simply readable). If you want to manage a data base, how many records will you be entering, how long will they be, what will you want to do with the information after it's entered?

This exercise is essential for several reasons. First, it will give you something to show a computer sales representative. The first-time buyer is best served by going to a computer store and asking a knowledgeable sales rep about specific software and computer recommendations. The sales rep should give you a dem-

Figure 7-1 Computer Shopping List

Type of Application	Capacity	Output Needed
Word Processing	Length of documents _____	Formal letters? Internal reports? How many pages a day?
Spreadsheets	Number of points in matrix _____	Internal calculations? Integrated informal reports?
Data-Base Management	Number of records _____	Mailing lists, etc? Outlines? Research?
Graphics	Types of graphs _____	Internal analysis? Formal presentations?
Communications	Smart terminal or remote access? Estimated hours on-line _____	Private network? PAMS? Information utilities?

onstration of different programs and equipment and even let you try them out yourself.

Second, you will start narrowing down your software selections. As you have seen specific software packages vary considerably based on how much information they can handle and what they can do with it. It is essential that you choose programs that can meet—and not unnecessarily exceed—your intended use and projected future needs.

Compatibility

Third, your shopping list will help you to make sure that your software programs are compatible with any computer equipment—called hardware—that you might consider buying.

You should understand that at this time there are few standards in the world of computers. The situation is comparable to the early days of the automobile, before manufacturers agreed that all cars should run on the same type of fuel. Eventually, maybe all computers will use the same operating system and process information in the same manner, but that's certainly not the case now.

Some brands of software are *machine-dependent*, meaning they can only be run on certain brands of computer. Software specifically developed and sold by computer manufacturers as part of a package with their hardware is typically machine-dependent. Try to run it on another computer and you will only get gibberish.

Other software packages will run on different computer brands and models, as long as they all have the same memory capacity and number of disk drives, process information at the same rate, use a certain operating system, etc. However, the software must be "configured" to the capabilities and specifications of the hardware. You can ask the software sales representative to do this for you. Or you can try it yourself, in which case you will have to enter information about the arrangement of the keyboard, terminal screen size, speed of the computer's central processor, printer's print wheel and spacing capabilities, etc.

In addition, software must be compatible with the computer's operating system, the basic program that gets the computer up and running. All computers must be "booted" (computerese for "primed") with an operating system before they can load and run any type of software and before they can successfully interact with printers, modems, and other peripherals. There are three major types of operating systems for personal computers: *DOS* (Disk Operating System), *CP/M* (Control Program/Microcomputer), and *Unix*.

Computer manufacturers commonly license operating systems from their publishers and then develop their own unique adaptations for their own hardware; for instance, Apple-DOS (Apple) and PC-DOS (IBM). In addition, software is limited not only by operating system but also by the version of the operating system.

Getting Down to the Hardware of the Matter

The fourth function of your computer shopping list is to determine how powerful a computer you need. A computer with too small a memory will not be able to handle powerful software, long documents, or hundreds of records. On the other hand, if your files are relatively short and software elementary, a huge memory capability will be underutilized and will be money wasted that could have been better spent elsewhere.

Lastly, the shopping list will insure that you can add on all the peripherals—printers, modems, hard disks—that you need. For instance, some computers cannot operate daisy-wheel printers, which would cause problems if you require absolutely perfect, letter-quality printing.

COMPUTER HARDWARE

When you walk into an appliance store and ask to see the clothes dryers, you will be shown various versions of the same basic machine: a rotating drum with a heater and blower. The differences between makes and models rest in the quality of manufacture and options: how hot the air is, how long the drum turns, how loud the buzzer is.

But what if the sales representative shows you (1) six different types of drums—one square, one round, one with slots in the sides, one made out of glass, and so on; (2) ten types of heating elements; (3) fifteen blowers; and (4) twelve venting systems? And imagine that when you get home you find that the parts don't work together, which really doesn't matter because none of them came with an electrical cord to plug the dryer in.

That's what it can feel like to buy a computer. In fact, the term "computer" is very misleading, especially for first-time buyers. If you walk into a computer store and ask to see a computer, you may be shown anything from a plastic box to what looks like a combination typewriter/TV. And all at widely varying prices.

Rather than think about computers, let's consider computer components. Several components can be enclosed in the same case or they can all be completely separate. Some can be added to expand the capabilities and functions of others. Actually, there are no absolutely right computers, only the right combinations of components.

Microprocessors

Microprocessors are the raw brain-power of the computer system. Microprocessors operate on a binary system, meaning all information is reduced to either a *1* or *0*, each called a bit. Individual characters are distinguished by the precise order of eight-bit combinations. For instance, the letter *A* equals 10000001, the letter *B* equals 10000010, and so forth. These eight-bit combinations, called *bytes*, are processed simultaneously along parallel paths in the microprocessor. Some microprocessors process 8 bits at a time, some handle 16, and others 32. The difference translates into how much and how fast the processor can sort, calculate, read, compare, and otherwise manipulate data.

Random Access Memory (RAM)

This is the system's internal memory. When data is entered from the keyboard or read off a diskette or cassette, the information enters the internal memory, there to be referred to and manipulated by the microprocessor. Data in the internal memory exists in a purely electronic state. If the system loses its power, the internal memory is wiped clean, and the data is lost—completely. Only when data is recorded on a diskette or cassette, called "writing" or "saving," is it stored for future retrieval.

RAM capacity is measured in kilobytes (one kilobye equals 1,024 bytes), and in personal computers ranges from 65K to over 500K. Since a software program must also be read into the system's internal memory, it takes up some of this capacity, leaving only the remainder for whatever specific data the user wishes to enter. Obviously, the more powerful and complex the software, the larger the computer's RAM must be. Some computers have built-in slots for installing additional circuitry panels to expand the system's RAM.

Drives

Drives are the mechanical systems that read and save information on a storage medium. There are three types of mediums: *tape cassettes*, which are identical to music tape cassettes; *floppy diskettes*, which resemble flexible "records" in permanent protective sleeves; and *hard disks*, which are hard plastic disks. Cassettes and floppy diskettes (for convenience sake called "disks" from now on) are manually inserted into slots on the computer that contain the drives. A hard disk, on the other hand, is permanently built into the computer system and is not interchangeable.

All disks have limited storage capacity, just as a record can only contain a certain number of songs. Hard disks have the greatest capacity (over 10 megabytes, or 10 million bytes) and are necessary for extremely large data bases. Hard disks also have the advantage of being able to contain numerous software programs, so that you can load programs without having to insert several different program disks.

Floppy diskettes vary in their capacity, depending on size (5 1/4-inch diskettes are most common for personal computers), whether both sides can be used, and density. Double-sided, double-density floppy diskettes can store up to 360 kilobytes. Cassettes' capacity is based on the length of the tape. Of course, since disks are interchangeable, there is no limit on how many a computer library may contain.

What type and number of drives your computer should have depends on the type of software you will want to use on it. Most business-oriented software packages require two double-sided floppy-disk drives—one to run the program disk and the other to run the disk that records the information you enter, called a *data disk*. A hard disk and one floppy-disk drive will also accommodate most business applications.

If you're not sure about how many or what type of disk drives you need, make sure any computer you consider purchasing has the capacity to install additional drives. Some equipment has room for adding an internal hard disk and/or attaching supplemental disk drives.

Disk drives are more prone to mechanical breakdown than any other part of a computer system, except printers. As with high-quality stereo tape recorders, the heads are extremely susceptible to dust and dirt, which is picked up off the disk surfaces. Therefore, keep your disks clean and, if you run the same disks every day, don't use them for more than six months, as they also tend to wear down. Periodic cleaning (once a year) of the drives either by a service representative or with a high-quality drive-head cleaning kit, is recommended.

Monitors

Monitors—also called *video displays* and *CTRs*—let you see what you and the computer are doing. Most monitors work on the same principle as a television tube, and in fact, with the proper connectors the family TV set can serve as a monitor for a personal computer. (Note, however, that computer monitors cannot be used as TVs, since they lack the ability to recognize and translate broadcast signals.)

There are two basic type of monitors: monochromatic and color. Monochromatic monitors produce a one-color image—white, green, or amber—on a black or green background. If you are going to use your computer primarily for word processing, spreadsheets, or accounting, you should get a monochromatic monitor; not only will it be cheaper than a color monitor, but it will also be easier to read. Whether green images or amber images are better seems to depend entirely on individual preference.

A color monitor is advisable if you are going to run graphics programs most of the time. Color monitors vary greatly in the degree of resolution and range of colors they can produce.

Important things to consider when choosing a monitor are how distinct, clear, and steady the images are; how fast the monitor can receive and display information from the computer (measured in bandwidth); the availability of contrast and brightness controls; and the physical size and weight of the monitor, since it is usually placed above or on the computer box itself.

Monitors eventually wear out as the phosphorus that coats the inside of the screen burns out. If you leave the monitor running but not in use, turn the contrast or brightness control down until the screen is completely dark.

Keyboards

It turns out your mother was right when she advised you to take that typing course in high school. Computer manufacturers continue to struggle with the problem of making computers useful for people who can't type. But until they come up with a model that can understand oral instructions or that can read brainwaves, typing remains the most practical way to communicate with a personal computer.

You can buy educational software that teaches you how to type *on the computer*. This is a good way to improve your skills and learn about the computer at the same time.

Computer keyboards are modified typewriter keyboards and use the QWERTY key layout (Q-W-E-R-T-Y are the fist six letters across the top row), although it is possible to reprogram the computer for the Dvorak layout. Additional features include:

Cursor and screen keys. There are four keys to the right of the main QWERTY section that move the cursor up, down, left, and right. Four more keys scroll the screen up and down, and jump to the end or beginning of the file. In their upper-case mode these keys double as numerical keys in an adding-machine layout.

Macros. These are keys that the user can program to stand for frequently used, longer strings of keystrokes. A common keyboard layout has 10 keys reserved as macros, F1 through F10, located to the left of the main QWERTY section. These can be expanded to 40 keys by using the prefix keys "Control," "Escape," and "Alternate." Under certain software packages the prefix keys are also used with standard letters to issue commands.

Mouse. The mouse is an option available on some computers and is a small, hand-held attachment with a wheel on the bottom and two buttons on top (the mouse's "ears"). By sliding the mouse on the desktop, you can move the cursor around the screen. The buttons are used with on-screen prompts to execute commands.

Printers

Since the days of the completely paperless office are still in the far future, the printer is the most important peripheral to the "thinking" parts of the computer system. It can also be the most expensive.

Printers fall into two major categories: *impact* and *nonimpact* printers. The impact category includes dot-matrix printers, which use a print head composed of tiny rods that strike the paper surface in different combinations to form characters; and letter-quality printers, which use molded, typewriter-like characters on daisy-wheel or spin-thimble spokes to form impressions.

The nonimpact category includes ink-jet printers, which form characters by spraying ink from the print head onto the paper; and laser printers, which use a laser beam to trace images on a light-sensitive drum. Toner adheres to the images etched on the drum and is transferred to paper, much in the same way a photocopier works. Both ink-ject and laser printers use dot-matrix methods to form characters.

Important factors to consider when selecting a printer include:

Cost. Printers can be very expensive—just how expensive depends on the type, features, and manufacturer. The nonimpact printers, representing state-of-the art technology, are at the high end in cost and the impact dot-matrix at the low. But, as you will see, cost must be balanced against the individual printer's capabilities and operation. The purchase of an inexpensive printer that does not produce the necessary quality of document in an efficient manner means that the entire investment in the computer system is threatened.

Print quality. Impact dot-matrix printers produce characters that can look distinctly "computerish." Documents produced by letter-quality printers, on the other hand, are indistinguishable from those typed on a typewriter. Thus, if you need to produce business correspondence and other text for presentation purposes, you should get a letter-quality printer. However, most letter-quality printers cannot produce good graphics, so if this function is important, you'll need a dot-matrix printer.

The sharpness of the image created by a dot-matrix printer depends on the density of the rod points on the print head. Impact printers range to a high of 75 × 75 point per inch. Nonimpact printers have much higher density: from 150 × 150 to 300 × 300, and they can produce extremely sharp characters that appear identical to those produced on a letter-quality printer. At the same time they retain strong graphics capabilities.

Speed. This is measured in characters per second (CPS). The letter-quality printers are the slowest, since they must rotate the daisy wheel or spin thimble to locate each character. CPS for letter-quality printers ranges from 20 to 200 but averages between 40 and 60. Compare this with impact dot-matrix printers, which average 250 CPS but can reach speeds of 600 CPS. Unfortunately, with dot-matrix impact printers the faster the CPS, the poorer the print quality. But if your business must produce hundreds of pages a day, it might be worth the tradeoff. Or it might be worth the extra cost of a nonimpact printer, which can produce near letter-quality print at 300 CPS.

Noise. The clatter of an impact printer, especially a letter-quality one, can make it impossible to hold a telephone conversation nearby. This can be remedied to a certain extent with a noise-reduction hood, a clear plastic case that fits over the printer. Or the printer can be located in a separate room or closet, although this can be inconvenient if single sheets of letterhead have to be hand-fed into the machine. Also, there is a limit on how long the cable from the computer to the printer can be without the signal suffering distortion.

Noise is not a problem with nonimpact printers, since the print head never actually contacts the paper.

Feed. There are two types of feed mechanisms. The first works on the pressure of the roller and is similar to the way a piece of paper is held in a typewriter (roller-friction feed). The second is through a *tractor feed*, sprocket wheels that lock into holes on the sides of continuous-form paper.

While the roller-friction feeds are designed for use with single sheets of paper, you can use them with continuous-form paper. The only drawback is that you have to stay right next to the printer to make sure the paper doesn't start feeding in crooked.

Compatibility. The printer receives the information it prints from the computer, and it sends back messages that let the computer know when the printing is finished. Therefore, compatibility between the printer, the computer, and the software is essential.

The printer has either a *serial* or *parallel interface* with the computer. A parallel interface means that data is transmitted eight bits at a time, similar to the way bytes are processed within the computer itself (see the section on Microprocessors on page 102). Serial interfaces require that the eight-bit blocks be broken down and each bit lined up one after another in a serial fashion. The important thing to remember is that serial printers must interface with a serial port (the place where the printer cable is connected to the computer), and parallel printers must interface with a parallel port.

Compatibility between the printer and the software package is essential in order to take advantage of the full scope of features each contains. A printer that has any of the extra features discussed below will not be able to use them if combined with a bare-bones software program, and vice versa.

Special features. These might include the ability to create different designs of type styles, underline text, print in boldface, and print sub- and superscripts. Proportional spacing (adjusting the width and height of characters to fit available space), adjustable pitch (amount of space between characters), and adjustable line height and space between lines are important features that lend a typeset quality to documents. All must be supported by the proper software package.

Maintenance. The printer, because of the mechanical nature of its operation, will probably be the first computer component to break down. Therefore, the quality of manufacture, warranty, and service options are important considerations in making a selection. Also, certain parts may need regular replacement, such as plastic daisy wheels which eventually deteriorate from the force of impact. Keep back-up wheels in stock in case an old one breaks.

Cables. One other note on printers: Unlike monitors and keyboards, printers do not come with their own cables to connect them to the computer. The printer cable is an extra expense and must be configured with the specific printer and specific computer in mind. Otherwise, the printer will not work, something that can cause terrible frustration to the computer owner who has carefully constructed and configured all the other aspects of the computer system.

Modems

Modems are what put you on-line with other computers across the nation. The main function of a modem is to translate signals that the computer produces into signals that can be relayed over telephone lines. It *mo*dulates and *demo*dulates the signals—thus the term *modem*.

Modems transmit signals at various speeds, measured in *bauds*. A modem operating at 300 bauds means that approximately 30 characters are transmitted every second over the phone line. One that operates at 1,200 bauds transmits approximately 120 characters per second. The faster rate translates into lower long-distance telephone bills, since the connect time required to transmit a block of data is less. And the slower rate will seem ponderous to computer users accustomed to the quick responsiveness of personal computers.

Modems also differ in how they connect to the telephone line. Older models sometimes had an acoustic coupling device that cradled the handset of a standard telephone. The quality of transmission was seriously impaired by the slight vibration generated by the modem's tone modulation. Today, almost all modems plug directly into the telephone wall jack, and there is no telephone set involved. The phone company requires that you inform them if you attach a direct modem to a phone jack.

Modems can either be separate pieces of equipment or be installed inside the computer. A stand-alone modem, which sits on the desktop near the computer, is connected by cable to what is called a *serial port* on the computer. As is the case with serial printers, modems require that data be broken down into bit-by-bit serial sequences rather than transmitted in the simultaneous eight-bit units used by the microprocessor. The serial port, sometimes called a *communications port* or *RS-232-C port*, is a panel inside the computer that does this rearranging.

Internal or *card* modems are built directly into the computer itself and include the serial port if one is not already present. Internal modems are convenient because you don't have to juggle an additional piece of equipment at the computer work station. On the other hand, internal modems must be specifically designed and installed inside the computer (something most owners should not attempt themselves), and if you ever decide to get a new computer, you will not be able to transfer the internal modem from your old one.

Special options on modems include auto answer and auto dial, a memory for frequently dialed numbers, and automatic switching between 300-baud and 1,200-baud speeds, and between pulse- and tone-generated dialing. However, there's no reason to buy these extra features if you don't have the proper communications software designed to operate them.

Useful Computer "Gadgets"

In addition to the basic computer components, you may want to consider some of the following extras to protect and enhance your setup.

Surge protectors. Electricity is a highly volatile form of energy. Sudden and severe increases in voltage occur on electrical lines quite often, caused by electrical storms, transformer blowouts, and generator switchovers. A very sharp, short increase (as high as 9,000 volts) is called a *spike*, and a longer but less intense jump is a *surge*.

Spikes and surges can wreck havoc on a computer. At the very least they will ruin whatever data is in the internal memory. They may even scramble data stored on disks in the drives. At the worst they will destroy the chips in the microprocessor.

Surge protectors absorb these increases and protect the computer, its peripherals, and software. They resemble multiple extension outlets and are plugged in between the computer and the wall outlet. Generally, the more expensive the surge protector, the more protection it will provide.

Buffers. Since a printer can't print as fast as the computer can transmit the signal, the printer has a small memory where it temporarily stores data. Once the printer has emptied its memory, the computer transmits another batch of data, then waits until the printer is ready again. This process means that while the printer is running, the computer is tied up feeding it small segments of the file being printed.

A buffer is a larger memory unit installed between the computer and the printer which receives and stores entire files for printing. It then slowly feeds the data to the printer and leaves the computer free for other uses.

Glare filters. It's almost impossible to arrange room lighting and the monitor so that all glare is eliminated from the screen. The solution is a clear, smoke-colored filter that fits on the monitor screen and traps all reflected glare. Glare filters are fairly inexpensive and certainly worth the price in terms of saving your eyesight.

SELECTING COMPUTER EQUIPMENT

Now that you have a rough sketch of the computer software and components that will suit your needs, you must start investigating specific computer makes and models. At this point you should talk to friends, family, business acquaintances, and anyone else who owns or uses a personal computer. Ask them about their equipment and software, what they like and don't like about it, what the repair record is like, where they bought their equipment.

Also, put aside time to visit local computer stores and browse through their offerings. Chat with sales representatives. Show them your "shopping list" and give them some general range of what you think you can afford for the entire system.

And remember that you won't be buying equipment, you will be buying support, too. The person who sells you the equipment is probably going to be the person who helps you install it and work through any problems in the first few days or weeks. A knowledgeable, patient, and accessible sales representative will prove invaluable.

Always test-drive different systems with the types of software you are interested in using. This is the only way to find out how "user-friendly" a system is, how quickly the computer responds, whether you are comfortable with the keyboard layout, how noisy and fast the printer is, how much noise the disk drives make, and so forth. Also, ask to see all the instruction and installation manuals for both the hardware and the software. These will be your only written references, and if you can't understand them, you lose an important resource.

After you have narrowed your selection down to three or four systems, consider the manufacturer. Is the company likely to go out of business, leaving you with "orphaned" equipment that can't be repaired? How much new software is being developed for this particular type of computer? How compatible is its operation with that of other computers? Does the manufacturer have a toll-free customer service line? Does it offer an unlimited warranty and service contracts?

As you narrow down both the equipment selection and the retail outlet, find out *exactly* what will be included in the purchase price. Try to get the sales rep to throw some "extras" into the price of the computer system, such as free or discounted software packages; free blank disks, printer ribbons, extra daisy wheels, other supplies; subscriptions to information utilities; classes on the computer and software operation, or several hours of training in your office. Also, find out if the supplier will configure cables and software for you and install the system in your office without charge.

HOW (AND HOW NOT) TO CUT COMPUTER COSTS

Discount and mail-order computer outlets offer hardware and software at between 10 percent and 50 percent off the retail price. They can do this because they don't provide any of the support services a retail outlet does. They don't help a customer select equipment; they don't configure or install equipment; they can't answer any questions about operation and compatibility; and sometimes they will not replace or repair faulty equipment. In fact, some manufacturers will not honor a warranty if the equipment is not bought at a retail dealer. Therefore, the first-time buyer assumes a high risk by shopping by mail or through a discounter.

Experienced buyers, on the other hand, can and do take advantage of the reduced prices, because they have the knowledge and experience to do much of their own research and installation. The same thing is true for buying used equipment. For instance, someone familiar with the way a disk drive is supposed to sound can spot an unusually noisy or laboring drive on used equipment. The novice might not.

One sure way to reduce the cost of computer equipment is to buy in quantity, ideally through a corporate purchasing department. If you work with a large client firm which purchases personal computer equipment for their employees, investigate the possibility of getting in on one of their orders. Besides realizing a significant price break, you will also have equipment that is identical and thus 100 percent compatible with your client's. (You must make sure, however, that the system meets your needs and is not designed strictly for large office networks.)

Quantity price breaks aren't limited strictly to big corporate orders. A complete business computer system and starter software package represent a lot of profit to computer retailers, who generally mark up hardware by at least 25 percent and software by 50 percent. Even if you can find only one or two other people to go in on a quantity order, you may still be able to talk the retailer down 10 percent or 15 percent.

THE COMPUTER IN THE HOME OFFICE

Deciding where to put computer equipment in the home office need not be a difficult or expensive task. All that's really required is a desktop for the computer and a stand for the printer.

You can also purchase any of the wide array of furniture especially designed for computer work stations, from expensive, hand-rubbed teak versions to inexpensive but functional models made of metal and formica. All have basically the same design: The monitor is placed on a shelf over the box that contains the computer "innards," the keyboard is put in front or on a drawer like shelf that slides under the desktop. The printer is on a separate stand, since its vibration can be detrimental to the other equipment. Another thing these furnishings all have in common is that there's rarely enough surface area to spread out papers, books, and other material you will probably be working with.

The monitor should be positioned so the light source is to the side of the screen and not directly in front of or behind it. Any other equipment that will be used in connection with the computer, such as a transcribing machine or telephone, should be within reach.

Several factors, however, are unique to the home-office computer and should be guarded against. They include:

Static

This is a particular problem with computers in the home, because residential carpeting often has higher wool content and a deeper pile than carpeting in traditional offices. Static electricity is generated any time two surfaces come in intermittent contact with each other, such as your feet and the floor when you walk across the room. When the air is dry, the static charge builds up until you touch something that is grounded or has its own charge. Unfortunately, this is sometimes an operating computer, and the result is a voltage spike that can erase the internal memory.

There are different types of antistatic devices, from floor mats to desk pads to sprays. You can also put a humidifier or ionizer in the office. Static isn't as serious a threat as a voltage spike that comes in over the electric lines, but it can be a nuisance and should be guarded against.

Heat and Cold

A computer generates heat when it is running; that is why you will hear a small fan anytime the computer is on. Be sure to leave plenty of space around the computer to allow for proper ventilation. Likewise, don't place your computer equipment near space heaters, radiators or hot-air ducts or in direct sunlight.

If your computer has been exposed to extremely cold temperatures (below freezing), let it warm up gradually before turning it on. Otherwise moisture will condense on the inside and possibly damage the circuitry. In general, your computer will function best if kept in the same room temperature environments that you find comfortable.

Airborne Pollution

This includes dust, smoke from cigarettes, cooking oils from frying and broiling, pollen from flowering house plants, even pet hairs. All can settle on disks and drives, and damage the disk heads that read and store data.

In general, computer equipment should not be exposed to smoke from cigarettes and cooking, which means keeping it in an area that can be sealed off from the rest of the residence. Specific actions to protect against pollutants are to keep the latches over the drives closed (with either an old disk or a cardboard insert in the slot); keep loose disks in a covered storage file; and cover the equipment with dust covers when it is not in use, and when vacuuming or otherwise raising a lot of dust.

Electrical Circuits

If the computer is on the same circuit with large household appliances, you may have problems maintaining a steady flow of current to the computer. For instance, when the refrigerator cycles on and off, it creates drains and surges on the current. If the circuit is overloaded, power will be lost completely and along with it any data in the computer's internal memory.

The only real solution is in the wiring. Don't use the same circuit for both computer equipment and anything else that creates a heavy drain on current, including appliances, air conditioners, space heaters, and humidifiers or dehumidifiers. If a separate circuit isn't available and can't be installed, consider purchasing an uninterruptable power source. This is a fairly expensive battery back-up system that takes over whenever the electrical current dips, is terminated, or fluctuates in any way. Installed between the computer and the wall outlet, it is always charged and ready to take over in case of a blackout. The power source will keep the computer system operating for only a limited amount of time, but it is sufficient to store on the disk whatever you are working on.

Children and Pets

The charming little creatures should not be allowed near the home-office computer. As harsh as this may sound, they can "dump" an entire day's work with a playful poke at the keyboard or a swish of a tail. Cats in particular are attracted to the warmth and whir of computers. When they rub up against equipment, the static electricity generated is sure to ravage the internal memory and may even cause harm to the microprocessor.

Personal Use

The temptation to use a home-office computer for personal use is great—after all, it's just sitting there and would be a great help in personal correspondence or personal finances. However, be aware that personal use of a computer located in a home office jeopardizes the exclusive-use requirement for home-office deductions. Also, the computer time spent on personal use cannot be included in calculating the expense deduction for the computer itself or its depreciation.

8

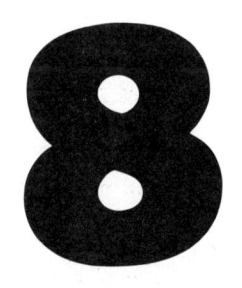

Suppliers and Servicers: Important Members of Your Home-Office Team

Office supplies, telephone, and delivery and repair services comprise the most significant overhead expense associated with home offices. Even in traditional offices, telephone service is usually the third major monthly expense, behind rent and salaries. In the home office, with its increased reliance on telecommunications, the phone bill is commonly *the* largest item on the monthly budget. It's also the most important to pay on time, since loss of phone service not only will leave you stranded but is extremely damning to your business image.

Large businesses hire office managers who are responsible for budgeting, purchasing, and keeping track of supplies and use of office services. But for someone working out of a home office, these important tasks must compete with the numerous other responsibilities involved in running a small business. Too frequently, supply and service oversight gets shuffled aside until the office runs out of stationery or until the phone bill drives the company into bankruptcy. But it doesn't have to be that way.

THE FIVE "Cs"

There are five "Cs" to keep in mind when buying supplies and services.

Confidence

Deal only with stable, recognized businesses. This is especially true when ordering office supplies over the phone or through the mail, since this area is prone to scams and fraud. Also, if the supplier goes out of business, it will be impossible to return defective items. Generally, if the company has a printed catalog and sells recognized brand-name goods, it is probably on the up and up. Of course, a referral or recommendation from a happy customer is the best evidence to go by. Be *extra* suspicious of any unsolicited phone calls offering unbelievable discounts on office supplies.

It's also important to have confidence in the quality of the supplies and services themselves. "Bargain" office supplies that end up tossed in the wastepaper basket because of grossly inferior quality are no bargain at all. The same thing is true of discount long-distance services with poor sound quality, and "overnight" courier services that deliver the package two days late. They may be less expensive than their competition, but unless they are reliable, the price is still too dear.

Cost

Again, the least expensive buy is not necessarily the best buy. There are ways, however, to find suppliers who give more for the dollar and still provide quality supplies and services.

First, check out the competition. Don't buy from the local office supply store just because it's the only one in town. Mail-order suppliers stock most of the same items and brand names and usually are much cheaper. (Some will pay for the delivery charges if the order is above a certain amount.)

The most important step in smart comparison shopping is to reduce prices to a common basis. For instance, two long-distance phone companies might offer competitive per-minute charges for their services, but Company X has an 800 access number and Company Y doesn't. In fact, calling Company Y's access number might be a toll call itself, and this cost must be added onto Company Y's price for a true comparative analysis.

Second, take advantage of sales and other price-reduction tactics. The best office suppliers are those who regularly reduce common items such as pencils, diskettes, file folders, and other standard office consumables. It also makes sense to buy in quantity if the supplier reduces the per-item cost, although the quantity has to have some realistic relationship to your actual consumption. Buying 200 typewriter ribbons for one machine, for instance, would not be wise; buying 12 at a time would.

Other price-reduction tactics arise from carefully studying the supplier or servicer's price structure. There are always discount times for making telephone calls; less expensive shipping rates; and "extras" that automatically get added on unless you specifically exclude them.

Convenience

Cost savings can be canceled out if it takes a great deal of time and energy to deal with a particular supplier or servicer. This is particularly true if yours is a one-person operation, where there never seems to be enough time to get everything done. If a long-distance phone service is always busy or has lines out of order, if a delivery service won't come to the office to pick up a package, or if a repair service demands broken equipment be brought to the shop, the burden of doing business with them might not be worth their lower prices.

Conservation

Effective use of supplies and services is an exercise in old-fashioned frugality. The first tenet is to hold down on consumption and waste. Place a three-minute egg timer next to your phone, and time long-distance calls; don't seal packages and envelopes until right before shipment, in case something else comes up that needs to be sent to the same destination; always put the top back on rubber cement, correction fluid, ink pads, and anything else that will dry out; don't express-mail or ship a package by air to destinations less than 100 miles away; don't use express services for anything being shipped on Friday; always report misdialed long-distance calls for credit or deduct their charges from the bill.

The second rule is to *recycle*. Use both sides of a sheet of scratch paper; reuse file folders when their contents are discarded or put in "deep" storage; save used boxes and large padded envelopes; erase old data files on cassettes and diskettes; put address labels on envelopes that have mistakes in typed addresses, and use them to pay bills; reclaim and reuse copier toner.

Credit

Office suppliers and servicers are often the first sources of credit for new businesses and generally are willing to open accounts with minimal investigation of business and personal information. Two notable exceptions are the local phone company, which will demand a security deposit, and the U.S. Postal Service, which probably has good reason to demand payment before performance.

Charge accounts with suppliers help establish credit records, and keep control over and substantiate business expenses. Instead of numerous petty-cash slips, there's an itemized statement paid by check at the end of each month. Items bought on credit are also easier to return, since the supplier doesn't have to go into its own cash to issue a refund.

If a supplier or servicer is reluctant to grant credit right off, agree to pay on a cash basis for a while *if* after a certain period of time, say three months, credit will be reconsidered. Once a good customer relationship is established, and once the supplier has come to include your business in its projected cash flow, extending credit won't seem like such a risk.

STOCKING UP—TYPICAL OFFICE SUPPLY NEEDS

Stationery

The very first supply purchase for a new business should be stationery, including letterhead, second sheets (either printed or plain), #10 business envelopes, and business cards. Commercial printers can typeset names, addresses, telephone numbers, and anything else that is to appear on the stationery. Or the printer can work with a logo or graphic symbol designed by a graphic artist. Since stationery is the most basic form of marketing and will represent the business in every piece of correspondence, the importance of the image it portrays cannot be dismissed. As a rule, a clean, understated design is preferable to a gaudy or hokey one.

The letterhead should display your business's name, address, phone number, and if applicable, your on-line utility and User ID number. If the company is incorporated, this should be made clear on the letterhead so that correspondents will be made aware of what type of business entity they are dealing with. Most often "Inc." or "Incorporated" is part of the business name anyway, so this does not present any problem. However, if you operate your business as a division of your corporation and use a different name (legally called a *fictitious name*) then "A Division of _____, Inc." should appear on the letterhead somewhere.

The business address shown on the letterhead presents some particular problems for the home office. Many people working out of home offices do not want their street addresses on their letterhead because they don't want business associates and sales representatives dropping by their residences unannounced. They also may want to conceal the fact that they are working out of home offices, either because they think it has a negative image or because they fear zoning restrictions. So, they use a post office box number supplied by the U.S. Postal Service or a private post office.

On the other hand, post office boxes have a somewhat negative image themselves because of mail fraud abuses and are considered by some as a dead giveaway that the business is run out of a home office.

On a practical level, there are four things to consider. First, the post office may not be convenient to the home office or have any boxes available anyway, so that greatly simplifies the decision. Second, UPS and courier services such as Purolator and Federal Express *must* have a street address to deliver packages. If the delivery route is small and the regular driver is familiar with your street address, he or she might deliver your package anyway, but this can't be relied on.

Third, post offices usually put mail in post office boxes earlier in the morning and more frequently during the day. Finally, if you decide to put both the street address *and* a post office box number on your letterhead or business card, the order is important. The Postal Service delivers the mail to the address shown immediately above the city, state, and ZIP code line.

The second sheet of your stationery can either be completely plain or display the company logo and name. Obviously, second sheets are necessary for correspondence that is more than one page long, but they also are handy as invoices and for memoranda.

There are three basic ways to print stationery. The most expensive is engraving, which creates a raised print image. Engraving is used primarily by law offices and other professionals concerned with presenting a very prestigious image. The second is thermography, which also creates a raised image but is less expensive than engraving. The third, least expensive, and most popular is offset printing. Almost all commercial printers have offset presses and will take jobs as small as a hundred sheets or envelopes.

The paper stock and color of ink you choose for your stationery depends on your personal preference and financial considerations. However, there are three things to remember about paper selection: Thick, heavy paper will show the impressions left by typewriter strike-over corrections; porous, bulky paper stocks absorb moisture easily; and dark or red-colored paper won't photocopy well. In addition, if you plan to use correction fluid, make sure your paper color matches one of the colors the fluid comes in.

Other printed stationery supplies might include small #6 3/4 envelopes 5 1/2-inch by 8 1/2-inch note pads, and adhesive mailing labels, although the latter can be run off on a copier if your need isn't great. You might also consider promotional brochures and presentation folders for marketing purposes.

Desktop Supplies

These include pens, refills, ink, pencils, leads, erasers, felt-tip markers, letter opener, rubber bands, paper clips, pushpins, stapler and staples, staple remover, scissors, utility knife, transparent tape and tape holder, ruler, calendar, ruled letter and legal pads, steno books, memo pads, telephone message pad, petty-cash receipts, columnar accounting paper, and graph paper.

Mailing Supplies

These include clasp or open-ended mailing envelopes, padded envelopes, cardboard flats and boxes, brown kraft wrapping paper, sealing or strapping tape, twine, rubber cement and thinner, ink pads, and stamps.

Filing Supplies

These include file folders and adhesive file labels, paper hole punch, file guides, hanging folders, expanding files, metal prong fasteners, index cards and index-card boxes, circular Rolodex-type file cards, and report binders.

Typewriter Supplies

These include carbon or cloth ribbons, correction ribbons, ink eraser and brush, correction fluid, correction tape, extra type elements or daisy wheels, plain white bond typing paper, drafting paper or newsprint, carbon paper, and onionskin or copy sets.

Copier Supplies

These include paper, plain adhesive labels, and toner, developer, oil, dispersant, concentrate, premix, or whatever other chemicals a particular copier may require.

Dictating Supplies

These include blank cassettes, cassette labels, and batteries.

Computer Supplies

These include diskettes or cassettes, library boxes, antistatic spray, head cleaners, printer ribbons, extra daisy wheels or spin thimbles, continous-form paper, preprinted forms, checks, postcards, and address cards.

Miscellaneous Supplies

These include light bulbs, window glass cleaner (for cleaning computer screens and copier windows), paper towels, paper cups, coffee, coffee filters, sugar or sweetener, nondairy creamer (or milk or cream), toilet paper, hand soap, plastic garbage-can liners, and cleaning supplies. It is also a good idea to keep a small screwdriver, whisk broom, and first-aid kit in the office.

STORING SUPPLIES

Ideally, supplies should be stored near the point of use: ribbons near the typewriter or printer; padded envelopes near the postage meter; legal pads on the desk. But while convenient, this approach is not very practical, since work areas usually can't accommodate both room to work and room to store supplies. Thus, while a very limited amount may be kept near the work area, most supply inventories will be stored in a central supply cabinet or closet.

A practical supply closet will have numerous narrowly spaced shelves so that loose supplies and boxes of stationery are not stacked on top of each other. Label the edge of each shelf with the general type of supply that is stored there. The closet should be relatively shallow so as not to hide items in deep recesses. It should be located where it does not occupy needed work area and yet is easily accessible.

The supply closet should not be exposed to extreme heat or cold, or have heating and cooling ducts running through it unless the duct work is adequately insulated. Most important, *paper supplies must be kept away from excess moisture and humidity*. Entire boxes of printed envelopes can become prematurely sealed if the gummed flaps get too damp. You can buy little cloth bags full of chemicals that will absorb moisture in the supply closet, but they are only effective if the closet is sealed.

After the initial stocking of the supply needs, a reorder pad should be posted near the supply closet with a pen or pencil tied to it. This way, whenever the last box of something is opened or supplies are low, just jot down the type of supply and the stock number off the carton. Periodically (say once a month), tear the list off and reorder.

LOCAL TELEPHONE SERVICE

Under current tax laws, business use of a general household phone line is deductible as long as adequate records are kept to substantiate the expense. This requires keeping a phone log not only of business calls but of nonbusiness calls as well, since the deduction calculation is a *percentage* of the monthly local service charge.

This is a major reason why most home offices have separate phone lines installed that are used exclusively for business purposes and are totally deductible. Other reasons are to avoid competition with other members of the household for time on the telephone and to get around the sticky question of how to answer a phone that rings both for the business and the private residence. Simply answering "Hello" may not sound businesslike enough, while answering with the business's name may confuse a caller trying to reach another member of the household.

At this point at least, there's no question about which supplier to choose for local telephone service for the home office: There are no competitors to the local telephone company. But you do have a choice about what type of service to get: residential or business.

Residential or Business Service?

Residential service is less expensive. Because of this, the phone company restricts its use to private residences only, since it figures that businesses would want to take advantage of the lower monthly service charge and run residential service into their offices. Theoretically, this restriction applies to the home office, too. However, there's little way the phone company can enforce the restriction if it doesn't *know* that the room the service is running to in the home is a business office.

Residential service can be listed only in an individual's name and includes, but does not require, a listing under that name in the telephone directory white pages. (Note: You'll pay a slight additional charge each month *not* to be listed in the phone book.)

The monthly charge for business service is more expensive than for residential service, although the difference is not as great as it used to be. In addition, business service includes a listing in the Yellow Pages under the business name. If you don't want your street address listed, you can specify a general neighborhood, such as "Morningside Area."

If you decide to convert your residential phone service to business service, you will be assigned a new phone number and be charged a one-time fee for the administrative and technical work involved in changing your number in the phone company's central office. If you add a separate line for the home office, you must either install the new wiring yourself (using either separate, single-line wire or multiline cable) or pay the phone company or a contractor to do it. The phone company is responsible for maintenance on the telephone line only up to the point it enters the building.

Also be aware that adding an additional line for a home office located in an apartment building may require the written approval of the building owner.

The phone company will require a deposit, usually equal to two months' estimated phone bills, for a new line, unless it is listed in the name of someone who already has a good telephone credit standing. Credit for a new line listed in your business's name cannot rely on your individual credit rating. However, if you pay your telephone bills by the time they are due, then the deposit, with accrued interest, will be returned in a year.

Telephone Service Options

Two common options you can order through most local phone companies are *call waiting* and *call forwarding*. If you are talking on the phone and have the call-waiting option, you will hear a beep on the line when another incoming call is attempting to get through. You can put whomever you are talking to on hold by pressing the disconnect button once, which also connects you with the second caller.

Call waiting is not recommended if the line is also used with a modem that has an automatic hangup feature, since the modem will interpret the beep as a loss of carrier and terminate its on-line link.

If you have call forwarding in effect, you can redirect all your incoming calls to another phone number anywhere in the country. Before leaving the office, you simply call the phone company and enter a special code plus the telephone number to which the calls are to be forwarded. When you return to the office, you turn the call-forwarding feature off in a similar manner.

You should be aware that with call forwarding you will be charged any additional toll charges incurred to relay your calls. For example, let's say your office is in Dallas. You go on a business trip and put your phone on call forwarding, entering the number of where you will be staying in Philadelphia. If someone in Los Angeles should attempt to call your office in Dallas and be rerouted to Philadelphia, you—not the party in Los Angeles—will be charged for the Dallas-Philadelphia call. So, obviously call forwarding can become very expensive, even though the basic monthly charge for the service is low.

Some local telephone companies offer more advanced services, such as a display that shows the telephone number of the person calling you—so you can decide whether you want to be "in" and answer the line. Another service monitors and stores the phone numbers of the last thirty people who called you, in case you failed to get a number or the caller didn't leave a message on your answering machine.

Ways to Hold Down Your Phone Bill

Ask a phone company service representative about optional types of service, such as optional toll and selective calling. With these services, for a flat fee each month you may talk for a specified time—from 60 minutes to 20 hours—to exchanges in your area which would normally be toll calls.

Order all your changes in telephone service and installation at once. This will save on those one-time charges incurred every time you ask the phone company to do something.

Call before 8:00 A.M., after 5:00 P.M., and on weekends and holidays when the rates are lower. Also, always dial direct rather than involve the operator (or even a computerized operator), since this increases the cost of the entire call.

Don't hesitate to ask for credit on wrong numbers and poor connections. After all, why should you pay for a service you didn't receive?

LONG-DISTANCE TELEPHONE SERVICE

Under the AT&T divestiture ruling, eventually all phone customers will have to choose a long-distance servicer (called a carrier) or be assigned one by the local company. But unlike local service, the long-distance phone service market is replete with competitors. All offer essentially the same thing—long-distance telephone calls at lower prices than those presently charged by AT&T. But just how much lower differs greatly, as do quality of transmission and extra features like operator assistance.

Choosing a Long-Distance Carrier

To compare long-distance charges among different available carriers, it's important to consider these factors:

Where are you calling? Many long-distance carriers don't service calls between numbers within the same area code, and some don't service calls between numbers within the same state. And just because a particular carrier's toll between, say, Boston and Washington is lower than another's, this doesn't mean it is the best choice for a user in Pittsburgh. Far more important would be to compare the charges for calls that originate from Pittsburgh.

Some carriers must add extra charges for calls to locations "off-net," that is, locations far away from their nearest receiving stations. This is because they have to lease lines from other companies to complete the last leg of the call, and these costs are usually passed on to the customer.

Therefore, it's essential that you compare the rates different carriers charge for typical calls *you* expect to make. Additionally, since discount carriers are not regulated by the government, their rates can and do change frequently, so a reanalysis is probably in order every year or so.

Local telephone costs. For example, if you must dial a local number to access the carrier before dialing the long-distance number, and if your local phone company charges per call or message unit, then these additional costs must be factored in. The cost for the local call will be incurred even if the long-distance number is busy or unanswered.

Local access charges are not a problem for AT&T long-distance users or for those living in areas that have converted to "equal access" as ordered under the AT&T breakup. They simply dial "1" before the area code and number in order to reach their primary long-distance carrier. Eventually, all phone customers will have "equal access." If, however, they wish to use a secondary carrier or to use their long-distance service while traveling or at another phone, they must use an access number and the local phone charge becomes a factor again.

How long are your calls? Since some carriers charge a higher rate for the first few minutes of a call and a lower rate therafter, the length of a typical call will influence ultimate cost. If you tend to talk for a long time on a call, say 20 or 30 minutes, you will benefit from the cheaper rates for additional minutes. If you make very short calls, you should consider a carrier that charges a flat rate.

How large are your monthly phone bills? Some carriers offer discounts for customers who run up large long-distance phone bills. These discounts may apply to the entire bill once a certain amount is exceeded, or only to that amount above the discount threshold. Discount percentages may increase as the bill gets larger, too.

On the other hand, some carriers impose a minimum monthly usage charge whether calls are made or not. These minimum charges are generally very low and shouldn't present much of a problem to the typical business customer.

How are calls billed? With AT&T, the charge for a long-distance call starts when and only if the person you're calling answers the phone; with most discount carriers, the charge starts when you finish dialing the long-distance number. Some carriers automatically back out 20 seconds or so to account for the time it takes the phone to ring at the other end, but this means that if you let the phone ring too long, and it goes unanswered, you will still be charged for the call. Likewise, if the call is answered by "Sorry, but your call cannot be completed as dialed" or "The number you dialed, 2-3-4-5-6-7-8, is not a working number," you will still be charged.

Similarly, long-distance carriers don't necessarily stop charging for the call at the precise moment you hang up. Some will round the length of the call up to the next full minute, some to the next quarter or tenth of a minute. You are billed accordingly.

Customer service and operator assistance. Wrong numbers, poor-quality calls, and other service problems must be reported to a customer service office that may or may not be available on a 24-hour basis. Few carriers can issue immediate credit for wrong numbers or poor-quality calls and instead require the customer to keep a record and deduct the charges from the monthly bill. Only AT&T has long-distance directory assistance, but anyone can call long-distance information at a cost, whether they subscribe to AT&T long-distance service or not.

Quality of transmission. Voice transmissions over some carriers' lines suffer from echoes, split-second delays, and interference from conversations on other lines. While these problems are annoying when trying to conduct a business conversation, they can be fatal to the transmission of computer data, which relies on the accurate relay of tones from one modem to another. If the carrier's line is going to be used to tie into an information utility or to link up with a computer network, the quality of transmission is vital and must be researched in advance.

TELEPHONE ANSWERING SERVICE

Legal and medical professionals often hire telephone answering services or exchanges—rather than install an answering machine—for two reasons. The first is for status: a good answering service will sound like a receptionist and not reveal the fact that the professional is not working out of a traditional, fully staffed office. The second is so they can be notified of important, even life-and-death calls, either by a mobile pager or by leaving a number with the service where they can be reached.

Telephone answering services are, obviously, more expensive than installing an answering machine. Just how much more expensive depends not only on what the service itself charges but on how far away its office is located from the home office. Incoming calls to the home office must be relayed to the service either through call forwarding or through a dedicated phone line. The charge for both methods increases significantly the greater the distance.

Answering services in major urban areas are sometimes combined with other administrative services, including mail and delivery drops, pager services, secretarial staffs, access to computers and conference rooms, and even entirely furnished offices used on a time-sharing basis. If you live in a suburban area, subscribing to such a service could provide you a "branch" office, help maintain a business presence in the city, and be a convenient place to work and meet clients.

ELECTRONIC MAIL

Electronic mail is essentially the transmission of any sort of communication electronically. Under this broad definition, there are two forms of electronic mail that have been around for some time: *telex* machines and *facsimile* machines. Telex machines convey text over lines leased from Western Union; facsimile machines transmit photographic images over phone lines.

The more recent usage of the term "electronic mail," however, applies to computer-to-computer transmissions of messages over telephone lines. Numerous on-line information utilities, such as The Source and Compuserve (see page 150 for a complete discussion of information utilities), and long-distance carriers, such as MCI, provide links by which you can leave a message in someone else's "electronic mailbox." The recipient can then call up and read the message on his or her computer terminal at leisure. The mailboxes are actually files stored according to the recipient's User ID number in the service's massive data banks.

The major advantage to electronic mail is speed: Messages are delivered in minutes rather than days. Furthermore, you save the time and cost of typing, copying, packaging, and posting a finished typed document, which for the typical business is estimated at between $8 and $10 per letter. When you send a document you don't have to rush to meet a 5:00 P.M. Post Office closing or a 6:30 P.M. courier pickup; when you expect a document you don't have to wait for the Post Office to open or the courier to arrive.

Electronic mail's advantage over phone calls is convenience: If the person you want to reach is busy or out of the office, you don't have to keep calling back. Instead, you leave the message to be picked up whenever convenient. The same message can be sent to numerous recipients at one time, eliminating tedious one-at-a-time phone calls.

Managers in large corporations that use electronic mail have noticed another important advantage: It seems to make employees feel less isolated and more a part of the corporate group. This can be especially important for telecommuters and other home-office workers who must keep in close touch with the central office and client's in-house staffs.

How Electronic Mail Works

Computer-to-computer transmissions are feasible only if the message sender and recipient both have computers (or in some instances a word processor, telex machine, or electronic memory typewriter), modems, and communications software.

Both parties must also subscribe to the same electronic mail service; the sender must know the recipient's User ID number, since "mailboxes" are not identified by name; and the recipient must regularly check for messages. A few of the services offer supplementary hand delivery to get around these restrictions. If the recipient does not subscribe to the electronic mail service, the company will print the message out at its nearest office and either deposit it in the U.S. Postal Service or have it hand-delivered by courier.

(Federal Express developed ZAPMail to get around the problem of *neither* party being on-line. The document is picked up by courier at the sender's office and carried to a Federal Express office, where it is transmitted over a facsimile machine to the Federal Express office nearest the recipient. The facsimile copy is then hand-delivered.)

To a novice telecommuter unfamiliar with on-line utilities, electronic mail can be overwhelmingly complex at first. You must dial the utility providing the electronic mail service; log onto the utility with your computer and choose the menu options to reach the right program; enter the User ID number of the person you want to send the message to; write and edit the message; and then command the program to send it. If you take a wrong step or enter a wrong code anywhere along the way, the entire process will fail, and you may have no idea why.

The best way to learn how to use electronic mail is to have a knowledgeable person walk through the system with you the first time. Most services have toll-free hot-lines that you can call to talk to a service representative. And the first time you use electronic mail, compose and send a brief message to yourself so you can get fully acquainted with the service.

The Cost of Electronic Mail

The cost of sending electronic mail depends on who is providing the service, the length of the message, and how it is sent. A message sent over a typical information utility, for example, would incur costs for the telephone call, the time logged onto the utility to compose the letter, and the "postage" charged by the utility to send the message, usually charged by blocks of characters. The utility might offer different postage rates depending on whether the message is sent express and whether carbon copies are sent to third parties.

The cost of receiving electronic mail includes the telephone call to get on-line, utility time to read the mail, and storage costs if the message is to be saved for future reference. You can lower the cost of sending and receiving electronic mail by cutting down on the amount of time you are logged onto the information utility. This is done by "uploading" and "downloading" your messages.

Instead of waiting until you are on-line to compose your message, write and edit it on your personal computer first. Then, after you log onto the information utility, it can be sent, or "uploaded," to the central computer in one quick step. Likewise, don't take the time to read your incoming messages while on-line. "Download" and store the messages in your own computer, disconnect from the utility, and read the messages at your own leisure.

U.S. POSTAL SERVICE

Although electronic mail is becoming an increasingly important method of delivery, it will never take the place of regular mail. The United States Postal Service will always be preferred for sending graphic materials, forms, legal documents, bulk advertising, packages, and even most business correspondence. No other delivery service is as widespread, competitively priced, and considering the volume handled, reliable.

The Postal Service has another impact on business operations in addition to simply delivering the mail. The daily routine of processing incoming and outgoing mail represents the two bookends of most people's business day. In the morning, the mail brings in correspondence, bills, payments, periodicals, packages, and solicitations, all requiring attention and some sort of action, even if it's just throwing a piece away. In the evening, the mail creates a sometimes hectic deadline for finishing letters, making copies, addressing envelopes, writing checks, packaging boxes, and dashing to the mailbox or Post Office before the last pickup.

As central as it is, the Postal Service is most often taken for granted and the target of complaints about poor service and increasing costs. There are, however, some very simple tricks to controlling postage costs. Regularly check the calibration of the postage scale (nine pennies equal 1 ounce); keep a wide selection of different denomination stamps (one-cent, two-cent, etc.) for additional ounces, rather than overposting with 22-cent stamps; avoid sending nonstandard-sized first-class mail; don't confuse certified mail with registered mail. Most of all, take full advantage of the different postal rates, which are structured according to the size, weight, and type of material mailed, and the cost and speed of delivery.

Types of Postal Rates

First-class mail. First-class applies to letters and postcards weighing up to 12 ounces. The first ounce costs more to mail than additional ounces; and postcards cost less than envelopes if they aren't larger than 3½ by 5 inches, which is also the minimum size mail the Postal Service will accept. First-class mail that in any way exceeds the 6½ by 11½-inch dimension maximum is subject to a surcharge and delivery delay, since it cannot be machine-processed.

The Postal Service sets the following delivery standards for first-class mail, but there are of course no guarantees: next day for ZIP codes in the immediate area if mailed before 5:00 P.M.; second day for ZIP codes within a 600-mile radius; third day nationwide.

As with all classes of mail, large quantities (200 pieces or more) of first-class mail posted at one time and presorted either by ZIP code or carrier route may qualify for slightly lower presort rates. Additionally, if the entire 9-digit ZIP code, called ZIP + 4, is used on quantity mailings of at least 250 pieces, an additional small postal discount may be applied.

Priority mail. This is first-class delivery for packages weighing over 12 ounces and under 70 pounds. The sum of the package's girth measurement (four sides) plus its length cannot exceed 108 inches. The charge for priority mail is calculated on its weight and how far away it is being sent. Distance is broken down into eight concentric zones emanating from the originating Post Office.

Express mail. Express mail is the Postal Service's overnight delivery service. Not all Post Offices can send Express mail, and some can send it only to certain other ZIP codes. Depending on how it is addressed, Express mail will be delivered to the recipient's address (guaranteed before 3:00 P.M.) or can be picked up at the recipient's Post Office (guaranteed before 10:00 A.M.). Same-day service is also available in some cities if the package is brought to and picked up at the Postal Service's airport facilities. Packages cannot exceed 70 pounds and the 108-inch, girth-plus-length dimension restriction.

Mailgram. This service is provided in connection with Western Union. Telephone messages called into Western Union and charged on the sender's telephone bill are printed much like telegrams and delivered anywhere in the country or Canada on the next day.

Only first-class, priority, Express, and mailgram mail are sealed against the inspection of the Postal Service. Items mailed under the following rates may be opened by postal employees.

Second-class mail. Second-class rates are restricted to magazines, newspapers, and other periodic publications. Generally, second-class mail is used by publishers to distribute their periodicals and requires a special permit. The cost of mailing is based on number of pieces, weight, percentage of advertising, and zone. Delivery can take anywhere from 4 to 15 days depending on distance, except in the case of newspapers and weekly newsmagazines, which get special treatment.

Third-class mail. Sometimes called *bulk* mail rates, these rates apply to identical copies of circulars, advertisements, and other *printed* promotional information that are being mailed to more than one person. Using bulk third-class mail rates requires paying an annual fee. Bulk rates are calculated by the pound, with a minimum per-piece rate. Discounts are available if the mailing contains at least 200 pieces and is presorted by ZIP code or carrier route. Non-profit organizations qualifying under IRS regulations also receive an additional discounted rate.

A piece of bulk-rate mail cannot weigh more than 16 ounces or, if presorted, be larger than 11½ by 13½ inches. Third-class mail can take anywhere from 4 to 21 days to be delivered.

Fourth-class mail. Fourth-class mail must weigh 16 ounces or more and less than 70 pounds. The girth-plus-length dimension cannot exceed 108 inches.

132 *Suppliers and Servicers*

Fourth-class mail is divided into several subcategories depending on what is being mailed. "Bound printed matter" rates apply to anything that is securely and permanently bound by glue, spiral binding, staples, etc., and are calculated based on weight and zone. "Special fourth-class" rates apply to books with at least 24 pages, 16-millimeter film, printed tests, printed music, sound and video recordings, and manuscripts, and are based on weight only. "Library" rates include the same items as special fourth-class rates but must be addressed to a library. "Parcel post" rates apply to anything else (except material the Postal Service considers dangerous or illegal) and are charged based on weight and zone.

Additional Postal Services

In addition to the postage calculated under the different rate categories, the Postal Service charges for special treatment for mail, including:

Registered mail. This service incorporates a system of receipts that are signed by every postal employee handling the mail from acceptance to delivery. It is designed to provide protection for valuable or very important mail, and also qualifies the item for postal insurance coverage for its full value up to $25,000 in case of loss or damage.

Only first-class mail or priority mail may be registered, and the Postal Service is very strict about how it must be packaged. No type of sealing tape, seals, or paper may be used that will not absorb a postmark impression, particularly at the intersections of flaps.

Certified mail. Certified mail provides proof of *mailing* with a dated mailing receipt and record of delivery at the addressee's Post Office. Certified mail does not include any additional insurance limits, is not handled any differently from ordinary mail, and is intended for first-class mail of no intrinsic value. It is used primarily for legal filings whenever proof of timely mailing is required.

Return receipt requested. This service provides proof of *delivery*. The recipient signs a postcard upon delivery, which is dated and mailed back to the sender. Return receipts can be used only with registered, certified, and insured mail. Delivery can also be restricted so that only the person named in the address can accept the item.

Insured mail. Insured mail, which is not the same as registered mail, is only available for third- and fourth-class mail, or for materials that fall under the classification definition of third- and fourth-class mail (books, advertisements, etc.) but which are mailed at first-class rates. The coverage limit for insured mail is $400.

COD. Collect on Delivery mail provides for money due on the purchase of merchandise to be collected by the Postal Service and returned by money order to the sender. Money collected on items mailed COD is limited to $400 and has to be paid in cash.

The Postal Service requires that COD merchandise must have been ordered by the customer. However, once the customer accepts delivery and pays the COD charge, the Postal Service is bound by law to forward payment to the sender. This means that if *after* COD charges are paid, you open a package and discover it doesn't contain what you expected (such as often happens in mail-order fraud schemes), the Postal Service can't return the money to you. Thus, COD shipments are inherently risky and should be avoided. Better to deal with suppliers that grant credit.

Special delivery. This supposedly means that a piece of mail is given expedited delivery when it is received at the addressee's post office. If the mailing address is within 1 mile of the Post Office or within the city delivery limits of certain Post Offices, the letter should be delivered immediately. Otherwise, special-delivery mail is handled as regular mail and isn't worth the extra charge.

In fact, some people believe that mailing something special delivery actually *delays* delivery because of the extra administrative tasks involved. In any event, whenever using special delivery always put the recipient's telephone number on the outside of the package and a request that the Post Office call and report that the mail is in. That way, at least it can be picked up at the Post Office rather than waiting for delivery.

Special handling. This service applies to the third- and fourth-class mail only and provides *preferential* handling to the extent practical during the transportation of a package. It does not include any sort of special-delivery service. Special handling is commonly used in shipping such items as baby poultry or honeybees.

Post Office boxes. No discussion of the Postal Service would be complete without mentioning Post Office boxes. Legally, they belong to the Postal Service, just as the mailboxes outside residences do, and cannot be used for any other purpose than delivering properly posted U.S. mail. That's why the United Parcel Service and courier services cannot make delivery to a Post Office box.

Post Office boxes are relatively easy to lease unless the Post Office doesn't have any available, which in some fast-growing areas is too often the case. A form must be filled out showing the renter's name, street address, and phone number; an annual fee is charged in advance and varies depending on the size of the box. The Postal Service can make you take a bigger or smaller box depending on the average volume of your incoming mail. If the volume is larger than any box can accommodate, the Post Office can require that you use and pay for a *caller service*, which means the mail is put in bags or trays and picked up at the desk or loading dock.

Additional information on the leasing and use of Post Office boxes is included in the section on business addresses on page 119. One important thing to remember however: If the rental of a Post Office box is to be tax-deductible, it must be used only for business correspondence and not for personal mail.

UNITED PARCEL SERVICE

Ranking right next to the United States Postal Service in low-cost, reliable, and widespread delivery service is the United Parcel Service.

UPS ground service usually takes from two to five days for delivery, except during extremely heavy shipping times like just before Christmas. Charges are calculated on the basis of weight and distance. Single packages cannot weigh more than 70 pounds, and the measurement of the package's girth plus its length cannot exceed 108 inches. Packages can be insured up to their full value. COD service similar to that offered by the Postal Service is also available.

UPS also offers overnight and second-day air delivery, although the overnight service is limited to certain areas. The air service also has restrictions on what types of material may be shipped, which exclude negotiable instruments, hazardous materials, art work, and extremely valuable items (since materials can be insured only up to $25,000). The same weight and size restrictions for ground service also apply to the air service.

UPS charges a small fee for coming to your office to pick up a package, although the fee doesn't increase if more than one package is picked up on the trip. If you typically have at least two pickups each week, you should open an account with UPS. With an account you will be charged a weekly fee equal to one pickup charge, but you can actually have an unlimited number of pickups, and the UPS delivery truck will automatically stop by your office each weekday.

Without an account, you will have to call a day in advance for pickup. You must be prepared to give the operator the package's weight, size, and destination. The operator will calculate the charges, and you must pay the delivery person, either by check or cash, when he or she comes for the pickup.

UPS must have a street address to make deliveries. If a Post Office box number is on the package, UPS will mail the addressee a post card requesting that he or she call UPS and provide a street address. Sometimes regular route managers will know this information already and go ahead and deliver the package, but this can't be relied on.

Always keep the boxes and packing materials that insured items, especially electronic equipment, are shipped in. Any claim for damage must be supported by evidence that there was some damage en route, and this can be determined

135 *Suppliers and Servicers*

only by a UPS inspection of the packaging. In fact, UPS will not accept insured electronic equipment unless it is adequately packaged, and this usually means in the manufacturer's original carton.

AIR AND GROUND COURIERS

Which came first? Did the business world really have a valid and increasing need for overnight deliveries, thus providing a ripe opportunity for express courier services? Or did the express courier services create the need? Perhaps businesses have simply come to plan around air-expressing things out at the last moment, rather than allowing more time for shipment, as they did in the days before Federal Express. Regardless of how the express courier market came to be, there's no doubt it is now an integral part of American business operations.

Door-to-door express courier services are expensive when compared to the Postal Service and UPS, and should be limited to unavoidable situations that absolutely demand timely, reliable delivery. But since these situations do seem to arise even in the best-planned offices, it's wise to become acquainted with the courier companies that service your area and how they charge.

All courier services charge on the basis of a package's weight, contents (whether general merchandise or business documents), and destination. Most have various premium services, such as Saturday delivery, and a few have a two-day delivery that's less expensive than overnight. The big difference between competitive services is how they transport packages—by air or ground.

Some air couriers, like Federal Express, have built their entire operation around their own fleets of airplanes and are appropriate only for packages that must be shipped via air. Other courier services, like Purolator, offer overnight ground transportation between certain cities in major metropolitan corridors. For example, a package sent from Washington to New York would go by air if shipped via Federal Express and by truck if sent by Purolator. Both would deliver it the next day, but of course the ground transportation would be considerably less expensive. So always ask how the package will be shipped, and in the case of firms such as Purolator, which offer both ground and air service, ask for the least expensive service.

Another factor affecting cost is whether the express courier service delivers directly to the area the package is destined for, or whether it subcontracts deliveries to a local courier. In sparsely populated rural areas particularly, local couriers must make the last leg of the trip, and the shipping cost includes both companies' charges.

Courier services all have essentially the same administrative procedure to request a pickup. You call the toll-free number and give the operator your name, address, and account number (if applicable); the package's destination (must be a street address) and weight; and the time of day it will be ready for pickup. If the shipment won't be ready before the courier comes through your area, or if you won't be at the office to hand it over, many services have drop boxes located outside national banks where you can deposit the package. However, find out the size of the box's slot opening to make sure your package will fit, and make sure you have blank bills of lading to complete and leave with it. Also, if a code must be entered before the box will open, find out what it is.

Since courier services are used primarily by businesses, sometimes a driver will think a residential address is an error and not come to the door. So always tell the operator that the office is in a home and which door the driver should knock at. Also, unless you prefer they not know, tell people who may be sending you packages to note on the bill of lading "Office in Residence."

When you send a package and it fails to arrive by the time the service has guaranteed it would, have the person who received it send you their copy of the bill of lading, which will show date and time of delivery. Then, when you get the invoice from the courier service, write a brief explanation on the invoice that you are refusing to pay the charge and return it along with the bill of lading as proof.

AIRLINES, TRAINS, AND BUSES

Sometimes it makes more sense to put a package on a commercial passenger airline, train, or bus instead of using a courier service. You will be assured of same-day delivery in the case of airlines and short-haul train and bus routes; you will know the scheduled departure and arrival times; and, if you live in an isolated rural area, you may have no alternative.

But the disadvantages are that you will have to take the package to the terminal yourself and arrange for its pickup at the receiving terminal; there is a far greater risk of misrouting or loss if any connections are required in transit; you must pay in advance for shipping charges; and the passenger carrier will accept no responsibility for delays.

REPAIR SERVICES

Nothing can throw an office into quite as much chaos as equipment breakdown. It's a well-known, although not scientifically documented, fact that office machines can sense when the operator is really desperate for something to be done, and that these are exactly the times that machines decide to quit. A copier will jam in the middle of a 100-page report that must get into today's mail; a computer will fail late Friday afternoon when you had plans to work all weekend to meet a Monday deadline. No amount of crying, screaming, swearing, or threatening will help.

Some equipment problems can be solved without having to call in a repair person, especially those recurring, simple malfunctions that you have watched the repair person fix before. This is why it always pays to ask questions and attempt to understand the basic operation of any piece of equipment.

Manufacturers' customer service representatives and technicians can also "talk" you through simple repair procedures or system tests on the telephone. Not only might you be able to fix the equipment yourself, but a chat with a disinterested expert will make you much more technically knowledgeable when and if you have to call a repair person in.

Types of Repair Services

There are three basic types of repair services: those operated or authorized by the manufacturer; those operated by or associated with the retail outlet where the equipment was purchased; and independent repair services.

If the equipment breaks while it is under a manufacturer's warranty, it will probably have to be shipped back to the factory or inspected and repaired by an authorized repair representative. (Always use the original carton and packaging when shipping equipment for repair, and fully insure the package in case of loss or further damage.)

Manufacturers' authorized repair representatives should be thoroughly familiar with the piece of equipment and have repair parts in stock. They also generally want to maintain their "authorized" designation, and so if you have a complaint about pricing or workmanship, you can threaten to complain to the manufacturer. On the other hand, authorized repair services may not be the most economical, and there may not be one in or near your town.

The retail outlet that sold you the equipment may also be an authorized repair service. However, sometimes retail shops will not service equipment that did not come from their stores. This is especially true for office supply outlets, computer stores, and telephone equipment sales companies that are heavily involved in leasing equipment.

Finally, there are the independent repair services that will work on almost any type of equipment with almost any type of problem, much in the same way a service station mechanic works on cars. Independents can be found by looking in the Yellow Pages or asking at a retail outlet that sells the same type of equipment. Employees of manufacturer's or retail outlet's service departments will sometimes operate independent repair services as part-time moonlighting businesses. The only potential problems with using independent repair services are that the quality of workmanship varies greatly, and you have very little recourse in case of shoddy work or lost equipment.

How to Choose a Repair Service

Deciding where and how to get a piece of broken office equipment repaired, assuming it is not under warranty or a leasing agreement, requires considerable consumer savvy. First, call a few local repair services, get a technician on the phone, and describe the symptoms—in detail. Although the technician will be reluctant to quote any repair estimates without seeing the equipment, you will be able to get some comparative prices on "what if" diagnoses. Sometimes a busy repair shop will not want to be bothered with small jobs, and so they will quote outrageous prices to drive the business away. Better to learn that on the phone rather than after you have taken the equipment to the shop.

Also ask what minimum charges are involved with their even looking at the equipment. Commonly, repair shops charge just to take the equipment apart and put it back together again. This charge may or may not be applied against the cost of actually fixing the equipment. Also, if the repair person must come to your office to fix heavy equipment, find out beforehand whether you are charged for travel time.

Because the time involved in fixing office equipment is usually crucial, ask how long it will take to fix it; assuming, first, that parts have to be ordered; and, second, that they don't.

After gathering this comparative information from different repair services, you may determine that it's just not worth the cost to get the equipment fixed. This is particularly true for older equipment that is probably going to continue to have problems. The price to repair it might better be part of the purchase price of newer, more sophisticated equipment.

Service Contracts

If you do decide to get the equipment repaired, you may want to get a service contract to cover future breakdowns. Service contracts are essentially health insurance for major pieces of equipment like personal computers, copiers, and office typewriters. For a fixed annual fee, a repair person will fix the equipment at your office whenever it breaks. Depending on the contract, you may have to pay for parts only, a minimum per-visit charge, or nothing at all. Typically, service contracts do require the customer to pay overtime charges if the service call is requested after hours or on the weekend.

The advantages to having a service contract are primarily economical: It provides protection against chronic or "catastrophic" equipment failure. You are also spared the travel time that most repair persons charge just to drive to your office, which can be significant depending on how far away you are. And contract customers are usually given priority over noncontract service calls.

Of course, if the equipment doesn't break down during the term of the contract, then the premium bought protection that wasn't needed and could have been invested in something else. Whether a service contract makes sense depends on the age of the equipment, since newer items shouldn't have as many problems as older ones and may be covered by warranty anyway; and the cost of a typical repair call. If you live far away from the repair service, travel time for *one* call could equal an entire year's premium and make a service contract a wise investment.

Repair Persons in the Home Office

One important final note about repairs: Always be very alert when repair persons are coming to the home office to fix equipment. They may be confused about a business located in a residence and not come to the door. Or they may not bother to knock but barge right in the front door, since they are accustomed to traditional offices. They may also unintentionally wander into the private areas of the residence looking for the office or a place to wash their hands.

If you work at home alone, be very conscious of your personal safety. While most repair persons are honorable individuals, you can never be too sure. Never admit a repair person into your home office whom you didn't call to fix a specific problem. Ask to see identification if you don't recognize him or her. Don't work in your robe or lounging clothes when a repair person is expected. Don't act too friendly, "chat" about your work, or reveal that you are alone during the day. You may want to ask a friend to come over or talk to a neighbor on the phone while the repair person is in the office.

MISCELLANEOUS SERVICES

Traditional offices generally hire janitorial services to do the cleaning and empty the trash. In a home office, these services are usually part of the general domestic routine: The office gets cleaned along with the rest of the house; the trash gets picked up with the household garbage.

However, if you hire a maid, cleaning service, or even your own children to do the cleaning, then the time spent cleaning the office is a deductible business expense. If you pay a trash removal or hauling fee, you can treat a portion of it as an indirect home-office deduction, based on the amount of trash generated by the office versus the rest of the household.

9

Information Resources:
Your Home Office Lifeline

Every active professional and business person fears being cut off from the flow of current information—and rightly so. Without knowing the most up-to-date developments and discoveries in your field, you can't make competitive business decisions. If you're out of date, you're out of luck.

It is this fear of "information isolation" that keeps some people from making the jump out of traditional offices and into home offices. They worry about being cut off from the office libraries, research departments, staff meetings, "water-cooler" conferences, and the other formal and informal channels of business intelligence.

Ten or even five years ago this argument had some merit. But the way businesses get information has radically changed since then. The widespread business use of personal computers and information utilities means huge banks of current information can be accessed by anyone with a telecommunications link, regardless of where the office is located. Technology can make the home office just as current, knowledgeable, and competitive as a traditional office. Maybe even more so.

But before exploring the high-tech world of computer-based resources, let's start with something more basic—the reference library.

FIVE REFERENCE BOOKS EVERY OFFICE SHOULD HAVE

Of course, each home office will require its own reference section for technical books and manuals associated with the specific type of business being conducted, but *all* offices need the following books for a functioning, businesslike operation:

A Dictionary

The more current the edition, the better. A 10-year-old dictionary will not have many of the terms that advanced technology has made commonplace, such as *bits*, *bytes*, *microprocessor*, and *RAM*. (On the other hand, older dictionaries do have a certain charm about them, since they include terms that have fallen out of popular use and been purged to make way for newer but not necessarily better words.) Also, make sure the dictionary has geographical and biographical references, or get separate dictionaries for these important categories of information.

The most important thing about a dictionary is that it be USED! A well-thought-out, carefully typed letter or presentation will lose all its effectiveness if words are misspelled or misused. Don't rely on "well, it looks OK" if you're not sure how a word is spelled. Take the time to look it up.

A Style Manual

This will be the resource for such things as how to set up a business letter; proper abbreviations, capitalizations, grammar, and word usage; how to punctuate; how to use italics, numerals, and symbols; how to format and organize a report; and so forth. A style manual will greatly assist in making your correspondence appear businesslike and your writing concise, clear, and correct.

An Almanac

A great reference for miscellaneous facts, such as what state produces the most honey and the exact sequence of events that led to Richard Nixon's resignation. Almanacs are updated every year, but depending on your need you don't have to purchase a new one each year.

Telephone Directories

Place a local directory under each phone set in the office, so one will always be handy when you need it. The home office should also have telephone directories from every city or area in which the business is active, now that it costs to call long-distance information. Out-of-state directories can be acquired, at a cost, from your local telephone company, or you can ask out-of-state acquaintances to send you their last year's directories.

A directory of 800 numbers, available from AT&T or at your local bookstore, will quickly pay for itself by making you aware of suppliers and servicers all across the nation that have toll-free numbers.

A ZIP Code Directory

ZIP code directories are available from commercial publishers and are useful for looking up ZIP codes, city spellings, and counties. A ZIP code directory will also list street names and large buildings or building complexes in multi-ZIP-code cities.

ZIP code directories also include state and city abbreviations, information on mail classifications and special services, Postal Service addresses, the areas served by the first three digits of a ZIP code, and more.

PRINT PUBLICATIONS

Periodicals and books fall into two categories: general interest and special interest. General interest periodicals provide information on a wide range of issues and trends and include local newspapers, national newsmagazines, and business magazines. Depending on the scope of news carried in your local paper, it might be valuable to subscribe through the mail to one of the large metropolitan dailies such as *The New York Times* or *The Wall Street Journal* to get more in-depth coverage of national and international events.

General interest periodicals are important for the home office because no business or profession exists entirely in a vacuum. The ability to spot and integrate unrelated events and trends can mean the opportunity to develop something new in your own field.

Special interest publications are valuable because they can offer more detailed information and updates in more limited areas of concern. They include magazines, books, and newsletters that focus on a particular trade or profession, and may be put out by commercial publishers or by associations. They also include publications that relate to specific aspects of a business operation, such as a magazine on personal computers or a tax-update newsletter. And remember, don't read these resources strictly for their news and features: The advertisements provide information on new products, suppliers, and servicers.

TRADE AND PROFESSIONAL ASSOCIATIONS

Joining a national association sometimes includes subscriptions to the association's publications. More importantly, it also includes the opportunity to meet others involved in the same type of business or profession, which can be an invaluable way to exchange information and generate business.

Other ways professional associations can assist members is by offering educational seminars, annual meetings, directories, group health and life insurance programs, travel discounts, and so on. Trade associations typically also hold trade shows where members can represent their companies at display booths and make pitches to potential buyers or "scope out" the competition.

An important new area of involvement for trade and professional associations is in electronic communications. An association may as a group establish its own computer network or subscribe to a certain informatin utility in order to facilitate the sending of electronic mail and the sharing of research or market data.

PERSON-TO-PERSON NETWORKS

These networks are the informal, physical meeting of people who have some common interest. A network may consist of people in the neighborhood who own and use personal computers in their businesses. They may find it helpful, especially when just starting out, to talk over and share their problems or successes with a certain type of software, or to exchange informatin on a new peripheral. They can also share equipment in case someone's temporarily breaks down.

A network can form for a specific goal, such as changing zoning laws, and disband when the object is achieved. Or it can be an ongoing association, such as a network that rotates day-care responsibilities for members who have young children at home. Networks of related but noncompetitive home-based businesses can be valuable sources of new business and resources for buying services and supplies.

Actually, networks exist everywhere, whether the people involved in them recognize it or not. Any time communications or transactions are repeated and form a pattern, a network is created. The advantage to acknowledging a network lies in making it members more conscious of their shared interests. This is especially important for people who work in home offices and who might feel that they are isolated from the business and professional world. Networks can also actively recruit and introduce new members, making the base of shared information larger and potential business contacts more numerous.

Finding a Network

Locating an existing network involves asking around. For instance, if you are trying to find a network of people who use the same type of personal computer as you do, ask the salesperson at the store where you bought your equipment or write the manufacturer. If you are looking for a network of people involved in the same trade or profession, ask a national association for its membership list in your area. Special interest publications might also have information about local clubs or organizations.

Creating a network is like trying to locate and organize any group of people: It takes a lot of work and dedication on the part of the organizer and at least passing interest on the part of the people being organized. The first step is to find one or two other people who are enthusiastic about the idea and who will help get it started. Then you must locate potential members.

Creating a Home-Office Network

For example, suppose you want to start a network of people who work at home in your community. You want to share information on suppliers and servicers, perhaps pool certain resources like mailing lists or time-sharing on business equipment, and lobby for an amendment on local zoning codes. But how do you find these home-based workers, who generally keep low profiles and are involved in a wide variety of business pursuits?

One of the best ways is to talk to your local telephone repair person, office supplier, UPS delivery person, and other suppliers and servicers. They are in a position to know where the home offices are located and who works out of them. Don't ask directly for names and numbers, since this might be considered an invasion of privacy. Instead, tell your suppliers and servicers that you are interested in having these other home-based workers *call you* and that the next time they happen to see any potential members, would they please give them your name and number.

Other ways to find members are to post notices on community and grocery store bulletin boards, and to ask the local paper, TV station, radio station, and cable company if they will run a community-interest item and/or short feature on the organizational efforts. Notices and announcements should include a date and place for a first meeting, perhaps a dinner meeting at a local restaurant, and your name and number.

Assuming anybody shows up, the most important thing to do at the first meeting is to exchange names and phone numbers. A directory would be helpful if someone is willing to invest the time and expense in typing it up, running it off, and mailing it to members. After that, the network should remain an informal group of people who share interests depending on their own needs and desires. Any specific effort, such as lobbying for or against a proposed change in zoning laws, should be handled by ad hoc committee. Otherwise, there's no need for officers, dues, or procedural standards.

COMPUTER-TO-COMPUTER NETWORKS

For the home office with a personal computer and telecommunication capability, the opportunity to share common interests and information is not limited to a small geographical area. A computer network can encompass an entire region, an entire state, or even the entire nation.

Types of Computer Networks

Computer networks are common in the business world. Anytime you see an airline reservation clerk or bank teller turn to a video screen and punch in codes on a keyboard, he or she is establishing a link over the phone lines with the main computer at headquarters. The clerk or teller can request information on schedules, seating capabilities, account status, or whatever data the main computer contains. They may also be able to enter information—recording a ticket purchase or checking a transaction—which is then recorded in the computer's memory.

On a smaller scale, a network exists whenever a portable computer sends or receives information from the main office. For example, an executive for a retail clothing chain must spend several days each week traveling to outlets and evaluating their inventory records. Instead of just taking notes and then carrying them back to headquarters, she enters them each evening on her portable computer and transmits them over the phone line to her office computer. That way her staff can compile and have a complete report ready upon her return.

These types of business-oriented networks access central computers that often contain confidential information. For that reason they usually require the use of passwords to gain entry. Sometimes there is a common password for all users; at other times the passwords are unique for each user and must be coupled with a user ID number or proper name.

Public Access Message Systems. In contrast, another type of network popular among personal computer users requires no passwords and is open to everyone. They are the Public Access Message Systems (PAMS), or elecronic bulletin boards, as they are sometimes called. Run primarily out of people's homes or computer stores, PAMS are easy to find by asking a sales rep at a local computer store or consulting a PAMS directory at the public library. Computer manufacturers might also be able to refer you to one in your area.

PAMS work like this: You call the telephone number through your computer and wait for the computer at the other end to answer. When it does, you will have to log on, which involves answering a number of questions, and then you will be presented with a list of options. You may ask to see all the current messages that other people have left, which might include a running debate on the federal deficit or the pros and cons of a new software release; you can leave a message, adding it to a "thread" that has already developed or starting your own; you may decide to copy a file onto your own computer disk; you can scan through "for sale" and "wanted" classified listings; or ask to "chat" with the person running the PAMS (called the "sysop," short for "systems operator") if he or she is available. The only charge is the cost of the telephone call.

PAMS are operated and utilized primarily by computer hobbyists and thus tend to focus on computer-related information, such as hardware repair or free software. However, there are also PAMS that carry religious messages, sexually oriented PAMS, and ones that are run by businesses to keep in touch with customers and field representatives.

(Note: You may also have heard about Local Area Networks or LANs. These are computer links *within* large offices or office complexes, and do not involve the local telephone company's lines. LANs require special wiring that can transmit computer data in binary form and without modems. LANs are a breakthrough for establishing office-wide computer networks, but they don't have much relevance for the home office—at least not at this time.)

Smart Terminals

Airline reservation desks and bank branch offices most often use "dumb" terminals to link up with the central computer. That means that the clerk or teller has no ability to store any of the information received or to edit the information sent before it is transmitted over the phone line. The terminal consists only of a video screen, keyboard, and of course, the modem (discussed in more detail on page 108). There is no computing capability at the terminal end.

A home office with a personal computer, however, will benefit from a "smart" terminal, meaning that its personal computer can interact with the computer at the other end of the telephone line. Smart terminals, achieved with communications software, can drive the various features of its modem, store information received over the phone line, edit messages before transmitting them, and program combinations of keystrokes to execute long, frequently used strings of commands. Some communications software also allows other terminals to access your computer and data files over the phone.

Any sort of computer link, whether through a dumb or smart terminal, requires two things. First, data must be sent and received with the same electronic parameters, meaning that each end of the link must be using the same rates of data transmission, protocol, parity checking, data bits, stop bits, and duplex functions (technical terms that define how computers "talk" to one another). Second, there can be only one command structure. The command structure, determined by the type of communications software, is the way you instruct the computer to perform certain functions, such as find a file, send a file, or receive one.

It is not necessary that the two computers in a computer-to-computer link use the same communications software, as long as the person at the terminal end understands and can utilize the command structure of the computer at the other end. That's why the PAMS are identified by the type of communications software used by the host computer, and why users tend to be people who own and operate the same type of personal computer with the same type of communications software. Learning a lot of different command structures inhibits a freewheeling perusal of PAMS, something that can be overcome by using an information utility as discussed later.

Computer Networks and the Home Office

Computer networks have great significance for the home office. Telecommuters—employees who work at home—can be plugged into company mainframes through dumb terminals, or they can work independently on personal computers and then transmit their work to employers over the telephone lines. Independent businesses affiliated with national franchises or trade associations can keep instantly updated on product lines, rates, membership directories, national or regional meetings, etc. If a business caters primarily to one major client or deals with one major supplier, a computer link can greatly facilitate the frequent exchange of information and data.

Home-office workers who travel constantly can let their personal computers "operate" the office in their absence. By carrying a portable computer or dumb terminal with you on the road and having the personal computer in the home office on remote access, you can keep in contact with incoming messages on your main computer, send information from the portable unit to your main computer, and instruct it to relay that information to someone else.

The PAMS are also important resources for locating computer-related items and information, much of it free or at reduced prices because sellers are dealing directly with buyers and incurring no advertising costs. They can also be utilized as marketing outlets, with the home office-based business placing its own ads in the classified section. Finally, the home office can become a PAMS operator itself. Although operators cannot charge a fee for access to their systems, they can freely advertise their own goods and services on the boards.

INFORMATION UTILITIES

No doubt about it, *the* most exciting technological development for the home office and for small businesses in general is the emergence of the information utilities, or videotex, as the industry is sometimes called. There are thousands of information utilities, defined here as any on-line computer service that charges a fee, either to the user or advertiser. They vary considerably in size and focus. Some are extremely specialized and available only to members of certain professional associations or within certain geographical areas; others offer diverse, consumer-oriented services to anyone who subscribes.

Types of services available through an information utility are divided into two major areas: *passive* and *interactive*. The major passive services are reference data bases; the interactive types include electronic mail, bulletin boards, and other functions that let the user "talk back" to the utility.

Reference Data Bases

Reference data bases are the core of information utilities. Somewhere, someone has compiled a data base on almost anything you could ever need to research: the names of the *desaparecidos* who have disappeared in Argentina; the genealogy of thoroughbred race horses; reviews of New York City restaurants; common rose viruses—you name it.

Information utilities that cater specifically to professionals provide valuable research tools through their constantly updated data bases. A doctor seeking to diagnose an unfamiliar illness in a patient can get on-line with a medical data base, describe the symptoms, and request it to select articles, abstracts, and textbook studies that might relate to the condition. A lawyer needing the most recent precedents in a specific area of the law can do the legal research much faster and can gain much more current information through a legal data base.

There are specialized data bases on energy technology, education, finance, economics, government, engineering, psychology, chemistry, electronics, and corporate annual reports, just to name a few.

For the general consumer, information on airline schedules, stock quotations, news, weather, sports, movie reviews, dating services, and auto repair is available through one or more information utilities, along with just about any other subject imaginable. Instead of buying one set of encyclopedias, you can access the complete text of five or six different sets entered in a reference data base.

In some cities, instead of consulting the local newspaper you can consult a data base that provides up-to-date entertainment schedules, information on which retailers have merchandise on sale, what tonight's specials are at local restaurants, and so on.

If you are wondering why all this information is available over computers, the reason is simple: Newspaper, magazine, and book publishers record and store text as computer data in the normal print publishing process. It's no big deal for them to make these computerized publications available to information utilities, who then make them available to the public, all for a fee.

Software

Information utilities make available a wide range of software programs for subscribers: games (which are particularly popular), word-processing programs, spreadsheet programs, educational programs, accounting programs, and graphics programs. This means that you can try a particular product out before deciding whether you want to buy it for yourself. Or if your need is limited, you can simply "rent" the program while you are logged onto the utility.

Of particular interest are the programs that are directly related to the information compiled in the utility's data bases. For example, a stock-quotation data base combined with custom-designed spreadsheet and graphics software can allow a user to make his or her own technical projections.

Communications

Electronic mail. The large, general-consumer information utilities include electronic mail services. As discussed more thoroughly on page 128, a subscriber can direct correspondence or other types of messages to the "electronic mailbox" of another subscriber, to be retrieved and read at the recipient's leisure. The big advantages of electronic mail over a direct sender-to-receiver computer link are that compatibility is not a factor (you don't have to have coordinating communications software or know the command codes) and the transmission doesn't require that both computers be on and available at the same time.

Clubs and groups. Another type of communications service is the special interest groups, clubs, or conferences, which are essentially special-interest electronic bulletin boards that are accessed through the information utility. The clubs provide a forum for lively, ongoing debates, give-and-take of information, and often classified ads listings. Like PAMS, one member serves as the systems operator, or sysop, who oversees membership and the messages posted on the club's files. Unlike PAMS, messages are stored by the utility's mainframe, providing much larger storage capacity than a personal computer could. Membership is either open to any subscriber, or restricted and by invitation only.

As with reference data bases, there are special interest groups for almost every subject under the sun: from golfing clubs (where you might find information on where to get tickets to tournaments) to lawyer's clubs (including "Help Wanted" listings for paralegals) to cooking clubs (featuring an appealing recipe for cherimoya parfait). CompuServe, a large general-consumer utility in the Midwest, even has a special interest group devoted to people with computers in their home offices. All the clubs or special interest groups operate with the same modem compatibility and command system, so you have access to literally hundreds of them.

National bulletin boards. The information utility may feature a national bulletin board for the exchange of messages on topics of general interest to its subscribers. The national bulletin board also features a huge classified ads listing. All a user has to do is request a category of goods or services, and the listings of "For Sale" or "Wanted" appear. Both the special interest and national bulletin boards are excellent sources for used computer hardware, free software, and other goods and services.

Real-time communications. Since electronic bulletin boards can be accessed by only one member at a time, they rely on messages that are posted and then left for others to read sometime in the future. The only person you can "talk face to face" with, meaning exchange messages on the screen at the same time, is the systems operator.

So the consumer-oriented information utilities have what's called "real time," which is very similar to a CB channel. Any number of subscribers can get on the same channel at once. Whatever is typed in shows up on everyone's screen. They can "talk" back and forth and all around about whatever they wish. For example, one user types, "Hi, Chocktaw here. Anyone see 'Dallas' last night?" In a minute someone responds and types "Chocktaw, Headwind here. Yeh, Pam really told J.R., didn't she?" Chocktaw then asks Headwind to fill him in, since he missed the show.

Shop At Home/Bank At Home

Shop at home is like a mail-order catalog, except on computer. Users select categories of merchandise, view textual descriptions and perhaps a graphic representation, and then *order* the product over the computer. Charges are either COD or entered on users' credit cards. Quite often the products are offered at significant discounts.

Currently, the quality of graphic representations is primitive—limited by the graphics software and the receiver's monitor. But soon you will be able to run a wire to your television set and receive a *video* image over the computer-information utility link. This will mean that you will not only see a perfect picture of the product but actually see it demonstrated.

Bank at home offers bank customers (whose bank also subscribes to the utility) the opportunity to pay bills, transfer funds, and check on the status of their accounts electronically. While this service is now limited mostly to the largest national banks, it is expanding rapidly as more and more banks subscribe to the utilities.

Gateway Services

Since there are literally thousands of data bases covering tens of thousands of subjects, it has become very difficult to know exactly which information utility can best serve a business's need. Perhaps no *one* can if the business needs access to a wide range of research sources. This has lead to a new breed of information services: those that research and tap into other information utilities.

Some of these *gateway services* simply provide their subscribers with access to numerous utilities. This is useful if you need information from a wide range of data bases in numerous information utilities and don't want to have to pay the membership fees to join them all. You will, however, have to pay the gateway service for the costs incurred when you are actually logged onto a specific data base.

Other gateway services will research a particular subject for you and tell you where the best information is located. Or they may provide you with abstracts and then retrieve the entire text from the appropriate data base upon your request. In any event, you will pay for their research services in addition to their costs incurred when logged onto the information utility. It still may be worth it, rather than subscribing to numerous utilities and spending your time searching for the right information.

Selecting an Information Utility

When choosing an information utility, you must ask yourself, "What do I want to use it for primarily?" Do you want a specialized reference resource? Then a utility that specializes in your particular field or one that has access to an association's or publication's specialized data base (which is quite common) must be the choice. Do you want information of general interest? Then almost any of the major consumer-oriented utilities will do. Do you want communications capability? Then you must make sure the people you want to communicate with belong to the same utility.

Ease of use is another consideration. A utility that requires complex, contorted commands will inhibit you and cost money as you prod through layers of menus and make mistakes trying to reach your final program destination.

Support is also important. Can you call a toll-free number and get a friendly customer service representative who will help you with your first venture into the Alice-in-Wonderland world of an information utility?

Finally, cost must be considered. The cost of using an information utility is broken down into three categories:

Membership fee. This is a one-time fee charged to new subscribers. It is sometimes waived if the subscriber purchases a modem and/or software package from the utility. Free membership in an information utility might also be included with the purchase of a computer from a computer store.

Usage fee. This is based on the actual time you are logged onto the utility. Rates may vary, depending on the time of day and whether it's a weekday or weekend. Most utilities also charge a higher rate for data transmitted at 1,200 bauds than for 300-baud transmissions.

The utility will tell you how long you have been on the service when you log off so you can keep tabs on monthly use. Again, if you purchase hardware and/or software from the utility when you subscribe, you may receive a certain amount of time free, such as the first hour or the first $100 of use charges.

The specialized data bases generally have extremely high per-hour charges because they are intended and may even be restricted to professional and business use. The general interest utilities are less expensive, but may have a minimum monthly use charge.

Usage fees can be reduced by uploading and downloading with your personal computer. Instead of using the utility word-processing program to compose messages for electronic mail, use your own program and then simply log on and upload the file to the utility. The same thing holds true for reading your electronic mail. Download it to your personal computer, and read it at your own leisure without incurring a charge for being logged onto the system. Data-base files and messages on electronic bulletin boards can also be subject to downloading. (However, copyrighted material such as software programs may be copy-protected, meaning you can't download them.)

Telephone access. Besides the time on the utility, you may have to pay for the telephone link. Many of the major general-interest utilities have agreements with long-distance carriers to provide access to their mainframes from anywhere in the country. The charge is either totally or partially included in the utility's per-use fee.

If you live in a major metropolitan area that has a local access number to reach the utility's long-distance carrier, your telephone charges will be minimal. However, if you live in a rural area, you are probably going to have to make a toll call to reach the carrier, and this must be considered in evaluating overall cost.

Storage costs. Storage costs are incurred for such things as electronic mail messages that are left in user files or when users intentionally use the utility to store files too large for their own personal computers. In some instances the individual who initiates an electronic bulletin board discussion must pay for storing the file in the mainframe. Storage costs can be controlled by purging records as soon as possible and downloading onto the user's personal computer.

Using an Information Utility

When you subscribe to an information utility, it will provide you with all the necessary information for modem compatibility and the communication software command structure. It's a good idea to walk through your first call on paper before actually making it, deciding exactly what service you want to utilize and how to get there.

The utility will provide a telephone access number which will connect you with either a long-distance carrier or the utility directly. After the utility answers, you will be required to give your User Identification number and your password. Passwords, which are made up by users themselves and should never be revealed, confirm that you are in fact who you claim to be, and keep someone else from logging on and charging the use to your account number.

You then will be presented with a series of menus to narrrow down the service you actually want to utilize. Again, a walk-through is recommended so you don't spend time actually logged on the utility and desperately consulting the manual or flailing about within the labyrinths of the command structure. Once you become proficient, you may be able to access certain functions directly without having to go through the menus, thus saving time and money.

When you are through, be sure to properly exit the utility system and then disconnect your computer from the telephone access. These are two very important, separate steps. Failure to execute either one of them will result in extra cost, since neither system will correctly log when you stopped using their services but will instead wait three to five minutes before disconnecting you automatically.

10

Organizing Your Home Office

Fundamental to an efficiently operated home office, and to any office for that matter, is organization. But like beauty, organization lies in the eyes of the beholder. A desktop covered with loose papers and scribbled notes may seem like a hopeless mess to one person and yet make complete sense to another.

For the independent business person working at home, the prospect of organizing a home office is both a blessing and a burden. First, the tools of organization—the administrative systems that ensure records and files are easy to find, and the daily routines that make sure nothing slips between the cracks—can be customized to satisfy the personality and work processes of just one person. On the other hand, that person may not have the background to foresee all of the administrative tasks involved in operating an office, nor the expertise to design systems that work.

Good administrative systems must be effective, efficient, and flexible. The only *effective* systems are those *that are consistently adhered to*. No system, no matter how ingeniously designed, will serve its purpose if the *people* involved either won't or can't implement it properly. This applies to offices large and small, and to systems as basic as taking out the trash and as complex as maintaining a payables journal.

Effective administrative systems therefore must be relatively simple and an integral part of the daily work routine—second nature to the work itself. For instance, filing is a chore and a bore. Finding the time and energy at the end of a busy and exhausting day to file correspondence or return files to storage is more than most people can muster. Instead, it usually gets put off until the inability to find things becomes paralyzing.

The solution is to make the filing system part of the entire work process. For example, when vouchers, contracts, orders, or transmittals are prepared, type a number on each that corresponds to the subject's file number. Then, when the time comes to file a stack of documents, it's a simple matter of putting them in numerical order and slipping them into the same numerically ordered files. You could even enlist other members of the household or hire neighborhood children to help. Thus, one simple step at the beginnings of documents' lives greatly eases the onus of filing them later on.

Efficiency is achieved by designing systems that serve more than one purpose. The same calendar book can be used for making appointments and keeping track of travel and entertainment expenses, since both are related to the same entries.

Computerized systems are most amenable to multiutility. A computerized data base that contains the names, addresses, telephone numbers, and other business information on prospective clients will not only be the source of marketing reports but, with integrated software, can address envelopes, produce invoices, print up Rolodex files, or even automatically dial the telephone. Some computerized payables programs can post the payable, age it, ask if it should be paid when it becomes due, write the check, clear the payables account, and post the expense to the general ledger—all from one entry made at the time the original invoice is received.

Flexibility is a major requirement for administrative systems because it is inevitable that the business operation will change and grow, and any system that cannot change and grow with it will have to be thrown out and replaced by another. Since it's difficult to know just how the operation will change, it's difficult to build flexibility for the future into the initial systems. But a look at how traditional offices solve this problem, especially in establishing filing systems, is helpful and will be addressed later in this chapter.

Again, how a home office should be organized is totally up to the person who operates it. Whatever works for you is by definition the right way to do it. The following work routines and administrative systems are general suggestions only. To be successful for your home office, each would have to be adapted to your type of work and your personality. But, hopefully, they can serve as a starting point.

FOUR THINGS TO DO EVERY MORNING

Upon entering the office each morning, or whenever your day begins:

1. Turn off the answering machine (or cancel call forwarding, or tell the answering service you are in and receiving calls). Of course, if the business line runs into the residential part of the home, you probably continue to answer it even if you aren't "in the office." But you should get into the habit of always turning on the answering machine (or whatever) whenever you leave home, and turning it off when you return. Otherwise you'll never know what important business calls you missed.

2. Turn on the lights, dehumidifier, air conditioner, space heater, coffee maker, and any other equipment necessary to a comfortable office environment. Also turn on the copier, computer, electronic typewriter, and any other pieces of equipment that the manufacturer recommends be kept on during the day rather than repeatedly turned on and off. Generally, *electronic* equipment should be turned on and off once each day, since they have no moving parts and require very little electricity when not actually in service—in fact, for some equipment a major point of wear and tear is the on-off switch. Turn the contrast or brightness down on computer monitors to keep from burning an image in the phosphorescent screen.

3. Go through the incoming mail. The earlier the mail is received, the better, since it commonly contains something that will partially determine the day's agenda—perhaps information needed to complete a project or a query that must be responded to quickly. (For this reason, many home-office workers begin their days very early in the morning, hours before the Post Office opens. They need time to concentrate on their work *before* the mail brings its surprises and distractions.)

If the mail doesn't come until later in the day, schedule a check of the mailbox at the same time you take your lunch or midafternoon coffee break. This way you won't forget the mail or let it interrupt your work concentration.

4. Review the day's agenda. Working with the To-Do list you prepared the day before, add any new task that arrived in the morning mail or that occurred to you overnight. In the margin give each task one of three priority rankings: MUST DO for those that absolutely, positively must be done today; SHOULD DO for those that need to get accomplished but can wait a day or so; COULD DO for those that can simmer on the back burner. Note the telephone numbers of people to call right on the To-Do list.

Of course, any work needing completion to meet a contractual deadline deserves the highest priority. Also, tasks that require your calling or writing someone else should generally be labeled "Must Do." This will keep you from becoming a bottleneck. For example, if supplies need to be ordered, get it done right away so it's off your list and on someone else's.

In scheduling the day's agenda, group miscellaneous small tasks together. This will leave blocks of uninterrupted time for concentrating on the larger tasks. Whether these "concentration" time blocks are in the morning, afternoon, or evening depends on when you are most mentally alert. Some people can't function in the morning, and others start early and fade after lunch.

When a task is completed, cross it off the To-Do list with a bright, bold color, a sort of visual conquest and pride in accomplishment. Note any necessary follow-up action in a long-term planning book. For instance, if you wrote Mr. So-and-so a letter saying you would call him at the end of the following week, note his name and telephone number in your planner under next Friday.

FIVE THINGS TO DO EVERY EVENING

Right before leaving the home office at the end of the work day:

1. Straighten up. Throw trash paper that has accumulated on desks or on the floor into the trash can or in the scrap-paper bin. Sort work paper on the desk into work-in-process displays or to-be-filed trays. Put pens, pencils, staplers, rulers, and scissors away. Rinse out coffee cups and glasses, or take them out of the office. Put computer tapes and diskettes in their holders. Put dust covers on electronic equipment.

General straightening up before the end of the day has two important purposes: You won't have to face a messy office the next morning, which can seriously hamper a productive work attitude; and it gives you a chance to review the day's progress—what got done and what didn't.

2. Prepare the next day's To-Do list. Include the uncompleted items from the ending day's To-Do list; check in your long-term planner for appointments, deadlines, and follow-up actions; and then add anything else that routinely has to be done on that day, like weekly trash collection or monthly billings. Writing down the next day's agenda the night before will make it much easier to "get down to business" the next morning.

Save old To-Do lists. They can be very valuable as business records, for notes, telephone numbers, and addresses that get scribbled on them, and for tax record purposes to substantiate "regular" business usage of the home office.

3. Seal, stamp, and post the outgoing mail. Generally, it's easiest to wait and drop all of the day's mail off at the Post Office right before it closes or at a mailbox right before the last possible collection. When mailing anything that requires over-the-counter services at the Post Office, such as Express mail or registered mail, try to get there a half hour before it closes in case there's a crowd. If mailing in large quantities, alert the Post Office in advance and ask what time you need to drop your mail off in order for it to be processed and postmarked on that day.

4. Turn off all appliances and equipment, especially hot plates, coffee makers, and space heaters.

5. Turn on the answering machine, call forwarding, or the answering service.

SETTING UP THE FILING SYSTEM

Filing systems in small offices tend to be highly eccentric. As long as they work for the one or two people who need to store and find records, how rational they are doesn't matter. In general, however, there are three major mistakes that should be avoided when establishing a filing system: Don't make the categories of records too broad; don't make the categories too specific; and, especially, leave plenty of room for expansion.

Files are cumulative by nature, and the filing system must be able to accommodate this. When a new business or a new project is undertaken, it's very difficult to know exactly where it's going and how it will develop. At first it may suffice to just have one file labeled "Taxes," but as time passes there will be worksheets; federal, state, and local returns and correspondence associated with each year of operation; and perhaps payroll records, deposits, and filings.

Alphabetical filing systems are not recommended for two reasons. First, they can commingle types of records that really have no relationship to one another other than the fact that they start with the same letter of the alphabet, such as "Papers of Incorporation" and "Paper Supplies." Second, new files must be added throughout the entire system rather than primarily at the end. This means that if for some reason 10 new clients with names all starting with B were added, all the files from C to Z would have to be shifted.

The Key-Access Filing System

A numerical system with alphabetized "key cards" is much more desirable. The files are divided into not more than 10 basic categories, for example:

1000–1999: *Organizational and Legal Records*, including corporate or partnership records, business licenses, business tax returns, payroll records, government filings, legal forms, permits, insurance schedules.

2000–2999: *Operational Records*, including supplier and servicer catalogs and correspondence, equipment manuals and warranties, business invoices and receipts, activity logs, employee resumes, master order forms, invoices, and contracts.

3000–3999: *Financial Records*, including financial projections, journals and general ledgers, worksheets, bank statements, canceled checks.

4000–4999: *Marketing and Promotional Records*, including advertising copy and designs, printed brochures, mailing lists, general promotional correspondence, information on trade shows and conferences, new product or service development.

5000–5999: *Resources*, including information on professional organizations, networks, newspaper and magazine clippings, newsletters, software and manuals, data-base reports.

6000–6999: *Client (or Project or Product) Files*, including all correspondence, orders, contracts, billings, work papers, and anything else related to providing goods or services to specific clients.

7000–7999: *Chronological Files*, including a *duplicate* copy of each piece of correspondence generated by the business, filed according to month. The chron file is an essential back-up against lost correspondence, assists in billing by showing what work was accomplished over the month or week, and provides a record of regular business practice for tax purposes. It is simple to keep a file folder by the copier and put the chron copy in it each time correspondence is photocopied. Then at the end of the month it is filed and replaced with an empty folder.

File numbers are assigned from each category only when and if there's need. Say a public relations firm picks up a new client named Appleton. The new client file is assigned whatever the next available number is in that category, number 6051 in this instance. An index card is typed up, reading "Appleton: 6051" and put in an alphabetically filed card box. These are called *key-access cards*, and whenever Appleton's file needs to be retrieved, the card shows where it can be found. It is also a good idea to use the client's file number on all contracts, billings, orders, work papers, records, and even correspondence.

If the client's initial file begins to get too bulky and includes too many different types of records, it should be broken down into several files and assigned suffix numbers or letters. For instance, Appleton needs three separate files for correspondence, contracts, and billing. The key-access card would then show:

Appleton:	6051
Correspondence	6051-A
Contracts	6051-B
Billings	6051-C

(The chron files do not need to be included in the key-access cards, since they are filed chronologically and are not difficult to find.)

Punch two holes in the top of papers to be filed, and fasten them in the file folder with metal fasteners. Within a folder, papers are filed with the oldest on the bottom and the most recent on the top of the stack.

Leave empty space in the file drawer at the end of each major numbering section. This will let you expand each section without having to shift everything that follows. Also, don't fill up the top drawer of a four-drawer file cabinet and leave the bottom ones empty, since this will make it top-heavy and possibly cause it to fall over on you.

Storing Files

Eventually, your filing cabinets will get full, and it will become necessary to go through and pull out inactive files for "deep storage." Files that are rarely needed or that are only being saved for legal reasons can be boxed, and the boxes numbered and stacked in closets, in the attic, in the garage, anywhere out of the way. Don't pull the key-access card for a stored file; simply note on the card which numbered box the file is in and where the box is stored.

Most inactive files and duplicate files (like chron files) can be thrown out after three years. Some records are required under federal and state regulations to be retained a certain number of years. If the home-office business deals with the Security and Exchange Commission, the Federal Communications Commission, the Federal Power Commission, the Interstate Commerce Commission, or the Civil Aeronautics Board, to name a few, the agency should be consulted as to what records need to be retained and for how long. The same thing holds true for certain state agencies, particularly if the business is responsible for the collection and remittance of sales tax.

All businesses are subject to the following records retention requirements:

1. The Internal Revenue Service requires that invoices, receipts, and cost records that support ledger entries be retained for three years. The ledgers themselves, and other summarizing records such as depreciation records and financial reports should be retained indefinitely.

2. The Department of Labor requires that payroll and personnel records be retained for three years.

3. The U.S. Postal Service requires that offices using postage meters maintain and retain for at least one year a meter record that shows each day's register reading.

4. The Interstate Commerce Commission requires that all bills of lading, claims for damages, freight bills, and other shipping records for goods carried by common carrier be retained for two years.

In addition, all signed contracts should be retained indefinitely in case of future legal action.

Files that are to be disposed of can be tossed in the trash or shredded if they contain highly private information. Burning is dangerous and usually more difficult than imagined, since closely packed papers have little oxygen available and resist ignition.

One last note on the filing system. Keep personal correspondence and records completely separate from the business files. Commingling records in the same file folder or even the same cabinet can jeopardize the home-office deductions. The most common area of possible confusion lies in the tax records. The business's tax records extend only to the corporate return, the partnership return, or Schedule C, Profit or Loss from a Business or Profession. Form 1040—Individual Taxpayer Return—and other schedules and papers are personal records and should not be filed with the business records.

COMPUTER FILES

All computer data stored on cassettes, floppies, or hard disks is saved in batches called *files*, each of which has a unique name. File names have two parts. The main name is limited to eight characters; the last part of the name, or *extension*, is limited to three. For example, if you write a letter to Mr. Fred Lyons and want to save it for later revisions, you might name the file it is stored in "LYONS.FRD."

Although this sounds simple, disorganized computer data files can quickly lead to a desktop full of floppies or cassettes and no way to find the particular letter, record, or spreadsheet you need. True, the computer is great at retrieving information; but you have to help. You have to select the proper disk to insert in the drive—which becomes progressively more difficult as your library grows to 30, 40, and 50 disks. You have to instruct the computer what the specific file's name is—which, because of the length limitation, results in such creative condensing that the name might not be recognized six months later.

If you have forgotten which disk a file is stored on or what its name is, you can command the computer-operating program to display a directory of disk files by file name, Then you can scan the names displayed and hope something rings a bell. However, with hard disks that can contain hundreds and hundreds of files, you may have to read through screen after screen of file names. This can so numb the brain that you will probably forget what you're looking for.

The latest generation of operating systems have what is called a "treeing" capability for organizing file names. This allows you to create and call up subdirectories of files—such as all files related to a specific program or all files related to a particular client. Without treeing, all the file names on a directory are displayed in a random listing.

There are two other ways to help keep computer files easy to locate. First, set up a file naming system and stick to it. If correspondence files are named by the addressee's last name, don't suddenly switch to a first name or a company name. Also, unless you already have an internal clock in the computer, always enter "Today's Date" when you boot the operating system. That way you can sometimes find a file, which you can't recall by name but have some idea of when you stored it, by the date displayed next to the name in the directory.

Second, set up a system for your disks and stick to it. For example, keep all information relevant to your billings—your billing forms, accounts receivable, dunning correspondence—on one disk. Keep your marketing files and correspondence on another, and so forth.

Safekeeping of Computer Files

There is one universal rule for the safekeeping of computer data: *Always* make back-up copies of important data disks and all software disks. Disks get bent, melt, have coffee spilled on them, are rubbed up against other disks, get fingerprints on them, and just plumb wear out. Disks in the computer are subject to power surges and operator mistakes, which can cause an entire file to flit out of the computer like some electronic Tinkerbell and escape to Never-Never Land. If this happens to the only copy of a program that cost $250, it could ruin your whole day. If it happens to the only copy of a handcrafted client data base with 500 records, or a whole year's journal entries, it could ruin your entire business.

Back-up data disks can be stored in the office, somewhere else in the residence, or even in a bank safety-deposit box, depending on how much protection is desired and how much access is required. Software publishers recommend that you use the program back-up disk and store the original. But remember, no one knows exactly how long magnetic disks will last or how long the electronic data stored on them will remain stable. So you should check your software originals every once in a while to make sure they are not deteriorating. A good rule of thumb is to renew your back-up program disks every six months or so.

Another general rule is to conserve space on disk space by deleting unused files or unused portions of files. Disks can hold only so many bytes. If you suspect that a disk is getting close to its capacity, run the operating system's "Check Disk Space" command to find out how much room is available. If a file is just one byte too long to fit into the available space, the computer can dump the entire file, leaving you with nothing more than a fond remembrance of whatever information it contained.

Deleting unnecessary files on data disks should become part of your daily computer housecleaning routine. If a word-processing program creates separate output files to format and print a document, they can be deleted once the document is printed. Back-up files used to check spelling or integrate with other programs can also be erased after use.

The input file can be deleted if there is a "hard" copy of the document, and you don't expect you'll need any revisions in the future. If you have letter files set up for people you regularly correspond with, delete only the body of a letter you have printed, leaving the framework—the address, salutation, closing, etc.—for future letters.

Delete inactive records on data bases, or store them on a separate disk. This will not only open up more space on the active records disk but reduce the amount of time it takes the filing program to sort through the data base.

Usually little can be deleted from a program without interfering with its operation. Exceptions are the tutorial files that are sometime included in order to teach you how to run the program, and information files like "Menu." Once you are thoroughly familiar with a program, you can move from one part of the program to another with command codes rather than reverting to the menu. Also, you can delete the installation files, which help you configure your software to your hardware, once you have set up your working back-up disk.

LOGS

Telephone logs and appointment books (also called planners, diaries, and calendars) are important evidence to support home-office tax deductions (see Chapter 2). They substantiate regular business use, or meeting and dealing with clients, patients, and customers, and can be used to record business expenses. Logs are also valuable organizational tools.

The telephone log can be a simple ruled pad with columns marked "Date/time," "Who called/was called," "Phone number," "Comments." Or it can be printed, two-part forms bound in a spiral notebook. Whatever, it must be maintained, and this is best accomplished by keeping it next to the phone and with a pen or pencil tied to it. Using the phone then automatically becomes a two-handed motion: One hand holds the receiver and the other fills out the phone log.

Properly maintained phone logs provide a record of calls which, along with the phone bill, can be used to allocate expenses; a back-up record of phone numbers; and a place to jot down follow-up notations. If an employee or someone else in the home answers incoming calls when you are not in, insist that each call be recorded in the phone log rather than relying on memory or notes on odd scraps of paper.

Appointment books are essential not only for keeping track of meetings with clients, customers, patients, and suppliers but also for deadlines and routine tasks that tend to slip your mind if not written down. Entries in an appointment book might be as mundane as "take out the trash" or as vital as "filing deadline for license renewal."

Again, appointment books are best kept near the phone. A format that shows the entire week at one glance is better than day-by-day or month-by-month calendars. The former doesn't give a good overview of upcoming commitments, and the latter usually doesn't provide enough space for detailed notations.

Phone logs and appointment books should be saved for at least three years as back-up documents for tax deductions.

ADDRESSES AND PHONE NUMBERS

Index cards or Rolodex-type files are best for keeping office records of names, addresses, and telephone numbers. Because the cards are removable, old addresses and telephone numbers can be removed and new ones inserted, which is preferable to crossing out entries in telephone memo books. Pulled cards also serve as visual reminders of the day's necessary phone calls.

Keep a small pack of blank cards next to the phone to jot names and numbers down when someone new calls. Staple new contacts' business cards to the file cards instead of transferring the information. Also, record the following information, if applicable, on an individual's or organization's address card: their electronic mail utility and User ID numbers; the number assigned to their folder in the filing system; and your account number, if the card is for one of your suppliers or servicers.

In addition, important phone numbers and addresses should be recorded in a small telephone memo book that can be taken along on trips out of the office. Some appointment books and calendars have telephone sections at the back. Be sure to check through it once in a while to make sure all the numbers are current.

Addresses and phone numbers can also be kept on computer filing systems. However, it's advisable to also have the information in hard copy in case the system fails or the computer is being used for something else. Many computer filing systems can be programmed to print records on continuous-form index or Rolodex cards.

THE DAILY MAIL

Incoming mail brings all sorts of notices, correspondence, bills, periodicals, solicitations, and sometimes money (hurray!) into the office. The important thing is to keep control of it all: Several days of unopened, unfiled mail can build into an intimidating backlog.

Sorting Incoming Mail

The key is to sort the incoming mail *as it's opened* according to the following four categories:

1. Mail that gets thrown away goes immediately into the wastebasket. Be ruthless: if you can't think of why you should hold onto a piece of mail, trash it.

2. Mail that doesn't require any response but should be retained, like FYI copies, notices, and catalogs, go into the to-be-filed bin.

3. Mail that requires some, but not immediate, action goes into *specific and defined* temporary way stations. Examples are: invoices that need to be posted to the payables journal go into a special folder marked "Unposted Payables"; government payroll forms are put with the employee work records; business magazines and newsletters are stacked on a desk or table for later perusal. When the time comes to post the invoices, fill out the forms, and read the periodicals, they will be where they should be and not lost in stacks of miscellaneous papers on the desktop or the to-be-filed bin.

4. Mail that requires immediate action should be turned around right away or noted on the To-Do list. If a check comes in the mail, immediately fill out the deposit slip, and put it in the outgoing mail drop to be taken or mailed to the bank at the first chance. If a business inquiry arrives that might lead to future business income, acknowledge its receipt immediately, either by telephone call or quick letter, and promise to provide whatever information is desired by a certain date. Make a big "follow up" note in the long-term schedule. If a dunning notice from an unhappy creditor arrives, call immediately and explain why the payment is overdue, even if it's just because the cash isn't available right now. Credit relationships last a lot longer if the creditor feels the debtor is at least accessible and taking the situation seriously.

When opening a letter from an unknown person or organization, tear the return address off the envelope and save it. It's amazing how many people, and especially government agencies, don't include their return addresses on their correspondence.

Outgoing Mail

The letters that *go out* of the office are its major envoys out into the business world and will be judged against the business and professional standards of traditional offices. Informal, handwritten letters or poorly typed letters indicate that the office is less than businesslike and will create a serious prejudice against the operation.

With the availability of memory typewriters and word processors, there are no good reasons why you can't prepare well-typed letters. Word processors can also run spelling checks and eventually will even be able to query sentence construction. The investment in such equipment and software is relatively small when compared with the potential business that can be lost by not paying attention to these details.

Every piece of business correspondence should include the address of the person or business it is being sent to and the date of mailing. If merchandise or a noncorrespondence document, such as a manuscript or a contract, is being mailed, it should be accompanied by a cover letter. Otherwise, there will be no record of what was sent where and on what date.

If you regularly send material to the same addresses, it's probably a good idea to get preprinted transmittal forms, or run some off on the photocopier. The transmittal form is a simplified cover letter and should show your business's letterhead, a blank space for the recipient's name, a blank for the date, and several boxes designating different types of commonly mailed materials. Just fill in the blanks and check off the appropriate box.

After you finish typing a letter or completing a transmittal form, it should be routed to the copier. Make at least two copies, one for the chron file and one for the subject file. Then sign the correspondence (if necessary), fold it, put it in the envelope, and place it in a central mail drop. Don't seal or put postage on the envelope until right before the mail is taken to the Post Office or mailbox.

Don't mail nonessential correspondence such as FYI carbon copies immediately if additional correspondence will be going to the same address in the next couple of days. Wait and combine the items in one envelope and save on postage and stationery.

WORK IN PROCESS

Work-in-process papers and materials should be kept as accessible and visible as possible, and yet be organized. The first step is to furnish the office with lots of shelves, vertical files, trays, or banker's boxes, so that papers are kept neat, together, and off the work surfaces when not actually in use. Colored file folders or labels help distinguish different types of tasks at a quick glance.

There are two aspects to organizing work in progress. The first is the actual project file folder where all the papers, notes, and materials associated with the project are kept together. The second is actually a slot, shelf, tray, or pigeonhole that indicates a specific step in the work proces: "Needs Correspondence" or "Needs Research" or "Needs Billing" or whatever suits the particular business operation. The last step is "To Be Filed," indicating the completion of the project and the end of the active work process.

The project files are organized by where they are placed in the work-process slots. For example, you need to do research on market competition for a new game named Easy Street. Easy Street's file folder, with all relevant information, goes in the "Needs Research" slot until you get around to it. After you complete the research, you need to write the client a letter, and so Easy Street's file folder gets shifted to the "Needs Correspondence" slot.

You can take a project file straight through the work process in one sweep, or you can put aside time to tackle one specific step in the process for various projects at once. Tuesdays, for instance, may be your day to prepare and mail out bills for whatever projects are in the "Needs Billing" slot. However you approach work in process, the materials will be organized and obvious.

Maximizing Work Time

At the beginning of this chapter, you read about the importance of preparing each day's work schedule the day before, and about how to rank and group the day's tasks.

Other things to remember when scheduling tasks:

1. The best time to reach people by phone is right after they get to work, which is about 9:10 A.M. in most offices. This way you can catch them as they get their first cup of coffee and before they get involved in conferences or tied up on other phone calls.

2. Always coordinate your work schedule with that of others working in the home office or other members of the household. Put aside "Do Not Disturb" times for the tasks that require heavy concentration. If the children get home from school at 3:15 P.M., save the routine, simple tasks for late afternoon; if someone else working within earshot in the office is planning to do a lot of telephone calling that day, go to the library, or stagger your hours and work in the late evening.

3. Don't hesitate to put more tasks on your To-Do list than you think you can get accomplished. You'll be surprised to find that the more you have to do, the more you will do. As a wise woman in Tennessee once said, "If you really want something done, give it to a busy person to do."

4. Schedule breaks. Not taking *any* breaks leads to insidious mental and physical exhaustion. Not *scheduling* breaks means they will be taken haphazardly and disrupt the work routine. Instead, take a definite lunch break and leave the office, even if that only means walking into the next room. And don't take your work with you. Instead, read a newspaper, magazine, or professional journal. Promise and then reward yourself with a piece of fruit or juice at 3:00 P.M., and again leave the office to get it.

5. Avoid unproductive time in transit. Take along reference reading or a project file to work on during train, plane, and bus rides. If you have to drive, coordinate appointments so that two or three are scheduled on one trip. Take the time to develop new business leads in the area being visited.

Brushfires

Unfortunately, even the best scheduled day will fall apart if you have to spend time and energy putting out "brushfires"—those unplanned crises that flare up and have to be dealt with immediately. If you find yourself chronically falling behind on scheduled tasks because of brushfires, it's time to analyze why.

Everyday, write down the unexpected crises that sidetracked your day. After a week ask yourself why most of them erupted. Were they caused by unnecessary interruptions? Perhaps you should restrict other people's access to you during certain hours. Turn the answering machine on, and don't answer any calls. Learn to say "No," "Got to go now," "I'm afraid I can't help you with that now. Why not call So-and-So?"

Were they caused by someone else's failure to live up to a commitment? Terminate suppliers and servicers who aren't reliable. Notify tardy clients or customers that because of their delay, you may not be able to meet your contractual obligation. Do it in writing.

Are the brushfires caused by a heavy backlog of undone work, so that you always seem to be playing catch-up ball? The only remedy for this is to get even, which means either putting in extra hours or bringing in temporary help. The short-term sacrifice will be well worth it.

Finally, are the crises due to planning oversights? Perhaps you failed to estimate the necessary time, talent, supplies, or steps required to achieve a goal. Integrate what has been learned into the next project so that you will have more control over its progress. And be sure your pricing schedule reflects any increased costs.

FINANCES

Of all the systems used to organize a home office, none are as important as those that control invoices, receipts, bills, deposits, and petty cash. Strong financial records will keep control of business expenses and substantiate their tax-deductible status, accurately reflect business income, maintain good credit relationships, and help in the collection of receivables.

The initial step to good financial systems is to separate the business activity from personal finances by opening a separate business checking account. All business income must be deposited in the business account; all business expenses must be paid out of the business account. Any transfers of funds between the business account and personal finances—stockholder contributions, loans, advances, draws, salaries, reimbursements, and the like—whenever possible should be done by check and accurately entered in the business checkbook.

For most service-oriented home-based businesses, money comes in primarily by check. Sorting checks out of the incoming mail and immediately depositing them is a high priority on the daily To-Do list. Since most banks require a few days for funds to clear before you can draw on them, you will want the process to begin as soon as possible. Printed, two-part deposit slips will help avoid the surprisingly common mistake in small businesses of making a deposit and failing to record it in the checkbook.

If the business is in retail sales and commonly receives payment in cash, a cash-receipt system is necessary to keep track of income and to meet state and local sales tax requirements. A cash register or prenumbered receipt book with carbon copies will do.

Money will go out of the office either by check or cash. Since cash is more difficult to keep track of, it is not the preferred method. However, there will always be situations when cash is necessary.

Petty Cash

A petty-cash system starts out with a check written to cash in an amount that you expect will meet the next week's cash requirements, $100 for example. The cash is kept, along with a log, in an envelope or cash box in your desk drawer. Every time you take cash out of the drawer, record on the log the date, amount, and purpose. Always return receipts for purchases and any change to the petty-cash drawer immediately upon returning to the office. At all times the cash plus receipts in the petty-cash drawer should equal the amount of the original check. When cash starts getting low, a second check is written to petty cash in the total amount of the receipts, and the expense entry is based on the categories of the receipts.

For example, at the end of the week you look in the petty-cash drawer and find $9.10 in cash and $90.90 worth of paid receipts: $24.60 for gas, $9.75 for tolls, $36.10 for parking, $11.35 for office supplies, and $9.10 for a reference book. The check is written for $90.90 and posted according to the above expense categories. Cash on hand is back up to $100.

Purchasing items with a check is a better way to record the amount and type of expense, since it is entered directly in the checkbook when the check is written. Always request a receipt for the purchase showing the seller, date, amount (broken down into line items and showing tax, if any), what was purchased, and check number.

Credit Relationships

Using servicers and suppliers who will bill you at the end of the month rather than requiring immediate payment has the added convenience of allowing you to put off payment for a little while. Creditors usually allow from 10 to 30 days to pay from the date of invoice, and sometimes longer. Just how long depends: The local phone company will discontinue service fairly quickly once a customer gets behind; some long-distance carriers won't.

Credit is a precious commodity for businesses large and small and should be carefully managed. If for some reason you are going to fall behind in payments or have already, *don't ignore the creditor*. Don't avoid dunning phone calls: Instead, own up to the fact that you are late paying, and express your concern over the situation and your intention to make it current as soon as possible. Don't stop making regular payments, no matter how small they may be. They indicate your good faith. Most creditors will accept a reduced payment schedule if it is adhered to until the account is cleared.

Too often, small business relationships are ruined by sloppy payables systems. Invoices get lost or payments are overlooked. Invoices and statements should be sorted out of the incoming mail each day and filed in a special folder. If the business gets only between 10 and 15 bills a month, this folder can serve as the way to keep track of what's due and when, similar to how most household accounts are kept. But if there are more, the invoices should be posted once a week or so to a payables journal.

The Payables Journal

Pages in the journal are arranged alphabetically by creditor's names. Invoices are posted showing the invoice amount, date, date due, and type of expense, and then the invoices are filed in an accordian-type expanding folder. A scan through the payables ledger shows who is owed what and when.

When a payment is made, the check is also posted to the creditor's account, clearing or reducing the debt, and the invoice is marked "$(*Amount*) Paid on (*Date*) with Check (*Number*)." The paid invoices are then refiled in another expanding folder. At the end of the accounting period, the "Paid Invoice" folder closes down and goes to the bookkeeper for expense postings. A new one is started.

Receivables Journal

Receivables are set up essentially the same way. Whenever the business does its billing, once a month for instance, the amounts due and the date billed are posted to each client's or customer's account in the receivables ledger. A copy of the bill is filed in a "Receivables Due" expanding folder.

When payment is received, it is deposited and posted to the payer's account, clearing or reducing the amount due. The copy of the bill is marked "$(*Amount*) Received on (*Date*) with Check (*Number*)." Paid bills are refiled in a separate folder. The "Paid Receivables" folder is used for posting income at the end of the accounting period. (Note: If you barter your business services or goods in exchange for *anything*, whether for business or personal use, you must record the fair market value of the exchange as business income.)

Accounting software that computerizes the payables and receivables journals can take just about as long to use as posting the entries by hand. However, their major advantages are that the programs keep much more accurate records, can run different lists and aging reports, can often print checks and prepare billings, and may integrate automatically with a general ledger program.

HOUSECLEANING

Although it may not seem like part of keeping the home office organized, house—really office—cleaning cannot be ignored. An office's neatness is essential to a good business image and the morale of the people who work in it. In addition, dust is a serious liability to electronic equipment, and food crumbs can attract pests that will soon move on to eating paper and other office supplies.

Straightening up should be part of the everyday routine, preferably right before the end of the day. Wastepaper cans should be emptied as needed, but certainly in coordination with the residential trash-collection schedule. If the office generates a lot of trash, be prepared to purchase one or two extra outside trashcans for its use (which will be tax deductible if used exclusively for the office).

Heavy-duty vacuuming and dusting can be done on the same schedule as the rest of the residence. Be sure to cover electronic equipment with a sheet or dust cover before vacuuming to protect it from dust in the air. If an outside cleaning service or maid cleans the home and the home office, separate out the time spent on the office away from the rest of his or her hours and pay that portion through the business. The same thing applies to services that clean the carpet, upholstery, and drapes.

11

Home-Office Insurance

A home office represents an important investment of time and money, whether it's simply a spare bedroom furnished with household hand-me-downs or a specially built addition containing sophisticated computer equipment. This is because, in addition to its furnishings, the home office houses the business's resources and records. It may also be essential for meeting clients, customers, or patients; and it may be the work site for full-time or part-time employees. It is an integral part of a serious business pursuit.

Unfortunately, some home-office workers are shocked to find out after a fire or theft that *none* of this investment—the equipment, furnishings, or supplies—is insured under their standard homeowner's or tenant's insurance policies. In addition, homeowner/tenant's policies will typically *not* cover any personal liability or medical expenses associated with the home office.

The problem arises because many homeowners assume that their insurance policies cover their residence regardless of its use. They trust, based on a typical policy, that they are covered for the value of the structure and all the personal property contained in it against damage from certain perils, such as fire, windstorms, and theft. (Perils such as earthquakes and floods generally require separate policies or riders.) In addition, homeowners usually carry liability insurance for protection in case someone slips on an icy sidewalk, falls off a ladder, or otherwise is injured on their property.

WHAT THE STANDARD HOMEOWNER'S POLICY DOESN'T COVER

A careful reading, however, reveals that many homeowner's policies *expressly exclude* some or all of the following:

1. Dwellings that are not used *principally* as a residence. Under strict textbook interpretation, "principally" means 80 percent or more of the square footage must be for residential use.

2. Separate structures that are used in whole or in part for business purposes (i.e., in connection with a trade, profession, or occupation, no matter how often or whether exclusively).

3. Business property used in conducting a business on the premises, including all furnishings and equipment in a home office. (A 1985 update of the Insurance Service Office's standard homeowners policy, which affects about 40 percent of the nation's homeowners, extends coverage to business property, but only up to $2,500 for property located in the residence and $250 for property away from the residence.)

4. Business inventory or samples stored on the premises.

5. Losses from unauthorized use of business credit cards, business check forgery, or the business's acceptance of counterfeit money. (Losses on personal credit cards, etc., are often covered under homeowner's policies.)

6. Accidental damage to electronic components from sudden electrical surges, whether to business equipment or personal-use equipment.

7. Personal liability or medical payments to others for bodily injury or property damage arising out of any business pursuit. This means the insurance company will not pay for any property damage or bodily injury to office employees, clients, customers, patients, repair persons, suppliers, or servicers who are on the premises for business purposes.

8. Personal liability or medical payments for any injury to a person who is eligible for benefits under state workman's compensation, disability, or occupational-disease laws.

Clearly, the standard homeowner's policy leaves the home office extremely vulnerable. The picture for the tenant isn't any better, since the typical tenant's policy has all the same exclusions regarding personal property and liability associated with a home office.

HOME-OFFICE RIDERS

There are two approaches to insuring the home office. The first and least expensive is to purchase a rider to the homeowner's or tenant's policy. This route is available if not more than 20 percent of your residence's square footage is devoted to the business. It also requires that your business operation involves no unusually high liability risks, such as a lot of people visiting the office every day, numerous employees, or the use of heavy machinery or flammable chemicals.

Home-office riders are intended for small service business and professional offices that don't hire more than one or two employees and that aren't generally open to the public. The riders must state the type of business activity. Insurance coverage is then extended to include business furnishings and equipment, and personal liability associated with the named business.

However, home-office riders *won't* cover damage to electronic equipment from electrical surges and *expressly exclude* personal liability or medical payments for bodily injury to office employees. These risks require separate policies, which are covered under "Additional Types of Insurance Coverage for the Home Office."

SEPARATE BUSINESS COVERAGE

If more than 20 percent of your residence is used by the business, or if your business activity has a high liability risk, then you may be required to purchase a separate business policy to insure the structure, business furnishings and equipment, and liability associated with the business activity.

Note the words *may be required*: Many insurance companies give agents a great deal of leeway in interpreting square footage and high-risk business activities. So since business insurance is considerably more expensive than homeowner's, it's a good idea to find an insurance agent who has some discretionary powers in classifying home offices.

If you must buy a separate business policy, it will fall into one of several classifications depending on your business activity, including "storefront" operations, medical clinics, artist studios, beauty shops, private schools, and so forth. The type of coverage and its cost vary greatly depending primarily on liability risks: Insurance premiums for a caterer are greater than for an artist because of the caterer's liability for food poisoning; a veterinary clinic will pay more than a storefront because of the vet's liability if a customer is bitten by a sick animal.

Business policies apply *only* to business property and liability; in order to insure your personal property located in the nonbusiness part of the residence, you will have to purchase a separate tenant's policy, which will also include liability coverage for people who come to visit you for personal reasons. Under this arrangement, you are essentially considered to be renting out part of the residence from your business.

If you live in a flood plain, along the coast, or in a high-earthquake area, you probably have a separate policy to protect you against these particular perils. However, make sure your home office is also covered. For example, the National Flood Insurance Program requires two policies—one for the structure and personal property in the residential area, and one for business equipment and furnishings in the home office.

ADDITIONAL TYPES OF INSURANCE COVERAGE FOR THE HOME OFFICE

Worker's Compensation

As stated above, home-office riders and some business policies do not cover liability or medical payments for any injury to office employees arising out of their office duties. And depending on the state in which you live, separate worker's compensation insurance may be required by law. The rates for this insurance are based on the type of work the employee performs and the employee's annual salary. If the employer is a corporation, officers working in the office may be required to be covered under a worker's compensation policy whether they draw a salary or not.

Note that worker's compensation is not the same thing as state unemployment and disability insurance, nor is it included in most health-insurance plans. It is the employer's liability to pay for medical costs, loss of income, and other damages in case a business employee is injured on the job.

Computer and Software Insurance

Home-office riders and business policies will cover computer hardware against theft, fire, and other insured-against perils; however, they will not cover damage to electronic circuitry caused by electrical surges or accidental spills and drops. Nor do they cover the relacement cost of software programs damaged in any way whatsoever. (They will pay for the cost of the disk!)

Because computer hardware and software represent the single most significant expense in many home offices, it's advisable that they have full insurance coverage, available through several companies that specialize in computer-related coverage. The annual premiums depend on the stated value of the equipment and software, and the coverage is usually for full replacement value rather than their cash value at the time of loss or damage, unlike most homeowner's policies.

Separate computer insurance will also cover the equipment when it is away from the office (except when it is left in an unattended car). This can be especially important if you have a portable computer.

Business Inventory Insurance

A home-office rider will cover personal property used in actually conducting the business, but it will not cover inventory or samples stored on the premises. If you regularly keep inventory in the basement, attic, attached garage, or elsewhere in the residence, ask your insurance agent about a separate policy to cover its estimated value. If the inventory is stored in a separate structure, ask about coverage for both the structure and the value of the inventory.

Interruption of Business Insurance

No one can judge the replacement value of damaged or destroyed business resource files and records. Without them, your business operation will essentially come to a halt and with it the income it generated. Interruption of business insurance covers this potential loss due to fire or other similar disaster. It does not cover financial losses due to business factors such as a poor market economy or competition.

Health, Life, and Disability Insurance

One of the major benefits employees give up when they strike out on their own is the health-insurance package provided by most employers. For the independent small business owner or professional, replacing it is essential, not only because of the impact of illness, death, or disability on personal finances but because it can mean the end of the business itself and any equity that has been built. Health, life, and disability insurance can be bought under individual policies or in connection with professional and trade associations. Group policies are available to businesses with as few as two full-time workers. Premiums are based on the age of the covered individual and type of coverage.

Malpractice and Products Liability Insurance

These are specialized types of business liability insurance. They protect your business and you personally in case a patient, client, or customer is injured or harmed in someway and claims that you are to blame. Don't think that such insurance is limited to doctors, lawyers, and automobile manufacturers: it also can apply to individual consultants who advise clients on financial and business matters; to artisans and sales representatives who sell products for use in the home; and to many more types of home-based businesses.

TWELVE PRECAUTIONS THAT HELP PROTECT THE HOME OFFICE

1. Don't overload electrical circuits. Trouble signs are circuit breakers that flip off when a piece of equipment is turned on, and hot electrical plugs and sockets. Don't use extension cords that are made of a thinner wire than the cord on the electrical equipment. Always ground equipment that comes with three-prong plugs. For a highly electronic office, electrical fires are a major threat, and they are usually caused by the carelessness of the people who work there.

2. Keep a separate fire extinguisher, and install a smoke alarm in the office. (Of course, fire extinguishers and smoke alarms belong throughout the residence, since the entire structure is vulnerable once a fire gets out of hand.)

3. Don't position electronic equipment under water or drain pipes that run through the ceiling, in case of burst plumbing or other types of leakage. If this can't be avoided, keep a waterproof tarp near the equipment, and cover it when away for any period of time.

4. Don't empty ashtrays into wastepaper baskets. Better yet, don't allow anyone to smoke in the office, since smoke is as bad for computers and diskettes as it is for human lungs.

5. Always work with back-up copies of computer software programs. Store the original disks in a safe place in the residence or in a bank safety-deposit box.

6. Store originals of legal and other essential business documents, insurance policies, and the like in a bank safety-deposit box.

7. If the home office is separated from the rest of the residence by a door, install a deadbolt lock on it, and keep it locked when away from home. This way, if thieves break into the private section, they may be deterred from breaking into the office, or vice versa.

8. When away from the home office on vacation or long business trips, secure computer equipment, typewriter, and other electronic equipment. They are popular targets for thieves because they are very easy to resell. Some computer desks and typewriter stands have locking devices that attach to the equipment or enclose it in a locked cabinet. Also, don't broadcast the presence of valuable office equipment in your home office, as this can draw unwanted attention. Keeping a low profile is the best protection against theft.

9. Ask your letter carrier to hold your mail at the Post Office when you are away for more than overnight. Likewise, stop the newspaper delivery. Install electric timers to turn lights on and off, and ask a trusted neighbor to keep an eye out and/or request the local police to drive by on their nightly patrols.

10. Keep in good repair and install good lighting on all steps, walkways, and entrances that are used by business visitors or employees. Also put in handrails and carpeting on interior staircases. Clear snow and ice off sidewalks as soon as possible, even if the office isn't in a commercial area.

11. Keep children's toys off the floor in the office and entryways. Don't expose business visitors or employees to house pets that may bite, scratch, or ruin clothing.

12. Compile a list of all business equipment, including the manufacturer, model, serial number, and special options. Also list office furniture with a detailed description, or even better attach a photograph. Keep these inventories along with copies of sales receipts in a bank safety-deposit box to substantiate filing claims in case of casualty loss.

though limited water flow could erode significantly in a year's time.

12

The Home Office and the Community, State, and Nation

Like it or not, the decision to create and operate out of a home office is not strictly a private one. Ever since the first workers marched out of home-based shops and into factories during the Industrial Revolution, governmental agencies have enacted a plethora of laws and codes designed to keep where we work separate from where we live. Zoning restrictions, labor laws, building codes, and licensing requirements can bring a home-based business to a screeching halt, all in the name of protecting the greater good.

With the rapidly increasing number of people opting to work at home, many of these laws probably will change radically in the next few years. Already, federal labor restrictions prohibiting home-based manufacturing of certain types of apparel and accessories are under heavy attack and will probably be completely rescinded in the not-too-distant future. However, other types of legal restrictions, such as zoning codes, lease agreements, and cooperative and condominium bylaws, may get more restrictive as home offices become more prevalent. Thus, anyone considering setting up a home office should check out all relevant laws affecting a combined residence/office *before* making any significant investment or a career move. It can save a lot of grief later on and keep the home office from becoming a dead-end effort.

ZONING LAWS AND HOME-BASED OCCUPATIONS

Municipalities plan growth and determine land use through zoning codes. Some areas are zoned for single-family residences; some for commercial stores and offices; others for industrial use, and so forth. Besides defining the size and shape of lots, the size of structures, what facilities they must include, etc., the zoning codes dictate how the structure may be used. Once an area has been zoned for a certain type of use, no one can introduce a different use without getting special permission from the zoning board.

Working and living under one roof may combine two mutually exclusive types of land use and violate the zoning laws. Sometimes the violation involves setting up a household in an area that is zoned for commercial or industrial use. Common offenders are artists who set up studios in old warehouses because the space is cheap and provides abundant windows, sturdy floors, and freight elevators. If they try to move into the warehouse, they may be introducing a residential use in an area zoned only for industrial or commercial use.

Why should anyone care? For two reasons. First, it may not be healthy for the artists. Industrial zoning codes typically don't require structures to have bathrooms, kitchens, heating, or other facilities considered necessary for a minimum standard of living. Second, the municipality may not be able to provide the necessary support services associated with residential use, such as police protection, schools, trash collection, and so on.

Far more common are home offices that violate zoning laws by introducing a commercial use into a residential area. Anyone who creates an office in his or her residence and operates a business out of it must be concerned about this, because municipalities and local neighborhood groups are notoriously vigilant about trying to maintain the character of residential areas. They don't want the traffic, noise, and outsiders that commercial businesses attract. Nor do they want the noise, odors, and pollution that some manufacturing operations generate.

Like the artist who sets up a household in a warehouse, businesses located in residential areas can place increased strains on public utilities—water, sewage, trash collection—and on police and fire protection. Finally, the municipality may realize (and rightly so) that people operating out of their homes have a financial advantage over businesses and professionals who work out of traditional offices. The zoning restrictions are an attempt to provide protection for the high ratables in the commercial districts.

Common Zoning Standards

This is not to say that home offices are always absolutely forbidden in residential areas. After all, neighborhood "mom-and-pop" grocery stores and small-town doctor's and lawyer's offices where the owners live upstairs are not entirely things of the past.

Certain types of home offices may be allowed under residential zoning, but they are usually restricted by one or more of the following standards:

Type of profession. This is an extremely value-ridden, discriminatory restriction that is constantly challenged by professional associations. For instance, the zoning law may state that an architect can work out of a home office but not a psychologist, because the community fears the "shrink" would attract emotionally unstable persons into residential neighborhoods.

Some zoning laws name the types of professions that are allowed, some list the types that aren't. Obviously, the second method is preferable, unless you happen to be on the "not allowed" list. In any event, there's very little that can be done to get around this restriction, short of changing the law.

Type of business operation. Similar to restrictions based on type of profession, this is a little broader, since it usually deals with the type of business operation rather than the business itself. For instance, retail outlets are commonly banned from residential areas because of the public traffic they draw and because a "storefront" appearance would be incongruous with the rest of the homes in the neighborhood. A retail concern that markets entirely through mail order might also be covered by this restriction.

Area of the residence used for business. In order to keep the home-based occupation "incidental and subordinate" to the residential use, zoning laws will commonly restrict the amount of space for the home office to 25 percent or less. However, this does not take into account those home occupations that are space/time based. For instance, a day-care facility may involve much more than 25 percent of the residence but for only a portion of the day.

Off-street parking. Increased traffic is a major objection to home offices, particularly if there is already heavy competition for parking places. Therefore, the office is often required to provide its own off-street parking spaces for employees and the expected number of visitors, in addition to any that may be required for the household itself.

Employees. The zoning law may state that no one other than members of the household may work in the home office; or it may limit the number of nonhousehold-member employees who can be hired by the home-based business.

Sometimes the word "family" is used rather than "household member," which involves the complex question of what constitutes a "family."

This is a very common restriction. It is a tacit approval of family-run business and essentially says, "O.K., you and other members of your household can do what you please, but the business can't get so big that it needs to hire other people." Or it accepts the fact that a professional may need to hire a secretary or two.

Outside appearance. This restriction prohibits any changes in the outside appearance of the building or premises which would call attention to the home occupation, such as signs, lighting, separate entrance, and so forth. Sometimes a small sign, 1 foot by 1 foot square, can be posted, but the law may restrict what it can display (e.g., name and telephone number only) and where it can be placed (e.g., flat against the house at shoulder height).

Nuisance controls. These restrictions are intended to keep home-based occupations from generating excessive noise, vibrations, glare, fumes, odors, dust, smoke, and electrical interference, or from becoming a fire hazard.

Utilities. A fairly new standard that is showing up in zoning restrictions prohibits any home-based occupations that would place an unusual strain on public utilities, including water, sewer, electricity, telephone, and garbage collection.

Permit or No Permit Required?

Municipalities have two different ways of enforcing their zoning restrictions concerning home-based occupations. The first requires that every person who wants to work out of a home office must get a permit from the city *before* setting up shop. This involves filling out an application that typically asks such questions as how many persons will be involved or employed in the business; that you describe the type of business activity, materials and equipment used, and methods of operation; what alterations to the home or premises will be required; what rooms will be involved; and how materials will be delivered to the home office.

The applicant must also state that he or she has read the ordinances relating to home-based occupations and will not violate them. The application is evaluated, usually by the planning board, and either granted or denied after a public hearing is conducted.

The second method does not require a permit; the ordinances are in effect self-enforcing. A home-based business that is in violation of the zoning laws must be brought to the attention of the zoning or planning board *after* the business is in operation. This means that as long as no one in your neighborhood complains, you could be in violation, but the authorities might never find out about it.

That is, unless your municipality requires that all businesses operating in its jurisdiction have business licenses. Although business licenses are usually issued through the city's administrative offices or through the treasurer's office, the planning and zoning boards might routinely be sent copies of all license applications for business in residential areas. The license form itself might ask, "Is part of your house used for business?" or "Do you work at your residence?"

What Are the Zoning Laws in Your Town?

Obviously, you should be aware at least of what the zoning ordinances are in your area. You may think that finding out would be simple. You simply call the zoning board and ask. However, your questions will have to be fairly *specific*, giving the location of the property and describing the business operated out of the home office. This is not something everyone is prepared to reveal, especially if they suspect their home office may be in violation of the law.

Another route to determine whether or not a home office might run into trouble with local zoning restrictions is to find other home-office workers in your neighborhood and ask them if they have ever had any problems. Local real estate agents also are usually aware of what's allowed and what isn't, as are local architects and building contractors.

How to Get Around Zoning Law Restrictions

If an existing or contemplated home office is determined in some way to be a nonconforming use under the zoning laws, there are two options. The first is to hope the proper authorities don't find out, which means that no one—neighbor, delivery person, letter carrier, trash collector, telephone company, supplier, client, employee—either intentionally or unintentionally reports it. To this end, the best practice is to keep the business operation as low-key as possible. Don't talk about the home office unnecessarily, and advise employees not to either; use a Post Office box for business mail; try to arrange as many appointments away from the home office as possible; avoid giving a specific street address when people casually ask you where your office is.

But since hiding the fact completely that you and perhaps others work out of your home office is impossible, it's essential that you keep friendly relationships with those people who know or suspect what's going on and could potentially sound the alarm. Squabbles and feuds with neighbors should be avoided in particular.

If such vulnerability worries you, the second option is to seek a *use variance*. While different municipalities have different procedures, generally the local zoning board will have extensive forms that must be completed, showing the physical characteristics of the property and residence, and requesting full details about the intended nonconforming use. For a home office this means information on the type of business operation, office layout, who will work there, estimated number and type of visitors, parking facilities, deliveries expected, and so forth.

All property owners within a defined radius, say 200 feet, will be notified of the variance application and the date when it will be considered by the zoning board. The application and hearing date will also be advertised in the legal section of the local paper.

At the hearing, zoning board members will ask questions and listen to presentations from the applicant and other interested parties. To gain approval of a variance application, it is wise to have neighbors appear and voice support for your home office. If possible, it might also be wise to refer to another similar variance in the neighborhood and its success. (Although if there are already *too* many variances in a neighborhood, the board might turn down the application on those grounds.)

If the zoning board grants the variance, it may apply only for a limited time, or for a specific business, or to a specific property owner. Or it may apply to any commercial use indefinitely and be transferable with the sale of the property. Sometimes, if the nonconforming use defined in the variance is not utilized for a certain period of time (for example, if you or a subsequent property owner closes down the home office for two years), the variance expires. It all depends on the local zoning laws.

Rejected variance applications can usually be appealed to the municipal governing body or local court system. If you can prove that the zoning board's decision was arbitrary or based on the negative position of only one neighbor, you may get the decision reversed or at the least get a new hearing in order to get more neighborhood input. But if the rejection was based on widespread opposition from neighbors or on a clear threat to the residential environment, the only recourse is to get the law changed. This can be done through the courts or by legislative amendment.

Amending existing zoning laws is a complex procedure: In most municipalities it requires the approvals of the local planning boards and zoning boards, and the adoption by the local governing body. But it's not impossible. In older, middle-class residential neighborhoods with large homes and high property taxes, a good argument can be made that allowing home offices will help property values—that professionals and entrepreneurs are attracted to properties where they can work at home because of the tax advantages, business benefits, and lifestyle conveniences.

OTHER STATE AND LOCAL REGULATIONS AFFECTING THE HOME OFFICE

Municipalities quite often have building, safety, and health codes that apply to any structure where the public is allowed, where employees work, or where food for public sale is prepared. If a home offices is open to the public, for example, it may be required to have restroom facilities and fire exits. Caterers or foodstuff wholesalers may be prohibited from preparing food for public sale or consumption in any kitchen that also serves as a residential kitchen.

Some types of business activities require licenses from either the local municipality or state agencies. Operating a retail outlet, for example, may require a merchant's license from the municipality. The license may result in your having to pay annual renewal fees and increased rates for basic utilities like water and sewer service.

State agencies may refuse to license certain types of business that operate out of home offices that are not clearly separated from residential areas. For instance, many states specifically will not grant a booking or employment agency license to a business that operates out of an office that has a bed or sleeping facilities in it. This reaction to the old "casting couch" abuses means that employment agencies located in home offices must be in separate structures or on separate floors, with permanent partitions between the office and residential areas.

LABOR LAW RESTRICTIONS

The federal government still has labor regulations on the books that prohibit the hiring of home-based labor in seven industries: knitted outerwear, women's garment, embroidery, handkerchief, costume jewelry, button and buckle, and glove and mitten manufacturing. Excepted from the restrictions are the handicapped, those workers caring for invalids, and independent subcontractors. To one degree or another these labor regulations are also present in state labor laws.

The "homework" restrictions were originally enacted to prevent manufacturers from exploiting semiskilled, piecework laborers from working out of home-based "sweatshops," where state and federal labor officials couldn't effectively monitor minimum-wage, child-labor, and safety requirements. To a certain extent, this is still valid. Unscrupulous manufacturers *can* hide away underpaid, overworked illegal aliens in home sweatshops.

But the broad sweep of these restrictive labor regulations prohibits many other people who *choose* to work at home—because they have small children or live in isolated rural areas—from selling the product of their labor, regardless of what price they are able to negotiate and their work situations.

And in the case of independent subcontractors, an overwhelming burden is placed on the home worker to prove his or her status, something that based on legal precedent isn't assured simply because the work is done at home and paid on a piecework basis.

In 1981 the U.S. Labor Department rescinded the homework restriction on knitted outerwear, but the decision was overturned as a result of a suit brought by various labor unions, garment manufacturers, and state labor law enforcement officials. Their position was that it was impossible to protect home-based workers from violations of provisions of the Fair Labor Standards Act, including minimum-wage, worksite-safety, and child-labor laws. However, it is also evident that the decentralized structure of a home-based work force seriously threatens labor unions. Not only are they difficult to organize; home-based workers are also direct competition to union members who work on the employer's premises.

The Labor Department's restrictions on homework came to the forefront again a few years later when four New England women unsuccessfully tried to reopen the suit that had been initiated by the unions. But one important result was the introduction of a "Freedom of Workplace Act," specifically amending the Fair Labor Standards to allow homework. In 1984 the U.S. Senate's subcommittee on labor of the Committee on Labor and Human Resources held extensive hearings on the issue. As of early 1985, the Secretary of Labor was again backing a rescission of the homework restrictions, and based on the free-enterprise leanings of the Reagan Administration, the probability of this happening looked good.

The disturbing fact is that during the Senate hearings the unions raised the specter of the "electronic sweatshop," of oppressed word-processing and data-entry workers chained to terminals in their homes and lacking any of the hard-won benefits of collective bargaining. The AFL-CIO has called for a general ban on computer homework, and the Service Employees International Union, representing nearly 800,000 clerical and health workers, has specifically banned their members from doing computer homework.

The likelihood of federal labor restrictions on computer homework is slim, based on two factors. The first is the historical resistance of clerical workers to organizing and affiliating themselves with unions. The second is the Reagan Administration's leanings toward deregulation in general. Free, unfettered entrepreneurship is popular now, and any challenge to this economic ideology is not likely to prevail.

But a strong negative stance by organized labor on computer homework could have a dampening effect on the future of telecommuting programs. Major businesses could become wary of making significant investments in programs that might arouse union ire or eventually be the target of federal labor restrictions. Until some clear law is passed by Congress, the future for wide-scale home-based telecommuting will be up in the air.

CONTRACTUAL RESTRICTIONS ON THE HOME OFFICE

In addition to federal, state, and municipal laws, there are also contractual agreements that could affect your home office. Most lease agreements state for what purpose the tenant will use the apartment or house, usually that it will be used as a "private dwelling place." If the tenant begins to operate a business or profession out of the leased premises, he or she is technically in breach of the lease.

This might not cause any problems. The landlord may simply require an increase in rent to bring it in line with commercial-use rates prevailing in similar leases. However, if the premises are covered under a municipal rent-control law, the landlord would have good reason to try and terminate the lease, evict the tenant, and rent to someone else at a higher monthly rental.

An attempt to evict a tenant because of a home office might well succeed or fail partially depending on whether the lease includes a clause making residential use a substantial obligation of the tenant. Such legal language might read: "The character of the occupancy of the apartment and the use thereof is a special consideration and inducement for the making of this lease."

A tenant's ability to successfully fight lease termination based on a home office might also be influenced by whether or not the landlord was required to and could prove actual damages resulting from the home office. The incidence of other offices in the building or neighborhood would also affect whether or not the home office was a substantial departure from the residential character of the complex.

Condominium associations and cooperatives may also have restrictions against any commercial use of units in the complex. Or they may require that anyone who wishes to operate a home office must first get the approval of the governing board.

If you live in a leased apartment, condominium, or cooperative, have an attorney read over your lease, title, or association rules to determine if establishing a home office will violate them in any way.

13

A Matter of Personal Style

The preceding chapters of this book deal primarily with the "working" part of working at home. Setting up and equipping a home office, business services and suppliers, tax considerations, insurance—all are nuts-and-bolts considerations for a solid, businesslike operation.

However, it would be unwise to disregard the "home" aspect of a home office. After all, home is the place where we go to *retreat* from the pressures of work and the outside world. When we bring our work home, it can upset our sense of equilibrium. "Work" ceases to be a place, as in "I'm going to work" or "Where do you work?" It becomes a process that must be integrated with all the other processes that take place at home—sleeping, eating, relaxing, raising children, entertaining, pursuing hobbies.

How to successfully blend work and home life under one roof depends entirely on the individual. One person may need to start each workday precisely at 9 A.M. and end it precisely at 5 P.M., much as if the home office were across town rather than in the spare bedroom. Another may be more productive working in spurts; not getting anything done for several days and then working 36 hours straight to catch up. There just are no right or wrong approaches; it's just a matter of personal style. And that's one of the greatest freedoms a home office offers.

HABITS

A common response by people who work in traditional offices to the suggestion that they should consider working at home is, "No, I'd never be able to keep out of the refrigerator. I'd be fat as a pig if I stayed home all day." Or, "I'd never be able to get anything done. When I'm at home I like to sleep late, take it easy, maybe watch TV, or read. I'd just putter the day away." What they are describing is what they do on weekends and holidays, and that's what *everybody* likes to do on weekends and holidays, whether they work at home or not. Relaxing and dropping your guard a little is what time "off" from work means.

By contrast, a workday means getting up early, showering, dressing, gulping down breakfast, getting the kids off to school or day care, and going to the office. After eight or so hours juggling different work tasks, it's time to go back home, fix dinner, watch the TV, read, go out, or do some more work before going to sleep.

Again, such a routine could describe a typical workday no matter *where* the office was actually located. We all devise routines to help order our lives and accomplish long-range goals. Making the switch from a traditional office to a home office simply means substituting some steps in your routine with others.

Procrastination

The hardest part is getting started—trite but true. Everyone has problems getting started at one time or another. In a traditional office, there are outside remedies for procrastination: The disapproving glances from bosses and coworkers help motivate action when you'd really rather sit and stare out the window. Likewise, home offices that hire full-time employees have a built-in impetus to start work at a certain hour each day and keep the ball rolling until quitting time. But for the person working alone in a home office, procrastination can be a real threat to steady productivity.

The best way to avoid the trap of procrastination when working at home is to establish a morning routine. Get up at the same time in the morning, exercise, shower, dress, walk the dog, eat breakfast, drive the children to school—whatever. Accomplish these prework steps in a "bang-bang" manner, as if you had to catch a bus or train. Then, in the same rush, add one more step that *always* leads immediately into work, like picking up the morning mail at the Post Office or sitting down at your desk with your first cup of coffee. Suddenly, you'll find yourself already at work, without having to really think about it.

Another tip to overcoming procrastination is to mentally visualize yourself at work on a specific task. As you lie in bed in the morning, think about how you will phrase the opening sentence in a certain piece of correspondence, who you need to call today, how you will begin researching a certain project. Once you start concentrating on the details of your workday, you will naturally be moved to action.

Define the days of the week that are to be workdays, say Monday through Saturday morning. This is important not just to keep yourself on a steady work schedule but to let others in the household know when you will and won't be available for leisure or domestic activities.

Don't vary from the routine on defined workdays. Don't pick up a novel "just to read a few pages" before starting work; don't sit down in front of the TV or run domestic errands. Eat lunch at about the same time each day. If necessary, schedule specific breaks for nonwork-related tasks rather than letting them be free-floating.

This routine will be hardest to keep and yet most valuable in the weeks and months immediately after starting to work at home. Studies show that worker productivity falls drastically during this period, primarily because the worker must redefine "home" and "work." After several months, the new work routine becomes second nature, and productivity greatly increases.

Compulsive Behavior

We are all prey to mild forms of compulsive behavior at some time or another. We may eat too much when depressed or drink too much when celebrating. Hopefully, these are "sometimes" binges and are usually kept in check through common sense, character, and our fear of disapproval from the people around us—family, friends, acquaintances, and business associates.

A person alone at home during the day, however, doesn't have people around watching. Who's to know if he or she eats a whole box of doughnuts or starts drinking at 10 A.M.? And what's worse is that the kitchen and liquor cabinet are right down the hall and not down the street. Unrestrained, these excesses can turn into full-fledged addictions.

The following are some of the chronic compulsive-behavior problems that commonly confront people working at home and ways to combat them:

Eating too much. Don't skip breakfast or lunch. You may have been able to get away with this when you worked in a traditional office, but at home, with food readily available, odds are you will snack throughout the day to stem your hunger.

Exercise. Regular, vigorous exercise depresses the appetite. When the urge to snack strikes, run around the block instead of running to the refrigerator.

Don't keep junk food in the house. If it's not there, you won't be able to eat it. Instead, keep raw vegetables, fruit, and unsweetened beverages in stock.

Alcohol and drugs. Alcoholism or drug addiction is hard to hide in a traditional office, where the same group of workers see each other eight hours a day, five days a week. Unfortunately, it's all too easy to hide in a home office. *Anyone who has an active problem with alcohol or drug abuse should probably not consider working at home alone.*

Anyone who unwinds by having a few drinks or otherwise getting high at the end of a hard day should guard against two potential problems when working at home. First, don't let these patterns creep into the workday. Working in isolation and running a business create a lot of stress, and if you deal with stress by drinking or using drugs you will be headed for trouble. It's just too easy at a moment of frustration or anxiety in the middle of the workday to pour a drink or get high. This doesn't resolve the situation that caused the stress, in fact in the long run it will cause much more.

Second, don't let alcohol or drugs become the dividing line between work and leisure. When you work at home, it's sometimes hard to feel the difference between when the workday ends and the leisure time begins, since they both take place in the same general area. Getting high shouldn't be the basis for distinction.

Ways to protect against these insidious routes to abuse include substituting other ways to reduce stress and to mark the end of the workday. If you start to feel stressful, try pacing back and forth, or get a simple treadmill. Or manipulate something with your fingers, like worry beads. Call someone up and discuss the problem that's making you anxious.

At the end of the workday go for a walk, jog, change into different clothes, play records or turn on the radio, go out or have someone over for dinner, anything to contrast with "work." If these methods fail, resolve to keep alcohol or drugs out of the residence. Force yourself to admit you are developing a problem, and seek professional advice. Finally, consider going back to work in a traditional office. Nothing is worth the waste and damage caused by alcohol or drug addiction.

Workaholism. This is by far the most common type of compulsive behavior associated with working at home. To some extent it may be an unfair label. Most people who work at home are entrepreneurs or small business owners and must work longer hours than regular employees in order to give their business ventures an opportunity for success. This would be true no matter where their business operations were located.

However, it's clear the home office can lead to a lopsided, "all work and no play" lifestyle. Since the business is constantly staring you in the face, it's hard to ignore the things that need to be done. Clients and customers know you are available at all hours of the day and night and won't hesitate to call, or even drop by.

Workaholism is a danger because it leads to one-dimensional personalities—people who really have no contact with or appreciation of anything else in the world besides their work. They do not make good family or community members, and they have nothing to fall back on if something should prohibit them from pursuing their work. They also tend to lack broad perspectives about society, humanity, and themselves. Eventually, they burn out.

Therefore, just as it is essential to know how to make yourself start working, it's essential to know how to make yourself stop. And again, routine is the answer.

Institute a "quitting time" step in your daily routine. Perhaps it's taking the mail to the Post Office, walking the dog, watching the evening news, fixing dinner for the kids or for a housemate, calling your mother, meeting a friend for dinner. You could even try setting an alarm clock in the office. Whatever the signal, you should use it to knock off work and turn your attention to other people, community affairs, a hobby, domestic tasks, leisure activities. Your work will still be there tomorrow, and you will be able to address it with new enthusiasm.

Along the same lines, take at least one day a week off. If you don't, all the days will start to merge into one another, and you will find yourself never knowing exactly what day of the week it is.

Self-Image

When you first start to work at home, it's fun to spend the entire day working in your bathrobe and slippers. It's fun, that is, for about two days, and then it starts to get boring. Worse, it gets depressing. After all, the only times most of us stay in our bathrobes all day is when we're sick.

So, even though you might not plan to see anyone during the day, make it a habit to get dressed every morning. Keep up the same daily personal grooming routine as you had before—showering, shaving, brushing your teeth, putting on makeup. If you let yourself "go to pot" just because you think you don't have to worry how you look, you're wrong. *You*'ll know how you look. And when you look like a slob, you feel like a slob.

SOLITUDE

Some futurist writers, while admitting that many more people will opt to work at home in the next decade, sketch fairly bleak pictures of the home office. They describe them as isolated "work cells" that deprive workers of meaningful social contact.

But the fact is that the vast majority of people who work at home don't look upon their isolation as a bad thing. The solitude of a home office allows greater concentration and increases productivity. It frees you from the peripheral distractions, chitchat, and politics of traditional office environments.

True, traditional offices also provide friendships, camaraderie, professional feedback, even romantic liaisons. Some workers, especially young, single people just starting out on their careers, rely very heavily on office-based social contacts and would probably not be happy working alone at home full-time.

Older, more established workers are more likely to have other networks that they rely on for personal interaction—spouse, housemates, children, old friends, neighbors, civic and religious organizations. In addition, running a typical business, whether based at home or not, requires numerous daily contacts with clients, customers, and suppliers. There are business lunches, telephone calls, visits to clients' offices, visits to servicers' and suppliers' facilities, computer links, not to mention the people who drop by the home office itself.

There are several ways of dealing with social isolation if you are worried about spending too much time alone. Join some sort of organization or group that meets regularly, at least once a week. This might include an exercise club, sports team, civic committee, discussion group, or an informal network. Sign up for a course at the local college or technical school, either as a student or teacher.

Schedule two or three work-related appointments outside your home office each week. Meet friends or business associates regularly for lunch. Take advantage of leisure activities that require going out, such as visiting a museum or going to a show, instead of always staying in and watching TV or reading.

If possible, get a dog, cat, or other pet you can hold and stroke. Studies with the homebound elderly and prison inmates show that pets contribute significantly to easing loneliness and stress.

The point is that when you decide to work at home, you assume responsibility for shaping and directing your personal life just as much as you assume responsibility for your professional life. Instead of relying on the somewhat random social encounters associated with a traditional office, you are able to select and plan your personal activities. Your time and energy can be devoted to the close companions and social groups that *really* mean something to you. The opportunity for a *greater* degree of personal satisfaction is there for the taking.

OTHER MEMBERS OF THE HOUSEHOLD

People who live alone may have problems dealing with the solitude of a home office, but they don't have to juggle the competing demands of a multimember household. They don't have to deal with quarreling children who burst into the home office in the middle of an important business call. They don't have to cope with spouse and housemates who need their dirty clothes taken to the dry cleaner. But just as solitude can be handled, so can domestic responsibilities.

The "Honey-Do" Syndrome

The major symptoms of this syndrome is the often-repeated "Honey, please do this . . ." and "Honey, please do that . . ." Spouse and housemates seem unable to resist finding little domestic tasks for the home-based worker. If the other adult member of your household works during the day in a traditional office, he or she may not understand why you can't wash the clothes, clean up the kitchen, do the grocery shopping, and fix dinner "because you're home all day anyway." If the other member of the household is home during the day also, he or she may still request your assistance around the house or with his or her own work.

The Honey-Do Syndrome is caused when your spouse or housemate fails to take your home-based work seriously enough, perhaps because you don't appear to take it seriously yourself. If you don't keep regular work hours, how are they to know if you're "at work" or not? If you avoid work by puttering around the house sometimes, who can blame them for asking you to do "just one little favor" for them?

This is just another reason why it's essential to keep a regular work routine that starts and ends at certain hours. If possible, schedule your work hours so that they coincide with the time everyone else is out of the house. Also agree that certain times will be specifically set aside for nonwork activities, whether for domestic responsibilities or just to spend time with your spouse or housemate.

Incorporate the work schedule into an overall understanding between you and your family or housemate *prior* to creating a home office. They must support the concept of sharing the home with an office if the home office is to succeed. Also, spelling these matters out in advance will let everyone know exactly what they can expect and when it is not being lived up to.

Children

Typical Case: Young professional couple faced with the birth of their first child decides that rather than risk placing the child in day care, where he or she might not receive proper treatment, and rather than ask one partner to sacrifice his or her career (and paycheck), one of them will work at home while the child is young. That way they can have their baby and feed it too. It seems like a rational and even laudable course, and it's really too bad it probably won't work.

Anyone who decides to stay home and mix work with caring for a preschool child had better be prepared to do one on a part-time basis only. There simply isn't enough time in the day or energy in a human body to pursue both full-time. This is particularly true when the business, like the child, is young; it too will demand extra attention during its formative years.

A wiser and more realistic course is to have a babysitter come to the residence for at least four or five hours each day. This could be a teenager or elderly person whom you might not feel comfortable giving complete child-care responsibilities to, but who can be a good "mother's helper."

Or, depending on your type of work, you could arrange a piecemeal, part-time work schedule, including a few hours in the very early morning before the child awakes, an hour at nap time, and maybe a few hours after the child goes to bed at night. This, however, prohibits any extended periods of concentration and might not mesh with others' business hours.

Once the child is in school, you can maintain a more traditional work routine. You also will have fewer interruptions. The office located in a home with children *must* be able to be closed off from the rest of the residence. The children *must* be taught that you are not to be interrupted during work hours except in case of emergency, or unless you have specifically asked them to check in with you—for example, when they get home from school.

If you are thinking about working out of a home office, talk it over with your children first. Let them know that they will be expected to keep quiet during your work hours and that they may be asked to help out in the office once in a while.

But also help them understand, to the degree they can, that children whose parents work at home have a unique opportunity to understand what "work" is. They will be able to see the tools, the process, and the output. If they help out, they will appreciate the efforts and the rewards. For them, unlike their friends, "work" will not be an entirely alien place their parents depart for each morning and return from each night; it won't be a simplistic television sitcom where employees sit around plotting schemes against bosses who are either fools or swindlers. Work will be there, down the hall, part of their homes and their lives.

EMPLOYEES IN THE HOME OFFICE

When you hire someone to work in your home office, you are bringing them not only into a work place but into your private residence as well. A very special relationship will evolve, one that will require a great deal of tact on each side if it is to avoid two major areas of trouble.

The first concerns protecting the privacy of the employer's residence and private life. Home-office employees often have keys to the residence, overhear family conversations, know when you are away, and generally get an insight that is usually reserved only for close family and friends. If this is combined with any sort of animosity or resentment for the employer, the results can be disastrous. In addition, even the most kindhearted employees can unintentionally cause problems if they talk about what they know, especially if the home office is in violation of any governmental or lease restrictions.

The second area concerns protecting the employee. The prospect of too much familiarity in a home office can make some potential employees very nervous, especially if the employer is of the opposite sex. For this reason, many temporary employment agencies will not send their workers to home offices. However, other potential employees will find the degree of informality and flexibility associated with most home offices very appealing.

Unless the employee also doubles as your domestic, don't ask him or her to perform domestic tasks like cleaning the house or grocery shopping. This is nothing more than an abuse of the employee's status, since he or she will feel compelled to acquiesce and yet is sure to resent it and complain—perhaps to someone else—that it's not part of their job description. It will only cause problems in the long run.

Home-office employees should be kept as much at arm's length as possible. To this end, the more separate the office from the residence, the better. An office with a separate entrance that can be sealed off from the residence is best. But since this is impractical for many people who work at home and yet want to hire someone to help them, the division can be maintained through attitude. This doesn't mean staying completely aloof from your employee, it just means that both you and the employee understand that some things are business and some things aren't, and that you prefer to keep your private life to yourself. Make sure when interviewing a prospective employee that this point is made in a friendly but firm manner.

THE 24-HOUR PARTNERSHIP

Two or three generations ago, it wasn't uncommon for husbands and wives to work together. Small family-owned and family-operated businesses prevailed in corner grocery stores, neighborhood restaurants, family farms, and small-town professional offices.

Today, we look back on these husband-and-wife teams with fond nostalgia: Two people sharing hearth and family and united in a common financial enterprise seems idyllic. But most of us accept the modern-day maxim that today such 24-hour partnerships are doomed.

Today, separate careers are considered beneficial to domestic relationships. Each partner, it is felt, needs to have independent professional goals to sustain his or her sense of self-worth and accomplishment. Marriages or live-in arrangements between employees are even thought to be bad for good business relationships, evidenced by the overwhelming number of businesses with company rules against employing workers who are married to each other or living together.

Yet, it's hard to ignore the fact that independent careers place terrific strains on relationships and often account for their breakup. A husband, engrossed in a difficult project at the office, comes home exhausted and unable to pay any attention to his wife or children, who cannot share his concerns and feel ignored. A wife works late at the office, arousing suspicion and resentment in her husband, who wants a well-maintained domestic life like his parents had.

What's the solution? Well, it's certainly not a headlong retreat into the past. Too much has changed for us to unquestionably adopt our grandparents' attitudes and lifestyles: the role of women, the complexity of business, the financial demands on the family.

But for some couples—clearly not all—working together out of a home office could be a realistic and rewarding option. They could continue to work at different careers and simply share the administrative and support functions of the home office, or they could pool their work efforts in a common venture.

Potential Landmines

Whichever route you consider, beware of the following:

Role conflict. There are no totally equal, 50/50 partnerships. The best you can ever hope for, in either personal or business relationships, is that *on the whole* you and your partner feel you play equal roles. You may take the lead in financial decisions; your partner may control marketing efforts.

If you find yourselves fighting over business decisions, you must assign roles and responsibilities, just as a business of unrelated workers would. In our grandparents' day this really wasn't much of a problem: The man made all the decisions, and the woman helped carry them out.

This will probably not work today, especially if the woman has been out in the business world and assumed job responsibilities. A better idea would be to realize that each partner brings unique abilities and achievements to the business and to divide up the business functions on that basis. Each partner should be happy, at least in general, with the roles that he or she will play. (There are always those tasks that no one wants to do, like filing. Since they still have to be done, make sure that each of you takes one or two of these undesirable jobs so that neither will feel overly burdened.)

If you each are pursuing different careers and simply sharing the same office, the best idea is to hire a full- or part-time employee to assume the administrative tasks of answering the phone, filing, typing, and so forth. However, one partner will still have to assume the role of managing this person; otherwise, the employee will get caught in the middle when you have conflicting demands on his or her time.

Business problems invading your personal lives, and vice versa. Running a small business is like taking a ride on a roller coaster blindfolded. One day you're steaming straight ahead, making good progress, and the next it seems you've fallen off the edge of the world. And you can never see what's coming.

It's difficult enough to deal with this as individuals, and even more so as two people who eat and sleep under the same roof and whose common financial future is at stake. If you fight about the family finances now, wait until you go into business together.

The only solution is to make a sincere pact that each of you will try and put business problems behind you when you leave the office. In the same vein, leave your personal disagreements outside the office door. When these rules are violated, don't argue about it at the time: A person who is under stress and upset is not going to give a hoot about the fact that you don't want to hear about it. Instead, discuss it later. Explore how important *both* aspects of your relationship are and how each needs its own place.

Finding the Gold Mine

Is it all worth it? Why take a well-functioning personal relationship and put it under the extra pressure of being together 24 hours a day? Why subject it to the stress of a common business venture? And why redefine it and the roles each partner plays? Because the potential rewards are great—almost immeasurable.

Two people sharing a residence and a home-based business double the financial and tax advantages of the home office. They both can produce more, with a lower overhead and higher after-tax gain.

Working toward a common business goal, they can spend more active time together. They can truly share their respective accomplishments and achievements. A business success is cause for mutual celebration because each understands and participated in the efforts that went into capturing it.

Most important, a couple that becomes a good working team is hard to beat. Their devotion to and trust in each other, combined with the competitive advantages of a home office, make a mighty springboard for a new business venture. They can succeed using their own assets and their own labor, controlled in the way they see fit. They are on their way to making themselves and their family personally independent and financially self-reliant.

Appendix

CHAPTER 2

Business Tax Deductions Master Guide
Prentice-Hall, Inc.
Englewood Cliffs, NJ 07632

Master Tax Guide
Commerce Clearing House, Inc.
4025 W. Peterson Avenue
Chicago, IL 60646

"Tax Avoidance Digest"
Euler Enterprises, Inc.
Penthouse 11
4853 Cordell Avenue
Bethesda, MD 20814

"Business Uses of Your Home" (Pub. 587)
Internal Revenue Service
1111 Constitution Ave., NW
Room 2315
Washington, DC 20224

CHAPTER 4

So You Want to Start a Business
Prentice-Hall, Inc.
Englewood Cliffs, NJ 07632

Business Planning Guide
Upstart Publishing
Box 323
Portsmouth, NH 03801

How to Plan and Finance Your Business
CBI Publishing Company
51 Sleeper St.
Boston, MA 02210

How to Build and Maintain a Profitable Consulting Business
Howard L. Shenson
20121 Ventura Blvd.
Suite 245
Woodland Hills, CA 91364
(818) 703-1415

How To Play the Moonlighting Game
Facts on File Publications
460 Park Avenue South
New York, NY 10016

How to Write a Marketing Plan
1979 Center for Entrepreneurial Management
311 Main Street
Worcester, MA 01608

Small Business Survival Guide
Prentice-Hall, Inc.
Englewood Cliffs, NJ 07632

Women Working Home: The Homebased Business Guide and Directory
Women Working Home, Inc.
24 Fishel Road
Edison, NJ 08817

HOMEWORK Program for the Home-bound Disabled
Control Data Corporation
8100 34th Avenue South
Box Q
Minneapolis, MN 55440

Listing of Free Publications
Small Business Association
P.O. Box 15434
Fort Worth, TX 76119

Telecommuting Research Program
Electronic Services Unlimited
142 West 24th Street
New York, NY 10011
(212) 206-8272

Telecommuting Review: The Gordon Report
TeleSpan Publishing Corp.
50 West Palm St.
Altadena, CA 91001

CHAPTER 5

Double Duty Decorating
Scribners
597 Fifth Avenue
New York, NY 10017

The Successful Office: How to Create a Workspace That's Right for You
Addison Wesley Publishing Company
Reading, MA 01867

Sunset Add a Room Book
Lane Publishing Co.
Willow & Middlefield Roads
Menlo Park, CA 94025

The National Design Center
425 East Fifty-third Street
New York, NY 10022

Acoustic Panels
Noise Control Products
1468 West 9 Street
Cleveland, OH 44113

Back Issues on Do-It-Yourself Home Office Design
The Family Handyman
1999 Shepard Rd.
St. Paul, MN 55116

Back Issues on Do-It-Yourself Home Office Design
Mechanix Illustrated
1515 Broadway
New York, NY 10036

General Office Furnishings
Laminates Unlimited, Inc.
2720 Sisson Street
Baltimore, MD 21211
(301) 889-5553

Graphic Arts and General Office Furnishings
Sam Flax
111 8th Avenue
New York, NY 10011
(800) 221-9818

Hideaway Desk and Bookcase
Delmart
2199 N. Pascal
P.O. 64495
St. Paul, MN 55164
(800) 328-9697

Modular Office System
Phoenix Design 20
Tradex Corp.
Zeeland, Michigan 49464

Office Wall Systems
Lockwood Furniture Systems
1187 Third Avenue
New York, NY 10028

Suspended Lateral Files
Robert P. Gillotte & Co., Inc.
Post Office Box 5735
Columbia, SC 29250

Lundia of Houston
P.O. Box 55372
Houston, TX 77055

The Organizer Desk/Cabinet
The Brewster Company
Turk Hill
Brewster, NY 10509
(914) 279-4630

CHAPTER 6

Modern Office Technology
Penton/PC, Inc.
Post Office Box 95795
Cleveland, OH 44101

"The Dictation Book"
Association of Information Systems Professionals
1015 North York Road
Willow Grove, PA 19090

"The Office"
Office Publications, Inc.
1600 Summer Street
Stamford, CN 06904

Call Transfer Attachment
Phone-Sentry Corporation
127 East Mt. Pleasant Avenue
Livingston, NJ 07039

Reports on New Office Products
Datapro
1805 Underwood Boulevard
Delran, NJ 08075

CHAPTER 7

PC WEEK
Ziff-Davis Publishing
15 Crawford St.
Needham, MA 02194

PC World: The Comprehensive Guide to IBM Computers and Compatibles
PC World Communications, Inc.
555 De Haro Street
San Francisco, CA 94107
(800) 247-5470

Personal Computing
Hayden Publishing Co., Inc.
10 Mulholland Drive
Hasbrouck Heights, NJ 07604

Independent Computer Consultants Association
P.O. Box 27412
St. Louis, MO 63141

Computer Workplace: Ergonomic Design for Computing at Home
by Jan Wollman
Byte Books
Peterborough, NH 03458

Computer Output Supplies
Delmart Company
2199 N. Pascal St.
P.O. Box 64495
St. Paul, MN 55164
(800) 328-9697

Computer Supplies and Forms
Moore Business Forms, Inc.
P.O. Box 20
Wheeling, IL 60090
(800) 323-6230

CHAPTER 8

GTE Sprint Communications Corp.
(800) 521-4949

AT&T Long Distance Services
(800) 222-0300

ITT World Communications
(800) 526-3000

Western Union Long Distance Service
(800) 526-5303

MCI Communications Corp.
(800) 624-2222

"Paperwork Survival Guide"
Avery Consumer Products Divsion
777 East Foothill Blvd.
Azusa, CA 91702
(800) 528-6600

National ZIP Code & Post Office Directory
National Information Data Center
10014 Dallas Avenue
Silver Spring, MD 20901
(301) 565-2539

Complete Service Guide
Purolator Courier Corp.
3333 New Hyde Park Road
New Hyde Park, NY 11042

Easiclip Fastners & Display Files
Ames Color File Corporation
12 Park Street
Somerville, MA 02143

Expandable File Pockets
Redweld Filing System
Kruysman, Inc.
160 Varick Street
New York, NY 10013

Filing and Accounting Supplies
Accountant's Supply House
518 Rockaway Avenue
Valley Stream, NY 11582

Filing Supplies
Jeffco Industries, Inc.
205 Hallock Avenue
Middlesex, NJ 08846

Filing Systems
Tab Products Co.
55 Potrero Avenue
San Francisco, CA 94103

Safeguard Business Systems
430 Delaware Drive
Fort Washington, PA 19043

General Stationery and Office Supplies
The Reliable Corporation
1001 West Van Buren
Chicago, IL 60607
(800) 621-4344

Stuart F. Cooper Co.
1565 East 23rd Street
Los Angeles, CA 90011
(800) 421-8703

The Drawing Board
P.O. Box 220505
Dallas, TX 75222
(800) 527-9530

Legal Supplies
Charisma Legal Supply Co., Inc.
3344 Emeric Avenue
Wantagh, NY 11793

Legal-Size Binders
Circle West Corp.
P.O. Box 186
Elmont, NY 11003

Pads with Holes Punched for Filing
Hilton's Office Supply
610 Bissonnet #B
Houston, TX 77081

Recycled Cartridge Typewriter Ribbons
Southwest Ribbon Company
5501 North Lamar
Suite A-135
Austin, TX 78751
(512) 458-3229

CHAPTER 9

NewsNet
945 Haverford Rd.
Bryn Mawr, PA 19010
(800) 345-1301

National Alliance for Home-based Businesswomen
P.O. Box 95
Norwood, NJ 07648

National Association for the Cottage Industry
P.O. Box 14460
Chicago, Illinois 60614

Consultants News
Kennedy and Kennedy, Inc.
Fitzwilliam, NH 03447

Directory of National Trade and Professional Associations
Potomac Books
1518 K St. NW
Washington, DC 20005

Directory of Online Databases
New York Zoetrope, Inc.
Suite 516
80 East 11th Street
New York, NY 10003
(212) 254-8235

The Computer Data and Database Source Book
Avon Books
959 Eight Avenue
New York, NY 10019

The IBM PC Connection: Telecommunications for the Home and Office
Micro Text Publications/McGraw-Hill Book Co.
One Lincoln Plaza
New York, NY 10023

The Wall Street Journal
Dow Jones Publishing
22 Cortland Street
New York, NY 10017

BRS/After Dark
BRS
1200 Rt. 7
Latham, NY 12110
(800) 833-4707

CompuServe
CompuServe Information Service
5000 Arlington Centre Blvd.
Columbus, OH 43220
(800) 848-8990

Dialcom
ITT Dialcom, Inc.
1109 Spring Street
Silver Spring, MD 20910
(301) 588-1572

Delphi
General Videotex Corp.
3 Blackstone St.
Cambridge, MA 02139
(617) 491-3393

Dialog Information Retrieval Service
Dialog Information Services, Inc.
3460 Hillview Avenue
Palo Alto, CA 94304
(800) 227-1927

Dow Jones News/Retrieval
Dow Jones and Company
P.O. Box 300
Princeton, NJ 08540
(800) 257-5114

Knowledge Index
Dialog Information Services, Inc.
3460 Hillview Avenue
Palo Alto, CA 94304
(800) 227-1927

The Source
Source Telecomputing Corp.
1616 Anderson Road
McLean, VA 22102
(800) 336-3366

Special Interest Group for Home-based Businesses
Association of Electronic Cottagers
CompuServe Information Service Address: GO
   HOM 146

677 Canyon Crest Drive
Sierra Madre, CA 91024
(818) 355-0800

The Electronic Mall
CompuServe, Inc./L.M. Berry & Co.
875 Third Avenue
New York, NY 10022
(212) 223-2424

CHAPTER 10

Executive Planner
Baldwin Cooke Company
2401 Waukegan Road
Deerfield, IL 60015

Personal Travel Expense Records
Day-Timers, Inc.
Box 2368
Allentown, PA 18001

Toll Free 800 Directory
(Consumer & Business Versions)
AT&T Long Distance Services
2833 North Franklin Road
Indianapolis, IN 46219
(800) 242-4634

CHAPTER 11

Buyer's Guide to Insurance
National Insurance Consumers Organization
344 Commerce St.
Alexandria, VA 22314

Computer and Software Insurance
Safeware, The Insurance Agency, Inc.
2929 North High Street
P.O. Box 02211
Columbus, OH 43202
(800) 848-3469

CHAPTER 12

"Planning for Home Occupations"
American Society of Planning Officials
1313 East Sixth Street
Chicago, IL 60637

Information on The Freedom in the Workplace Act
The Center on National Labor Policy, Inc.
5211 Port Royal Road
Suite 400
North Springfield, VA 22151

Index

Accelerated Cost Recovery System (ACRS), 17-23
Accounting:
    computer software, 95-96
    journals, 174-75
    accounting systems, 159
Activity logs, 10, 159, 161, 167-68
Addresses and telephone numbers, 168
Adjusted basis, 19, 22
Alcohol and drugs, 199
Alcoves, 65
American Institute of Architects, 3
ASCII, 93
Associations, 144, 145, 149, 150, 153, 182

Bank at home, 153
Bauds, 108, 154
Brushfires, 172
Buffers, 109
Business address, 119, 134, 136
Business correspondence, 143, 170
Business entity, 119
Business income, 173
Business licenses, 190

Carpeting, 71
Casualty losses, 15
Cellular phones, 79
Certified mail, 132
Chairs, 68
Children, 27, 32, 113, 184, 202-3
Cleaning, 139, 161, 175
Coated-paper copiers, 85
COD, 133
Commercial passenger services, 136
Commissions, 13
Compulsive behavior, 198-200
Computer:
    compatibility, 100
    depreciation, 19
    discount equipment, 110
    disks, 70, 165, 166
    drives, 103-4, 112
    equipment, 184
    files, 165-67
    internal memory, 102
    insurance, 181
    keyboards, 104-5
    networks, 147-50
    sales representatives, 99
    service contracts, 138
    supplies, 121
    support, 110
    tax deductions, 17
    work stations, 111
Condominium, 194
Conference table, 68
Cooperatives, 194
Copiers (see photocopiers)
Courier services, 58, 120, 135-36
CPS, 106
Credit, 118, 169, 174
CTRs (see monitors)

Daisy wheels, 82
Data bases, 90, 150-51, 153
Day-care services, 10, 15
Desks, 64, 67-68
Desktop supplies, 121
Dictating/transcribing equipment, 83, 121
Disks, 103
Display, 68
Dot-matrix, 82, 105
Downloading, 129
Dress, 200
Dumb terminals, 148
Duplicating needs, 84

Eating too much, 198-99
Electric surges, 179
Electrical circuits, 58-59, 113, 183
Electronic bulletin boards, 147, 151-52
Electronic equipment, 160, 183
Electonic mail, 127-29, 151
Electronic sweatshop, 193
Employees, 188, 203-4, 205
Employees, 188
Entrepreneurship, 37
Equipment: (see also individual items)
    insurance coverage, 179
    lease or buy, 75
    second-hand, 76
    stands, 68, 86
Ergonomics, 54, 61, 68

Facsimile machines, 127
Fair Labor Standards Act, 50, 193
Fair market value, 19, 21
FICA, 40
Fifty percent rule, 17
Files:
    chron, 86, 170
    computer, 165-67
    storing, 164-65
Filing:
    as part of work process, 159
    cabinets, 65, 69, 164
    supplies, 121
    systems, 162-64
Fire extinguishers, 183
Flexibility, 31
Freedom of Workplace Act, 193
Freelancing, 37
Furnishings: (see also individual items)
    display, 170
    do-it-yourself, 62
    evaluating need, 61
    insurance coverage, 179
    miscellaneous, 71
    recycled household items, 62
    second-hand, 62
    stands, 111

Gateway services, 153
Glare filters, 109
Gross income derived, 23

Index

Half-year percentage, 21
Halogen lamps, 70
Health & safety regulations, 192
Home-bound disabled, 32, 51
"Honey-Do" syndrome, 202
Housemates, 202

Image, 57-58
Independent subcontractor, 31
   contract price, 42-44
   cost compared to employee, 40-42
   criteria, 38
   fringe benefits lost, 41
   legal entity, 38
   tax status, 39-40
   written agreement, 38, 44, 45-48
   under federal labor restrictions, 193
Industrial homework, 49
Information utilities, 97, 128, 150-55
Insurance:
   flood, 181
   health & life, 41, 42, 145, 181, 182
   interruption of business, 182
   liability risks, 180-81
   malpractice and products liability, 183
   riders, 180
   separate business policy, 180-81
   standard homeowner's/tenant policy, 179-80
Inventory, 182
   insurance, 179, 182
Investors, 11
Isolation, 57

Key-access filing system, 162-64
Kilobytes, 103

Labor law restrictions, 192-93
Labor unions, 193
Landscaping and lawns, 14
Layout:
   additions, 66-67
   bunker office, 65
   closet office, 64-65
   recessed spaces, 65
   separate structures, 66
   spare room, 63-64
   task-oriented works areas, 59
Lease/purchase agreements, 75, 137
Lease restrictions, 194
Lighting, 65, 70, 109, 111, 184
Local Area Networks, 148
Lofts, 63

Macros, 105
Mail:
   incoming, 160, 168-69, 173
   outgoing, 161-62, 169-70
   supplies, 121
Mailgrams, 131
Mail order businesses, 188
Marriage, 204-5
Microprocessors, 102
Modems, 97, 108-9, 127, 128, 148, 154
Monitors, 96, 104, 160

Moonlighting, 3, 11
Mortgage interest, 15
Mouse, 105

Neighbors, 190
Networks, 145-47
New construction, 58
Noise, 56, 106

Orphan computer equipment, 110

Parallel interface, 107
Partitions, 65
Passwords, 155
Payables, 174
Periodicals, 144
Personal liability and medical payments, 179
Pets, 201
Petty cash system, 173
Phone service, 59
Photocopiers, 83-86, 121, 138, 170
Photocopies, 120
"Placed into service," 18, 22
Platform, 65
Post office boxes, 119, 133
Postage meters, 86-87
Postage scale, 130
Postal rates, 130-32
Postal Service, US, 129-34
Printers, 96, 105-8
Priority mail, 130
Privacy, 56-57, 172, 203, 204
Procrastination, 197
Productivity, 1, 34, 44, 201
Public Access Message Systems, 147-48

Random access memory, 102-3
Real estate taxes, 15
Real-time communications, 152
Receivables, 174
Recovery period, 19, 22
Reference library, 143-44
Registered mail, 132
Rent-control laws, 194
Repair service, 136-39
   covered under lease agreement, 75
   printers, 107
   service contract, 76
Residential vs. business phone service, 123
Restrooms, 60
Risk, 38
Rollover exclusion, 23

Salesperson, 13
Salvage value, 19
Screens, 65
Security, 58, 139, 183
Self-image, 200
Serial ports, 107, 108
Service contracts, 138-39
Shelves, 65, 69
Shipping electronic equipment, 134, 137
Shop at home, 90, 152
Signs, 189
Small Business Administration, 3

Index

Smart terminals, 148
Software, 91-101
  accounting, 95-96, 175
  available through information utilities, 151
  back-up disks, 166, 183
  communications, 97, 128, 148
  cost, 99
  data-base management, 94-95
  graphics, 104
  insurance, 181
  integrated, 97
  operating system, 101, 166
  spelling checkers, 92, 170
  spreadsheets, 93
  support, 98
  versions, 98
  word-processing, 91-93
Solitude, 200-1
Spouses, 202
Static electricity, 112
Stationery, 119
Storage, 60
  inventory, 10
  supplies, 122
Supplies, 120-22
  conserving, 118
  copier, 86
  desktop, 120
  filing, 121
  mail order, 117
  mailing, 121
  quantity discounts, 117
  storage, 69
Surge protectors, 109
Sysop, 148

Taxes:
  activities related to trade or business, 9, 11
  condition of employment, 9, 13-14, 50
  deductions:
    business use of personal phone, 77
    computers, 113
    direct home office expenses, 15
    home office limitation, 14, 23
    indirect home office expenses, 3, 15, 42-43, 56
    real estate taxes, 4
    self-employment tax, 9, 43
    storage area, 10
    straight business expense, 15, 17, 19, 43
    telephone service, 122
    travel expenses, 4, 9
  dependent care credit, 27
  depreciation, 16-23, 25, 27
    personal property, 19-22
    real property, 22-23
  exclusive use, 9-10, 14, 27, 55, 165, 172
  FICA, 40
  gain on sale of home office, 19, 23-27
    long-term capital gains, 25
    recapture, 25
    taxed as ordinary income, 25
  gross income derived, 14
  hiring family members, 27
  hobby pursuit, 11
  home office as rental property, 14
  investment tax credit, 19
  meeting and dealing, 9, 12-13
  net square footing, 15
  principal place of business, 9, 11-12
  regular use, 9, 10, 161, 167
  self-employment tax, 4, 9, 43
  separate structure, 9, 13
  straight business deduction, 75
Telecommunications 3, 74, 142, 149
Telecommuting, 32-33, 49, 193
Telephone answer services, 127
Telephone answering machines, 52, 79-80, 160, 162
Telephone service:
  access to information utilities, 154
  directories, 144
  equal access, 125
  local, 122-25
  long distance, 125-27
Telephones, 76-79
Telex machines, 127
"To-Do list," 160-61, 169, 171
Trash removal, 139
Typewriters, 83
  service contracts, 138
  supplies, 121

Unadjusted basis, 19, 21
Unemployment and disability funds, 40, 44, 181
United Parcel Service, 134
Uploading, 129
Utilities, 15
Utility links, 58-59

Video display (see monitors)
Videotex (see information utilities)

Walls covering, 71
Warranties, 137
Windows, 71, 74
Work breaks, 160, 171
Work in process, 58, 170-72
Work-at-home employees, 48-51
  finding work-at-home programs, 51
  reimbursements, 50
  tax status, 49
  telecommuting, 49
  written employment contract, 49-50
Workaholism, 199
Worker's compensation, 179, 181

ZIP codes, 144
Zoning, 145
  new construction, 66
  permits, 189
  restrictions, 187-91
  use variances, 190